# THE AUTHORITY OF INTERNATIONAL LAW

# The Authority of International Law

*Obedience, Respect, and Rebuttal*

BAŞAK ÇALI

OXFORD
UNIVERSITY PRESS

**OXFORD**
**UNIVERSITY PRESS**

Great Clarendon Street, Oxford, OX2 6DP,
United Kingdom

Oxford University Press is a department of the University of Oxford.
It furthers the University's objective of excellence in research, scholarship,
and education by publishing worldwide. Oxford is a registered trade mark of
Oxford University Press in the UK and in certain other countries



First Edition published in 2015



Published in the United States of America by Oxford University Press
198 Madison Avenue, New York, NY 10016, United States of America

British Library Cataloguing in Publication Data
Data available

Library of Congress Control Number: 2015951017

ISBN 978–0–19–968509–7

# *Acknowledgements*

The book has been on a journey that has transcended three jurisdictions whose relationship with international law is quite different. Writing started in London and continued in Geneva. It was completed in Istanbul. I like to think that this journey has inspired part of its creation. The other—I hope main—inspiration has been the result of thinking about, researching, and practising international law in domestic contexts for the past decade.

My interest in the authority of international law sharpened as I undertook my Economic and Social Research Council -funded research project 'The Judicial Legitimacy and Authority of Supranational Human Rights Courts: A Comparative Analysis of the Perception of the European Court of Human Rights' (Grant No: RES-061-25-0029). Whilst this research agenda aimed to reach an empirically grounded understanding of the authority of the European Court of Human Rights and its judgments in relation to parliaments and national courts, it quickly became clear that each and every actor I met in these domestic contexts was seeking to grapple with the doctrinal relationships they thought they had or did not have with law and legal institutions above and beyond the state. It was striking that most views domestic actors held, even within the same jurisdiction, were inconsistent with one another. The struggle to find a midway solution between loyalties to domestic law and to international law was what brought them together. A few took short cuts, but most of them searched for a way to reconcile what they took as multiple legal authorities demanding their attention and action. Due to promises of anonymity, I am not able to thank my judge interlocutors in London, Ankara, Karlsruhe, Dublin, Sofia, and Strasbourg openly. I am grateful to them all.

The struggles I found in the course of the empirical investigation of 'their reasons' to respect or disregard international law led me naturally towards a more rigorous and systematic analysis of the authority of international law. Could we develop an account of the authority of international law that is both sound and workable? I wanted this analysis to be both practically relevant and legally defensible for those that grapple with the authority of international law as a matter of political and judicial practice. This book, therefore, is squarely located in the field of practice-oriented legal doctrine. It is concerned with how we move from the theoretical analysis of the authority of international law to a doctrinal analysis here and now. But I hope that the book will also be of interest to those who are occupied with questions of authority from the legal philosophy perspective.

I am one of those lucky ones to have benefited from support both institutionally and individually on the journey of this book. I owe all of them great gratitude.

University College London's Department of Political Science was my institutional home between 2003 and 2013. I was granted exceptional support during the periods I trekked across Europe from Diyarbakır to Dublin for long conversations with parliamentarians as well as constitutional and high court judges discovering the intrinsic and difficult relationships between the sociology of the authority of international law and the legal theory of it. Along this road, I benefited from the excellent research assistance of Alice Wyss, Anne Koch, and Nicola Bruch.

During this research leave from UCL, I was lucky to have been welcomed into the multidisciplinary research programme on the legitimacy of international law and institutions—first as a fellow of the Norwegian Academy of Science and Letters under its 'Should States Ratify Human Rights Conventions' Research Project at its Centre for Advanced Study and subsequently as a regular visitor to Pluricourts in Oslo. My encounters with a lively academic community of law, philosophy, and political science scholars with a sustained interest in the legitimacy and authority of international law have enabled me to better clarify my views and to interact with political scientists and political philosophers concerned with the authority of international law from the perspective of its justifiability to domestic democratic polities. For the opportunity, the welcome, and the prompt midday smørbrød, I thank, in particular, Andreas Føllesdal and Geir Ulfstein.

A number of audiences in London, Florence, Copenhagen, Nottingham, Madrid, Geneva, and Reykjavik have given me feedback that pushed me to develop and improve my work on the authority of international law. In particular, but in no particular order, I wish to extend my thanks to the late Kevin Boyle, Richard Bellamy, Dino Kritsiotis, Nigel Rodley, Françoise Hampson, and Mikael Madsen. My new home—Koç University Law School in Istanbul—was extremely supportive as I turned into the final straight and gave me space to complete the manuscript. My particular thanks go to Zeynep Elibol for helping to relieve my marking load when time was of the essence. Cem Tecimer, my student research assistant, offered nothing but outstanding help with formatting the manuscript and interpreting my occasionally haphazard footnotes. Seçil Bilgiç offered much help with organizing the bibliography. Rachael and Sam tackled this particular Turk's ability to forget definite and indefinite articles or confuse pronouns. Their editorial suggestions have not only made the book's language better, but its arguments clearer.

My Oxford University Press editors Merel Alstein and Emma Endean were kind and patient when delays occurred—in particular when organizing my move from London to Istanbul via Geneva. I also would like to thank my two anonymous reviewers for encouraging me to write the book for the broader international law audience rather than solely for the Council of Europe space.

Finally and, most importantly, my family has supported me without question when it mattered the most. Very special thanks to Sam again, to my son, Ara, who patiently played beside me without disruption on many early mornings and post-crèche evenings, to my parents Gülseren and Erdal, my sister Göksu for always being there, and to Margaret who made the trip from Sheffield to Istanbul many a time to support me during long working hours.

I dedicate this book to Kevin Boyle, who offered me enthusiastic support during its inception, but could not see its completion.

# *Contents*

# *Table of Cases*

# *Table of Instruments*

## INTERNATIONAL INSTRUMENTS

### UN Conventions/Treaties

**UN Declarations/Resolutions**



**Other International Instruments**



## REGIONAL AGREEMENTS

## NATIONAL LEGISLATION

### Ireland



### Italy



### United Kingdom



### United States

# Introduction

'To deny that international law exists as a system of binding legal rules flies in the face of all the evidence.'[1]

## Mr Hirst and Mr Davis

On 10 February 2011 an unusual motion was brought before the House of Commons—the lower house of the British Parliament. The motion, by David Davis, Member of Parliament for Haltemprice and Howden (and former shadow home secretary), proposed:

'That this House notes the ruling of the European Court of Human Rights in *Hirst v the United Kingdom* in which it held that there had been no substantive debate by members of the legislature on the continued justification for maintaining a general restriction on the right of prisoners to vote; acknowledges the treaty obligations of the UK; is of the opinion that legislative decisions of this nature should be a matter for democratically-elected lawmakers; and supports the current situation in which no prisoner is able to vote except those imprisoned for contempt, default or on remand.'[2]

In the subsequent vote, 234 votes were cast in favour of this motion and 22 against. They also voted against narrowing the scope of section 3 of the Representation of the People Act 1983 that states convicted prisoners do not have a right to vote. This motion had been brought forward in the midst of the political upheaval created by a culmination of cases brought before the European Court of Human Rights by convicted prisoners. The first of these, by Mr Hirst, was in 2001—ten years before Mr Davis took to the floor.[3]

[1] Hans J Morgenthau, *Politics Among Nations: The Struggle for Power and Peace* (2nd edn, New York: Knopf 1954), 249–52.

[2] HC Deb 10 February 2011, vol 523, col 493 available at: http://www.publications.parliament.uk/pa/cm201011/cmhansrd/cm110210/debtext/110210-0001.htm.

[3] *Hirst v UK (No 2)* (2004) 38 EHRR 40.

When the Chamber of the European Court of Human Rights reached a decision on this case in 2004 and found that the existing law on voting violated the right to vote for prisoners, the British government appealed to the Grand Chamber of the Court. A year later in 2005, the Grand Chamber agreed with its lower chamber. It held that the ban, by virtue of its blanket nature, prevented Mr Hirst from voting and that this was incompatible with Article 3 of Protocol No 1 (the right to free elections) of the European Convention on Human Rights.[4] In particular, the Court held that the 'general, automatic and indiscriminate disenfranchisement of all serving prisoners, irrespective of the nature or gravity of their offences' made the British law on prisoner voting incompatible with international law.[5] This judgment was followed by thousands of new applications from convicted prisoners. In 2010, the European Court of Human Rights delivered a third judgment—the case of *Greens and MT v United Kingdom.* The Court told the UK government to change its legislation to remove the blanket ban within six months of this judgment becoming final.[6] The UK got an extension to this by intervening in a similar case against Italy.[7] The UK was unable to revise the law after the extension, leading to further violation cases against the UK on the right of prisoners to vote.[8]

It is in this context that British members of parliament rebelled against the request from the European Court of Human Rights that the UK amend its legislation on prisoner voting. Mr Davis highlighted this in his opening remark, exclaiming that '[the debate] gives this House [not the government] the right to assert its own right to make a decision on something of very great democratic importance, and to return that decision to itself'.[9]

Aside from illustrating the distaste members of parliament had for permitting prisoners to vote[10] (the Prime Minister said the idea made him 'physically ill'),[11] this highly visible public debate was a rare example of the authority of international law being questioned in a transparent manner. These discussions, which mostly take place in closed United Nations' sessions, were played out in the UK's newspapers, radio phone-ins, television news bulletins, and current affairs shows—not to mention in taxi cabs, hair dressing salons, and across dinner party tables. What made the Hirst debate (or, as

[4] *Hirst v UK (No 2)* (2006) 42 EHRR 41 [GC].

[5] *Scoppola v Italy (No 3)* (2013) 56 EHRR 19.

[6] *Greens and MT v UK* (2011) 53 EHRR 21.

[7] Ibid.

[8] *Firth and Others v The United Kingdom* of 14 August 2014 (not yet reported); *Mc Hugh and others v The United Kingdom* of 10 February 2015 (not yet reported).

[9] HC Deb 10 February 2011, vol 523, col 493.

[10] Ibid. cols 493–586.

[11] HC Deb 3 November 2010, vol 517, col 921. The Prime Minister's words available at: http://www.youtube.com/watch?v=DjzmvvozHuw.

many commentators called it, the Hirst saga) so attractive was that a question so rarely debated in international law circles became part of everyday conversation: what happens when international law—backed up by an authoritative interpretation of a competent court—collides with an omnipotent parliament?[12] Granted, the expansive interpretive role of the European Court of Human Rights, which interprets the European Convention as a 'living' instrument[13] rather than based on the original intent of its drafters in 1950, was a main cause of this collision. In its original submissions, the UK argued that Article 3 of Protocol 1 did not in fact cover the right to vote and even if it did, the decision to remove voting rights from prisoners came under the wide margin of appreciation of states.[14] If the European Court of Human Rights had followed the British government's interpretation of international law, both international law and domestic law would have happily co-existed. But it didn't. How do we then make sense of David Davis's challenge to the *Hirst* judgment?

Mr Davis's opening remarks illustrate the two ways in which authority collided here. First, it was not possible for an interpretation of international law, even one offered by a court mandated to do just that, to force itself on a parliament. There is nothing new in this.[15] It is an observation about how international law works. To be enforced at all, international law relies on the co-operation of domestic authorities, be these executives, parliaments, or courts. It is not a self-enforcing system.[16] When international law demands anything from domestic legal and political orders it is simply down to the implicated domestic order's own internal decisions to execute that international law for it to have domestic or international effect. This is very clear in the Hirst affair. If we accept that the international rule says that there shall be no blanket bans on convicted prisoners voting, the only way to enforce the international law in a country where there is such a ban would be for its parliament to amend legislation.[17] International laws, even those with the most

[12] The UK Parliament is omnipotent in the sense that under UK Constitutional Law Parliamentary primacy is a central principle of separation of powers.

[13] *Tyrer v United Kingdom* (App nos 5856/72) (1978) 2 EHRR 1, 15–16; *Saadi v United Kingdom* (2008) 47 EHRR 427.

[14] HC Deb 10 February 2011, vol 523, col 493.

[15] For a classical statement of this, see Leo Gross, *States as Organs of International Law and the Problem of Auto-Interpretation* (Berkley: University of California Press 1953).

[16] International law comes close to having direct effect in the case of European Union law before European Union member states' domestic courts. Even then, however, it is not clear whether international law can be automatically enforced. See Neil Walker, 'Beyond boundary disputes and basic grids: Mapping the global disorder of normative orders' (2008) 6(3–4) *International Journal of Constitutional Law* 373.

[17] This flows from the duties of cessation of a violation and the duty of non-repetition of a violation if it is continuing. Draft Articles on Responsibility of States for Internationally Wrongful Acts,

inter-state characteristics (for example, the principle of non-intervention in internal affairs of a state, as banned by Article 2/7 of the United Nations Charter), also rely on the same principle. Without states either taking action or refraining from taking action, we cannot enforce international law.[18]

Second, David Davis was mounting a deeper account of this collision between the authority of international law and domestic orders. On one hand his motion recognized 'the treaty obligations of the United Kingdom'. At the same time it asserted that whether prisoners may or may not vote was an issue for the UK Parliament alone. He further argued that this was because of the 'great democratic importance' of prison voting as an issue. Put another way, Mr Davis was asserting that Parliament had the right not to respect this particular decision of the European Court of Human Rights as part of its treaty obligations because Parliament had the exclusive authority on voter regulation. Mr Davis went a step further, however. He put forward a theory on the displacement of the authority of international law. The greater the democratic importance of an issue, the less compelling the duty to follow treaty obligations is. Mr Davis's first assertion alone is enough to infuriate most, if not all, international lawyers. It is hoped that the second provides additional motivation for readers to follow this book through to the end.

These two ways of talking about the authority of international law are distinct. The former states a fact well known by both international and constitutional lawyers. The latter makes a fundamentally disputed normative assertion about when international law ought to enjoy any form of authority in domestic legal orders. Mr Davis is not only saying that no-one, as a matter of fact, can force Parliament to comply with this ruling. There is not much to dispute there. He is also saying that neither he nor Parliament should be expected to respect the authority of international law in this matter. Is this assertion correct? How does one know whether it is correct or not?

This book is interested in the second and deeper challenge mounted against the authority of international law by domestic legal orders. How do we make sense of Mr Davis's claim that the UK Parliament has ultimate

Pt 2, arts 29–30 in ILC, 'Report of the International Law Commission on the Work of its 53rd Session' (23 April–1 June and 2 July–10 August 2011) UN Doc A/56/10 available at: http://www.org.un/law/ilc reprinted in James Crawford, *The International Law Commission's Articles on State Responsibility: Introduction, Text and Commentaries* (Cambridge: Cambridge University Press 2002).

[18] There are, of course, domesticated international laws. Some countries in the Council of Europe, for example, have domestic laws that allow for more direct application of the European Convention on Human Rights. If the European Court of Human Rights delivers a violation judgment, that judgment as a domestic matter of criminal, civil, or administrative law may lead to an automatic procedural right to re-trial.

authority over interpretations of international law? Do we analyze this claim as essentially a deep power struggle between the United Kingdom—a powerful nation, a heavyweight player in international law, one of the drafters of the European Convention on Human Rights—and the European Court of Human Rights? Do we analyze it as the ultimate assertion of state sovereignty over international law? Is it best to approach Mr Davis's parliamentary motion from the perspective of a lack of democratic legitimacy of international law and its interpretive processes? Or do we take it as an instance of dualism winning the battle against monism?

## The Methodological Approach of this Book

There are a variety of analytical frameworks and intellectual traditions through which we can make sense of these questions. Normative understandings of the authority of international law in academic literature and every day political debate are wide and varied. These range from the standard consent-based approaches to international constitutionalist approaches (which hold that some international laws may be hierarchically superior to domestic laws as a matter of form, function, or substance)[19] and from domestic democratic approaches (which refuse to acknowledge any significant further authority above and beyond 'we, the People')[20] to pluralist approaches (which hold that international law's authority is an open-ended question).[21]

In addition to these different and, at times, rival theories about the authority of international law over domestic systems, enduring conceptual questions remain concerning the authority of international law. Rival accounts may not only disagree about the normative reasons for the authority of international law, but also the conceptual nature of that authority. What is the nature of the authority of specific international laws? Are we to understand

[19] See generally Bardo Fassbender, 'We the Peoples of United Nations: Constituent Power and Constituent Form in International Law' in Martin Loughlin and Neil Walker (eds), *The Paradox of Constitutionalism: Constituent Power and Constitutional Form* (Oxford: Oxford University Press 2007); Jan Klabbers, Anne Peters, and Geir Ulfstein, *The Constitutionalization of International Law* (Oxford: Oxford University Press 2009); Mattias Kumm, 'The Cosmopolitan Turn in Constitutionalism: An Integrated Conception of Public Law' (2013) 20(2) *Indiana Journal of Global Legal Studies* 605.

[20] Martin Loughlin, 'Why Sovereignty?' in Richard Rawlings, Peter Leyland, and Alison Young (eds), *Sovereignty and the Law: Domestic, European and International Perspectives* (Oxford: Oxford University Press 2013); Armin Von Bogdandy and Ingo Venzke, *In Whose Name? A Public Law Theory of International Adjudication* (Oxford: Oxford University Press 2014).

[21] Nico Krisch, *Beyond Constitutionalism: The Pluralist Structure of Postnational Law* (Oxford: Oxford University Press 2010).

international laws as pre-emptive directives? Is the authority of international laws independent from their content? Is international law's authority better conceived as persuasive authority? Do we have to first subscribe to a thicker view concerning the nature of the international system, as international constitutionalists or normative pluralists do, in order to decide whether an international law has authority or not? Is the authority of international law ultimately tied to whether it conforms with important values such as human rights?

These questions have important implications for deciding which of a number of rival theories explains the authority international law really enjoys over domestic orders. None of these questions, however, are settled in the literature. Rather, many commentators operate with implicit conceptions of the authority of international law, either directly borrowed from domestic law or domestic legal philosophy, or from standard consent theories of international law, when they set out to criticize or provide support for why it should have authority over domestic legal orders.

The methodological approach of this book is inspired by two important traditions in law: conceptual analysis and practice-based analysis.

As a matter of conceptual analysis the book is first and foremost a call to return back to the drawing board. It calls for a systematic survey of our contested working understandings of the authority of international law. It queries why we import concepts from domestic law and our mainstream international law wisdom that sees the authority of international law as essentially stemming from the binding qualities of international law. It then focusses its efforts to develop and defend a practice-based and doctrinal approach to the authority of international law. The book is interested in Mr Davis's request to UK parliamentarians and the predicament domestic political authorities are in when faced with international law they find unattractive, objectionable, or unacceptable. This practical and doctrinal approach to the authority of international law is also interested in how lawyers and judges in domestic courtrooms can best conceive and respond to the authority of international laws they encounter.

This book proposes that, in order to understand the authority of international law over domestic systems, we do not only interrogate how different theories assign or query the authority of international law and decide which one, on balance, has stronger arguments. We must get a stronger grasp on the concept of authority as it applies to international law and then develop an account that best fits with its concept and its broader practice. This is needed in order to make sense of examples such as the challenge to the authority of an international court judgment mounted in the UK Parliament. The fundamental assertion I make is that, despite the many theories on the authority of international law that exist, it is not clear whether we have a sufficient understanding of the concept of authority as it applies to contemporary international law and what legal doctrinal consequences should follow from it in every day practice.

How do we then mount a conceptual analysis of the authority of international law? Here I do not seek to engage with a high level philosophical discussion. Rather I employ conceptual analysis in its most common sense usage. In Aristotelian terms, conceptual analysis is an attitude that seeks to better understand our common parlance and practice.[22] This attitude both concerns the directionality of analysis and its purpose. First with regard to directionality, conceptual analysis starts from common opinions rather than metaphysical, high-level theoretical questions. Second, with regard to purpose, it seeks to resolve problems and puzzles that arise from these very common opinions. The reason for engaging in conceptual analysis is its potential to clarify or re-organize a debate and in so doing contributing to overall knowledge. As Coleman explains, conceptual analysis is 'to retrieve, determine or capture the content of a concept in the hope that by doing so, we will learn something interesting, important or essential about the nature of the thing that the concept denotes'.[23]

Legal conceptual analysis in this book, therefore, is about uncovering 'the most salient features' of the concept of the authority of international law in contemporary terms.[24] My key focus is to understand what is at stake when we engage in discussions about the authority of international law over actions of state officials, be they political or legal.[25] In this respect, I am primarily focussed on the practice of international law rather than the idea of international law. Foremost, I seek to understand, paraphrasing Raz, *our concept* of the authority of international law and not *the concept* of the authority of international law.[26]

There are three central aims of legal-conceptual analysis discussed. The first is to offer a fulsome treatment of what really flows from a concept, its nature, and scope. In the international legal field this involves asking

[22] Aristotle, 'Nicomachean Ethics' in Jonathan Barnes (ed), *The Complete Works of Aristotle: The Revised Oxford Translation*, vol 2 (Princeton: Princeton University Press 1984).

[23] Jules Coleman, *The Practice of Principle: In Defence of a Pragmatic Approach to Legal Theory* (Oxford: Oxford University Press 2001) 179.

[24] Ibid.

[25] Throughout the book, I follow Waldron's usage of state officials as agencies of the international legal system rather than its subjects. Jeremy Waldron, 'Are Sovereigns Entitled to the Benefit of the International Rule of Law?' (2011) 22 *European Journal of International Law* 315–43.

[26] Joseph Raz, *Ethics in the Public Domain: Essays in the Morality of Law and Politics* (Oxford: Oxford University Press 1995) 237.

questions such as whether authority as applied to international law is a distinct concept from authority applied to domestic law. The second is to take a legal concept and distinguish centrally conceptual claims from centrally normative theories. This is at once a fundamental challenge and a main purpose of legal-conceptual analysis. Conceptual analysis is committed to striving to achieve neutrality amongst competing thicker normative theories. This is helpful when the treatment of the concept brings clarity to how different normative or social theories use the concept. The third is to use conceptual analysis as an aid to better the doctrinal analysis of authority claims of international law over state officials, be they parliamentarians or judges.

The conceptual analysis of law is often placed under the tradition of the descriptive jurisprudence of international law.[27] Normative jurisprudence has often been skeptical of conceptual analysis. There are long-standing debates about whether conceptual analysis can be separated from normative legal analysis and whether those that are committed to conceptual analysis are in effect merely developing yet another normative analysis of the same concept.[28]

A central objection to legal conceptual analysis is the fallacy between conceptual and normative analysis. If law is essentially a normative concept, how can we maintain a distinction between what is conceptual and what is normative? I shall turn to this objection in Chapter 5 of the book. For the moment it shall suffice to say that I do not support what may be termed as a 'clean distinction' between conceptual and normative analysis. In fact, if what is at stake is a practical understanding of the authority of international law, it is undeniable that conceptual analysis must include some normative criteria. I nevertheless maintain that the distinction is possible. The core and essential characteristics of a concept can be set out without adopting a thicker normative theory about and around it. That is, a conceptual analysis of the authority of international law may be compatible with a number of thicker normative theories about the authority of international law. This is a cautious claim however. I do not argue that conceptual analysis can be compatible with *all* normative theories about the authority of international law.

Throughout this book I hold that the mere fact that conceptual analysis delves into normative questions does not mean that conceptual analysis alone can shape and inform one's approach to a field of inquiry. Conceptual

[27] Jules L Coleman and Jody Kraus, 'Rethinking the Theory of Legal Rights' (1986) 95(7) *Yale Law Journal* 1335; HLA Hart, *The Concept of Law* (2nd edn, Oxford: Clarendon Press 1994).

[28] See for example Stephen Perry, 'Interpretation and Methodology in Legal Theory' in Andrei Marmor (ed), *Law and Interpretation* (Oxford: Clarendon Press 1995); Brian Leiter, 'Beyond the Hart/Dworkin Debate: The Methodology Problem in Jurisprudence' (2003) 48(1) *American Journal of Jurisprudence* 17; Charles Lowell Barzun, 'Legal Rights and the Limits of Conceptual Analysis: A Case Study' (2013) 26(2) *Ratio Juris* 215.

analysis and normative analysis have different purposes. The former is an inquiry directed at uncovering the most salient features of a concept. The latter is an attempt to develop a fulsome normative treatment of a legal issue. Conceptual analysis seeks to generate neutral knowledge that has wide appeal amongst substantive theories of a normative concept. This does not mean it always succeeds. This is, however, the defining purpose of conceptual lines of inquiry. I, therefore, do not posit conceptual analysis as a rival to or replacement for normative analysis. I see it as a necessary methodological step towards better understanding a murky field.

The second methodological commitment of the book is to a practice-based analysis of authority. I define the practice of international law by looking at the kinds of relationships between international law and state officials as well as the actual norms within the contemporary international legal system. I seek to put forward an account of the authority of international law that best represents what the diversity of international law asks from domestic legal orders and offer an account of best fit with what most state officials can reasonably recognize as the demands international law has over them. Here, the broader conceptual methodological commitments of the book are aligned with that of constructive interpretivism.[29] The book aims to shed more light on how we may understand *existing* authority relationships in international law in a more conceptual, but also a more coherent way that links the practice of international law as closely as possible to a conceptual understanding of that practice.[30]

When analyzing the relationship between domestic political orders, judicial orders, and international law, the book holds that, despite the proliferation of international law in the past four decades or so, international law and domestic legal and political orders continue to have different purposes validated by different types of social, political, and moral concerns. Whilst these concerns overlap at times, as in the case of human rights law and constitutional rights or domestic criminal law and international criminal law, this does not make domestic law and international law one single unified body of law. Rather, international law and domestic law are best conceptualized as intersecting realms of law. State officials are, by and large, aware of how their purposes intersect and, for the most part, operate in accordance with the cognitive framework of differentiation. For this reason, it is best to

[29] Ronald Dworkin, '"Natural" Law Revisited' (1982) 34 *University of Florida Law Review* 165.

[30] Here I use constructive interpretivism as an umbrella concept whose common starting point is to make sense of an existing practice rather than an ideal state of affairs. It is sometimes also called a 'practice-based' theory. See Charles R Beitz, *The Idea of Human Rights* (New York: Oxford University Press 2009).

characterize this book as 'empirically informed'.[31] As a matter of description of the current state of international law, the assumption of the distinctiveness of domestic law and international law offers the best grounding for analyzing the authority of international law as a practice. This functional approach may be contrasted with a historical evaluative one. The book does not approach the authority of international law as a concept that has 'evolved' over various epochs—though it is perfectly possible to approach it in this way. Such a focus is beyond this work.

## The Core Argument of the Book

This book poses a specific question about the UK Parliament's response to the *Hirst* judgment: Did the United Kingdom fail to fulfil any duty authoritatively imposed on it by international law by voting in favour of David Davis's motion? Or, more generally, how does international law impose authority over domestic systems? If so, what is the nature and the scope of that authority?

In response to these questions, the central arguments of the book are twofold. First, the existence of international law as our imperfect institution to regulate our co-habitation in the form of separate, but independent political entities brings with it a prima facie duty of minimal deference to international law. Minimal deference involves the 'attribution of presumptive weight'[32] to international laws that are duly consented or provisionally consented treaties, established customary international laws, and non-consensual systemic norms of international law, or general principles. Furthermore, the political and judicial organs of a state are not similarly situated with regard to the authority of international law. Judges, in particular, are entrusted with interpretive authority. They must, therefore, seek to harmonize how political officials act domestically and as part of the international collective of states. This implies that domestic judiciaries have a duty to not always follow their legislatures when interacting with international laws and their authority.

[31] This is a notion often used in the political theory of existing arrangements. The term 'empirically informed' suggests that theoretization is not based on abstract principles, but are informed by existing institutional arrangements. See Richard Bellamy, 'Interview' in Morten Ebbe Juul Nielsen (ed), *Political Questions: 5 Questions on Political Philosophy* (London: Automatic Press 2006) 20.

[32] Aileen Kavanagh refers to minimal reference in these terms when discussing the duty of deference of judges to the legislature. She further distinguishes minimal deference from substantive deference. See Aileen Kavanagh, *Constitutional Review under the Human Rights Act* (Cambridge: Cambridge University Press 2009) 181.

Second, minimal deference to international law is not, in and of itself, action-guiding or conclusive. International laws encompass variable forms of authority relationships with domestic orders depending on the capacity of the specific international laws to impose duties themselves. Specifically, these authoritative relationships range from overriding authority to qualified authority and rebuttable authority. This general duty to take international law into account at the very least includes a deliberation about what kind of an authority structure a specific international law imposes on state officials.

Throughout this book, I define the *authority that a particular international law possesses* in domestic orders as the capacity of a particular international law to impose duties or to confer powers on state officials.[33] I use the notion of capacity to make distinctions about how a regulation is formulated in international law. The capacity of a particular international law, therefore, has to be assessed by the logic through which it instructs domestic authorities to act (or to refrain from acting). In everyday practice, international laws have different kinds of capacities when imposing duties or conferring powers on state officials. In other words, different international laws have different 'authority structures'. What the authority structure of a particular international law shows is which international laws require absolute obedience and which may be respected in other forms and gestures. In this definition 'capacity' means the legal-normative capacity of international law. It does not mean 'capacity' in an actual sense or in a moral-normative sense. The capacity of international law to impose duties is a function of the necessity for international co-operation in the international system and the general duties that domestic legal orders have to support, respect, and advance an international system for better co-operation.

International law's capacity to impose duties on states is independent from what Mr Davis or Mr Hirst think that capacity is. I aim to set out a conceptual account that can stand up to the objections of actors that do not act with self-interest. The definition of authority as the capacity to impose duties further differentiates authority based on the binding nature of international legal agreements and actual compliance with international law. A piece of international law may well be legally binding, but it may not enjoy authority in the sense that it does not have the capacity to impose a specific pre-emptive duty or the duty it imposes could be rebuttable by other considerations. The binding nature of international law, therefore, is a necessary, but insufficient condition for the authority of international law over domestic orders.

[33] Here I am following a conventional definition of authority. In literature authority and legitimate authority are often used inter-changeably. See for example Joseph Raz, *The Morality of Freedom* (Oxford: Oxford University Press 1986).

Conversely, the authoritativeness of international law is not sufficient for compliance. States may violate international law or they may respect international law for other reasons—such as self-interest, for example.

## The Contribution of this Book

This book is foremost a contribution to how we may go about understanding the authority of international law over domestic state officials in the context of the contemporary international legal order. My primary reference point is international law here and now made up of a diverse range of treaties in force (ranging from trade, human rights, environment, to international crimes), operating alongside judicial and quasi-judicial institutions interpreting international law side-by-side with states. The contemporary condition of international law has the qualities of both dense and widespread forms of regulation in different issue areas and regions. My central aim is to provide a framework that is able to account for international law not only made up of a range of laws regulating strictly inter-state matters, but also as a body of law that overlaps or conflicts with domestic law from time to time.

The book contributes to existing debates on the authority of international law in four distinct ways. First, it focusses the debate on the authority of international law towards the kinds of duties state officials have towards particular international laws. This practice-informed and practice-oriented focus enables us to see debates on authority as concrete and practical problems of everyday decision-making. This book demonstrates these different relationships between international law and state by drawing on examples of particular international laws and their authority structures. By zooming in on specific international laws, the book shows that it is not the type of international law (i.e. international human rights law, trade law, or UN law) that determines the authority of international law conceptually. It is the authority structure of the particular international law and the duties that law imposes. For example, the argument would not hold that international human rights law has more authority than other branches of international law simply by virtue of a presupposition that the former has a higher normative importance than the latter. This sets me apart from constitutionalist approaches that assign a constitutional value to human rights in the international system. In the same vein it also does not hold that all international laws of a ius cogens character impose the same duties on domestic institutions.

Second, on the conceptual level, the book is critical of often highly demanding concepts of authority and legitimacy being imported from standard domestic political and legal theory to identify the shortcomings of the authority of international law. It asserts that very strong notions of authority such as the right to rule and the corresponding obligation to obey are inadequate to understand the authority relationships between domestic orders and international law. The analysis that I develop, in particular, radically departs from existing debates that present the authority of international law vis-à-vis domestic legal orders from a 'winner takes all' perspective. Instead, I argue that the conceptual structure of the authority of international law is inherently relational and the duties of obedience that international law imposes on domestic orders come in different strengths and forms. There is no ultimate winner in the sense that either international law or domestic authorities have the ultimate authority in each and every case of authority competition. This does not, however, mean that we lack the means to decide when and how the authority of international law should figure in the domestic legal order. In that respect, the relational quality of international law is not about empirical observations telling us that states sometimes respect international law and sometimes do not. It is an argument about under what conditions international law has *a claim to authority* such that it must be respected by state officials and in what form such respect should take place.

Third, on a more theoretical level, the book is critical of the gap between standard consent-based accounts of authority prevalent in mainstream international law and self-interest and identity-based theories of compliance and, hence, authority prevalent in international relations approaches to international law. It holds that neither of these approaches offers a descriptively accurate conceptual structure to capture the diversity of authority relationships that exist between international law and domestic orders.

Fourth, the book is critical of the debate between international constitutionalists and normative pluralists as they relate to the authority of particular international laws. The focus international constitutionalists have on substantive general principles may obscure the fact that a general principle might nevertheless have a weak authority claim on domestic legal systems. Normative pluralists, on the other hand, may place too much emphasis on the indeterminacy of the authority of international law, leaving a large doctrinal vacuum for state officials to engage with the authority of international law.

This book puts forward a novel account of the authority of international law that is not ultimately tied to formal state consent, the practice of states, or domestic institutional frameworks and cultures. It further defends the account it provides against blanket challenges to the authority of international law from arguments based on democratic authority and sovereign self-interest. Arguing that prior consent, compliance, and domestic institutional structures do not exhaust the questions of when international law has overriding authority over domestic orders, the book offers a framework to analyze the authority of international law as a relational concept. In doing so, the focus is shifted to the analysis of the kinds of duties international law imposes on domestic orders and the kinds of obedience it demands from domestic courts, executives, and parliaments in return.

## The Proliferation of International Law

So far what I have articulated may at first sound to some as a project aimed at undermining the existing authority of international law. Franck remarked in 1995 that international law has entered its 'post-ontological' phase.[34] International law now impacts on virtually every area of public policy. In addition, we also have an increasing number of international institutions and courts interpreting international law. This is most notable in the fields of international human rights law, international trade law, international criminal law, and the international law of the sea. How does the account of relational authority I develop here square with the consolidation of an international regime?

The proliferation of international law makes the systematic conceptual analysis of the authority of international law in domestic systems all the more relevant. The view that equates more international law with more authority operates with a consent-based understanding. That is, if states consent to a particular international law, the authoritativeness of that law must flow from this consent. Therefore, more international laws, more authority. On the contrary, I show that consent is neither a necessary condition for all international laws, nor is it a sufficient condition for the authoritative quality of international laws that require consent. States may aim to consent to the creation of international laws in many policy areas—including areas where domestic regulation already exists. But it does not flow from this that all international laws create strict obligations to obey. If it can be shown that a particular international law does not include a pre-emptive duty, for example, as in the case of facilitating free trade, the consent to be bound by international trade law can sit comfortably with states arguing that they can challenge international free trade laws based on domestic social and environmental policy objectives.[35]

[34] Thomas M Franck, *Fairness in International Law and Institutions* (Oxford: Clarendon Press 1995) 6.

[35] See for example WTO, *United States: Standards for Reformulated and Conventional Gasoline-Report of the Appellate Body* (29 April 1996) WT/DS2/AB/R; WTO, *United States: Import*

There is a second sense in which the proliferation of international law makes it more pressing to revisit the conceptual structure of its authority. Contrary to the consent view, which assumes that the authority of international law consolidates over time (i.e. more consensual international law, more authority), an opposite view holds that the increase in the number of international laws in effect undermines the authority of international law. Proponents concerned about the undemocratic rise of international law most forcefully articulate this criticism.[36] Is it really the case that international law is a deeply undemocratic structure, which lacks the legitimate authority to impose duties on states? In what follows I will show that theories that value democratic legitimacy (either because they center on the principle of the political equality of individuals or because they offer a much more deliberative and advanced form of law making) are isolationist. This is because they ignore or underplay the value of international co-operation and the indirect benefits such co-operation brings to individual-level benefits. Instead of insisting that domestic procedures are more deliberative—and, therefore, superior—we ought to think about the duties that domestic authorities have in making international law more deliberative—and enhance its legitimacy repertoire.[37]

If exceptions are consistently carved out to respect the authority of international law—thus making this respect partial—what prospect, if any, does international law have in pulling for compliance? Would these exceptions not open the floodgates for abuse where states, which have ratified treaties, simply refuse to follow them arguing that the obligation to obey in a strict sense simply does not exist? In response to these legal-policy considerations in positing the authority structure of international law as having relational content, I submit that a more accurate conceptual account of the authority of international law (including potential cases for its rebuttal) would lead in effect to better or more entrenched compliance.

*Prohibition of Certain Shrimp and Shrimp Products-Report of the Appellate Body* (12 October 1998) WT/DS58/AB/R.

[36] Kristen Hessler, 'Resolving Interpretive Conflicts in International Human Rights Law' (2005) 13(1) *Journal of Political Philosophy* 29; Steven Wheately, 'A Democratic Rule of International Law' (2011) 22(2) *European Journal of International Law* 425.

[37] This is without any prejudice to many existing ways through which international law is currently made more deliberative, including parliamentary assemblies in international organizations with central law making abilities (eg the Organization of American States and the Council of Europe), the participation of non-governmental organizations in drafting of new international standards (eg the development of the Declaration of the Rights of Indigenous Peoples), and processes for public participation in the negotiation and implementation of international agreements (eg the UNECE Convention on Access to Information, Public Participation in Decision-making, and Access to Justice in Environmental Matters).

A second line of criticism towards the argument as a whole may be considered. That is that the argument is state centric. It approaches the authority of international law only as a matter of obedience or as some form of respect or rebuttal by state officials. Given the proliferation of international regimes and the heightened conflicts between different legal orders that are not national in character, does this book cast its net too narrow? What about the authority of international law over individuals (explicit in the case of international criminal law or implied in most international human rights law)?[38] And how do we make sense of the authority of international law over international organizations?

Here, I think the best response is to say that the authority of international law over state officials is and will remain the core case of the authority of international law. Whilst it is correct that individuals may now be directly subject to the authority of international law and that non-state entities, such as the European Court of Justice and the UN Security Council, have authority competitions, this does not warrant side-lining the core case—namely understanding the authority of international law over political and judicial state officials.

The debates on clashing regimes (focusing on the European Court of Justice and its treatment of Security Council Resolutions or WTO decisions and the relationship between the European Court of Justice and the European Court of Human Rights) are of course lively and important.[39] They, however, often focus on a sui generis set of European courts and generally only discuss how judges distribute the authority of international law.[40]

Rather than starting from a specific judicial phenomenon, this book focuses on the standard case for the authority of international law—the relationship between domestic legal orders and international law. In this sense, whilst the literature, (in particular on the authority of the European Union law over domestic legal systems), is helpful in understanding multiple legal orders, I submit that there is also a general need to develop more in depth studies of

[38] Samantha Besson, 'The Authority of International Law-Lifting the State Veil' (2009) 31(3) *Sydney Law Review* 343.

[39] See generally Steve Peers, 'Banana Split: WTO law and Preferential Agreements in the EC Legal Order' (1999) 4(2) *European Foreign Affairs Review* 195; Joseph H H Weiler (ed), *The EU, the WTO, and the NAFTA: Towards a Common Law of International Trade* (Oxford: Oxford University Press 2000); Marco Bronckers, 'The Relationship of the EC Courts with Other International Tribunals: Non-committal, Respectful or Submissive?' (2007) 44(3) *Common Market Law Review* 601; Juliane Kokott and Christoph Sobotta, 'The Kadi Case-Constitutional Core Values and International Law-Finding the Balance?' (2012) 23(4) *European Journal of International Law* 1015.

[40] Schaffer echoes these points in his review of Krisch's work on the pluralist structure of postnational law (n 21). See Gregory Schaffer, 'A Transnational Take on Krisch's Pluralist Postnational Law' (2012) 23(2) *European Journal of International Law* 565.

the standard case—the relationship between state officials and international law. I shall return to the implications of the core case for authority relationships between international law and other entities in Chapter 5.

## The Structure of the Book

The book is composed of five chapters and a conclusion. In the first chapter, I review the multiplicity of debates on the authority and legitimacy of international law in order to show that existing discussions on the authority of international law start from diverse premises on the nature and scope of the authority of international law. Here I start by discussing what I call the 'standard view of the authority of international law'. I explain why international lawyers have traditionally assumed a benign neglect for compliance deficiencies in international law and have not revised their views of its authority, which have been largely based on the binding nature of international laws that generate authority claims. In particular, I show that the view that advocates an absolute authority for international law is in effect a legal-policy position rather than a conceptual position on the nature of the authority of international law. Having said this, this view should not be taken as wholly unfounded. International lawyers have largely adopted this standard position as a defensive strategy against the critiques of international law.

The chapter then turns to how constitutionalism, fragmentation, and pluralism debates intersect with the authority of the international law. It asks whether they shift the attention from the standard approach. This discussion shows that this burgeoning literature has been surprisingly silent on the conceptual underpinnings of the authority of international law and has not adequately questioned the standard assumptions of authority or advanced our understanding of the relationship between authority and compliance. The final task of Chapter 1 is to discuss the two types of attacks that have been mounted against the standard view. These are the self-interest accounts of compliance and the skepticism political theories have displayed about the legitimate authority of international law. The chapter argues that to defend the authority of international law requires a significant shift away from the main arguments of the standard view criticized in this section. The core assumption that binding laws have authority may seem to offer a good legal policy solution, but it is not robust enough to counter some of the charges levied at the standard account by democratic legitimacy and self-interest based sovereignty accounts.

Chapter 2 presents the core argument of the book. It first discusses how we may go about identifying the conceptual characteristics of international law's authority. It argues that discussions on the authority of international law are largely modelled on discussions of the authority of domestic laws. It questions whether our concerns with the authority of law in a single state adequately carry over to the international realm. Chapter 2 then looks at how we can systematically think through the authority of international law as having the capacity to impose duties and confer powers on state officials. It illustrates the different types of duty that may be imposed on domestic authorities by international law. The chapter develops, first, the notion of the relational authority relationship and, second, the differentiated duties of obedience, respect, or rebuttal as a conceptual scheme that makes best sense of the authority of specific international laws.

Chapter 3 tackles the authority relationship between domestic political authorities and international law. It discusses the basis on which we ask political state officials to have a minimal duty of deference to international law and whether this demand stands up against its critiques. This chapter first focuses on the range of hybrid reasons that ground the legislature's duty of minimalist deference. In particular, I discuss the jurisdictional authority of international law over domestic political organs alongside consensual and participatory forms of authority. Chapter 3 then discusses the range of criticisms against the static and dynamic authority of international law and represents a forceful defence of the view that no political authority can argue for the prima facie right to ignore international law.

Chapter 4 visits the relationship between international law and the domestic judicial organs of a state and argues that the monism and dualism framework fails to explain the dialectical relationship between domestic courts and international law. The chapter discusses how the relationship between domestic courts and international law has been traditionally discussed through the interpretive framework of monism and dualism. It points out that there are two variants of this: a constitutional and an ideological variant. It further holds that neither is satisfactory as they are unable to account for different types of authority relationships between domestic courts and international law. The chapter argues that domestic judges need to have a reflective understanding of the authority of international law and be sensitive to the kinds of duties imposed by international law. It also discusses how this account affects the relationship between judges and political officials and our understanding of domestic law.

Chapter 5 evaluates the normative and legal-policy implications of the account of the authority of international law provided in the book. It argues that the relational authority of international law is an improvement upon the standard view of the authority of international law. The standard international law account of authority creates unrealistic expectations and leads to different kinds of authority relationships being under-analyzed. The adjustment of the authority paradigm from absolute authority to relational-authority also finally shows that international law is not insensitive to values such as democratic legitimacy or internal self-determination or subsidiarity.

The concluding chapter sets out the limits of the argument put forward here and the conditions under which the relative authority of international law can be transcended or completely eroded. The limits of this argument are drawn by two important factors: the structural condition of authority competition between domestic institutions and international law and the interpretive condition of international law encompassing a wide range of general principles, which may be subject to more than one reasonable interpretation.

# 1

# Authority and International Law: The State of the Field

'There need be no mystery about the source of obligation to obey international law.'[1]

## Introduction

The standard view amongst international lawyers is that international law has a claim to authority by virtue of its legally binding qualities. Major international law textbooks and studies repeat this but rarely delve deeper.[2] A variety of methodological and disciplinary perspectives have queried whether this is indeed the case.[3] In recent year a variety of international lawyers have argued that the authority of international law is better conceived through the prism of constitutionalism and relative normative authority of international laws based on how they figure in the constitutional hierarchy of international law.[4] Others have argued the opposite, holding that international law's authority is

[1] James Leslie Brierly, *Laws of Nations* (6th edn, Oxford: Oxford University Press 1963) 54.

[2] For earlier influential statements, see Louis Henkin, 'International Law: Politics, Values and Functions: General Course on Public International Law' (1989) 216 *Recueil des Cours* 1, 46; Ian Brownlie, *Principles of Public International Law* (6th edn, Oxford: Oxford University Press 2006). For a more recent restatement, see Andrew Clapham, *Brierly's Law of Nations* (7th edn, Oxford: Oxford University Press 2012). For a similar observation about the standard view, see also Thomas Franck, *The Power of Legitimacy Among Nations* (New York: Oxford University Press 1990) 187.

[3] Andrew T Guzman, *How International Law Works: A Rational Choice Theory* (Oxford: Oxford University Press 2008); Mattias Kumm, 'The Cosmopolitan Turn in Constitutionalism: On the Relationship between Constitutionalism in and Beyond the State' in JL Dunoff and JP Trachtman (eds), *Constitutionalism, International Law and Global Government* (Cambridge: Cambridge University Press 2009); Eric A Posner, *The Perils of Global Legalism* (Chicago: Chicago University Press 2009); Jan Klabbers, Anne Peters, and Geir Ulfstein, *The Constitutionalization of International Law* (Oxford: Oxford University Press 2009); Nico Krisch, *Beyond Constitutionalism: The Pluralist Structure of Post-National Law* (Oxford: Oxford University Press 2010).

[4] Klabbers (n 3).

a matter of open contestation between different authorities domestically and internationally and that normative pluralism is the home for the authority of international law.[5] International lawyers that hold a will-based theory of authority or with a rational choice bent have questioned the idea of international law having any authority in the first place.[6] The authority of international law has also come under attack from political philosophers committed to democratic constitutionalism. Political philosophers have queried whether the term authority is the right one to use when discussing claims made by international law on individuals, pointing to the lack of legitimate democratic procedures in international law.[7] They have also asked what authority, if any, international law can have over democratic states.[8] Domestic constitutionalists have asserted that the authority of international law is dependent on what the domestic constitution in question thinks it is.[9]

It would not be accurate to claim all of these accounts as part of one big debate on the conceptual structure, normative underpinnings, and practical consequences of the authority of international law. Rather there are multiple debates, often with dramatically different starting points and conclusions about the nature and scope of the authority of international law. The debate draws from diverse intellectual traditions ranging from rational choice theory to constitutionalism, legal pluralism, and domestic political philosophy. With the exception of Grotius-inspired international constitutionalists, who hold that the authority of international law draws on constitutionalist values of the international legal order,[10] most of these accounts support the popular conclusion that the authority of international law is weak or suspect.

[5] Krisch (n 3). [6] Posner (n 3).

[7] Allen Buchanan, *Justice, Legitimacy, and Self-Determination: Moral Foundations for International Law* (Oxford: Oxford University Press 2003).

[8] Buchanan (n 7); Kristen Hessler, 'Resolving Interpretive Conflicts in International Human Rights Law' (2005) 13(1) *Journal of Political Philosophy* 29; Richard Bellamy, *Political Constitutionalism: A Republican Defence of the Constitutionality of Democracy* (Cambridge: Cambridge University Press 2007).

[9] Armin von Bogdandy 'Pluralism, Direct Effect and the Ultimate Say: On the Relationship between International and Domestic Constitutional Law' (2008) 6 *International Journal of Constitutional Law* 397.

[10] See representatively Bruno Simma, 'From Bilateralism to Community Interest in International Law' (1994) 250 *Recueil des Cours* 217; Bardo Fassbender, 'The UN Charter as the Constitution of the International Community' (1998) 36(3) *Colombia Journal of Transnational Law* 529; Christian Tomuschat, 'International Law: Ensuring the Survival of Mankind on the Eve of a New Century, General Course on Public International Law' (1999) 281 *Recueil des Cours* 9; Erika de Wet 'The International Constitutional Order' (2006) 55(1) *International and Comparative Law Quarterly* 51; Anne Peters, 'Compensatory Constitutionalism: The Function and Potential of Fundamental International Norms and Structures' (2006) 19(3) *Leiden Journal of International Law* 579.

For an international lawyer, the popularity of this conclusion amongst a wide and disparate audience is at best uncomfortable. Why is the standard view of the authority of international law under sustained attack? Are mainstream international lawyers that hold that the binding quality of international law confers authority on those laws engaged in an intellectual exercise that is regarded as having either no or limited effects on domestic legal orders? Is the claim to authority merely a fiction believed by mainstream international lawyers alone? Why do rational choice theorists, domestic political philosophers, domestic constitutionalists, and even some international lawyers themselves find the authority of international law suspect?

In this chapter I have two aims. The first is to set out the key tenets of existing approaches to the authority of international law. I start this review with what I dub 'the standard view of the authority of international law' (hereinafter the standard view) in mainstream international law. Whilst the most well-known feature of the standard view is that the authority of international law is based on state consent conferring binding qualities to international law, I aim to show that there are two more salient conceptual features of the standard view that are under explored: the decoupling of the authority of international law from its enforcement and from its neutrality. Most notably, the standard view depicts the authority of international law as an either/or concept. This is a 'take it or leave it' account of the authority of international law. In addition this view is a formal one that seeks to avoid further value judgments about the nature of the international legal system and whether we ought to differentiate the duties imposed by international law.

My second aim is to review the recent critical contributions to our understanding of the authority of international law. These contributions come from diverse traditions. Some stem from international law scholarship and others from the neighbouring disciplines of political science and political philosophy.

What is common in these contributions is their attempt to provide a *general attitude* towards the authority of international law, either in the form of support or skepticism. They, however, fall short of offering a doctrinal account about the very reach of the authority of international law over domestic legal orders. In addition, both the proponents of the authority of international law and its sceptics employ conceptions of authority that differ from each other. It is not just that the descriptive and normative senses of the term are conflated in these debates, but also that the normative debates centre on different conceptions about what having a claim to authority entails. The fact that multiple conceptions of authority are at work is not a problem in and of itself. It, however, shows the need for further conceptual analysis.

This critical overview of the existing debates on the authority of international law returns us to the central question posed in this book: what kinds of conceptual underpinnings should inform our understanding of the authority of international law? What is the best description of the authority of international law in relation to domestic authorities? Chapter 2 is an undertaking towards answering these questions.

## The Standard View: Consent as the Basis of Binding Quality

The standard view on the authority of international law is surprisingly lean and simple. In the words of one of the most sophisticated modern international lawyers, '[A] state is not subject to any external authority unless it has voluntarily consented to such authority.'[11] In other words, the source of the binding authority of international law is the acceptance of that authority by states. Once it can be shown that a state has consented to a piece of international law, it enjoys authority in the domestic system in that international law has the legitimate right to impose duties on domestic legal orders and demand observance in return. The standard view of the authority of international law sees international law as having practical authority, not persuasive authority.[12] This means that international law provides states with reasons for action (or inaction) rather than advice that states are free either to take or to set aside. International law's authority is action-guiding because states confer a binding quality to it through hypothetical or actual consent.

On first analysis, linking the binding nature of international law to consent of states seems straightforward. This distinguishes international law from political statements, conversations, or the actions of states, as well as from what states or other actors may wish international law to be (international law *lex ferenda*).[13] The only international law that has a claim to authority is the one that can be shown to be binding on states. Other types of law, most notably soft law, may still be observed by states. The crucial difference, according to the standard view, is that soft law enjoys persuasive authority

[11] Louis Henkin, International Law: Politics. Values, and Functions (1989) 216 Recueil des Courrs D'Academie de Droit International Law 9, 27.

[12] On the distinction see Grant Lamond, 'Persuasive Authority in the Law' (2010) 17(1) *Harvard Review of Philosophy* 16.

[13] Jan Klabbers, 'The Redundancy of Soft Law' (1996) 65(2) *Nordic Journal of International Law* 167, 181.

rather than practical authority.[14] A state may follow soft law because it is persuaded by the merits of the regulatory proposals. A state that does not follow soft law, however, does not become a violator of international law because of disrespect for its authority.

Over the years consent-based theories of international law have proved adaptable to the changing nature of the international legal order.[15] International lawyers have come to employ flexible definitions of consent. The influence that it has on international legal practice is important and it continues to inform the 'standard account'.[16] This is despite sustained criticisms and important queries as to whether general consent is indeed compatible with the individual autonomy of states.[17] As Duncan Hollis puts it, 'Notwithstanding criticism of Article 38 and state consent, most international lawyers rely on them as international law's operating framework'.[18]

The proponents of the standard view have put forward source-sensitive theories of consent. Consent can be explicit or tacit,[19] individual or general.[20] Consent-based theories of authority have an easy, straightforward position when dealing with ordinary treaty law and place all ordinary treaty law as made binding through the explicit consent of states.

For consent-based theories of legal obligation, a treaty that has been ratified by a state automatically has the quality of binding law (subject to reservations)[21] and, therefore, enjoys authority. For example, it is not controversial to prove how binding Article 20 of the 1961 Vienna Convention on Diplomatic Relations is against state parties. This grants a diplomatic

[14] Christine M Chinkin, 'The Challenge of Soft Law: Development and Change in International Law' (1989) 38 *International and Comparative Law Quarterly* (1989) 850.

[15] Henkin (n 11); Brownlie (n 2); Bruno Simma and Andreas L Paulus, 'The Responsibility of Individuals for Human Rights Abuses in Internal Conflicts: A Positivist View' (1999) 93(2) *American Journal of International Law* 302, 307.

[16] Brierly, for example, was skeptical about whether consent can assign binding qualities to international law. As he put it 'consent cannot of itself create an obligation; it can do so only within a system of law which declares that consent duly given, as in a treaty or a contract, shall be binding on the party consenting'. James Brierly, *The Law of Nations* (Oxford: Oxford University Press 1950) 54.

[17] Anne Peters, for example, holds that the current system is no longer governed by individual consent, but by a majoritarian system. Anne Peters, 'Global Constitutionalism Revisited' (2005) 11 *International Legal Theory* 39, 51.

[18] Duncan B Hollis, 'Why Consent Still Matters—Non-State Actors, Treaties, and the Changing Sources of International Law' (2005) 23 *Berkeley Journal of International Law* 137.

[19] *SS 'Lotus', France v Turkey,* Judgment, (1927) PCIJ Series A no 10, ICGJ 248 (PCIJ 1927), 7 September 1927, Permanent Court of International Justice (historical) (PCIJ).

[20] On the use of general consent, see Louis Henkin, *International Law: Politics and Values* (Dordrecht: Brill 1995) 28.

[21] Cf Vienna Convention on the Law of Treaties (adopted 23 May 1969, entered into force 27 January 1980) 1155 UNTS 331 (VCLT 1969).

mission and its head the use of the flag and emblem of the sending state on the premises of the mission, including at the residence of the head of the mission, and on their means of transport in any ratifying state.[22] A state that has signed, but not ratified this treaty is assumed to be in a transition phase between fully binding obligations and obligations not to act in full disrespect to the spirit of the treaty.[23] A state that has entered reservations compatible with the object and the purpose of the treaty accepts the binding quality of international laws minus the provisions to which it has entered reservations.[24]

The binding quality of customary international laws has always proved more difficult to illustrate.[25] In the case of customary international law the very binding nature of the law hinges on the interpretation of evidence of state practice and opinio juris about which there may be reasonable disagreement.[26] Under customary international law the silence of states to crystallizing norms of international law point to their tacit consent. This is because the binding quality of the nature of law not only depends on intentional actions (be this actual practice or legal motivation accompanying the practice) by states, but also on the reactions of other states. The standard view also operates with general consent rather than individual consent in the case of custom formation.[27] The lack of a final interpretive authority in the international system often means that most 'would be custom' norms are not confirmed by anyone in the international legal system, consequently making their authority more suspect in the domestic order.[28] For the standard view, however, this is not a problem concerning the authority of international law per se. The problem is simply the empirical verification of the binding quality of a customary norm. States are assumed to know and be bound by custom, even if

[22] Vienna Convention on Diplomatic Relations (adopted 18 April 1961, entered into force 24 April 1964) 500 UNTS 95. Available at: http://untreaty.un.org/ilc/texts/instruments/english/conventions/9_1_1961.pdf.

[23] VCLT 1969 art 18. [24] VCTL 1969 art 19.

[25] *Jurisdictional Immunities of the State* (*Germany v Italy: Greece Intervening*) [2012] ICJ Rep 99 (*Jurisdictional Immunities*).

[26] Michael Akehurst, 'Custom as a Source of International Law' (1975) 47(1) *British Yearbook of International Law* 1, 26–7. There is also disagreement on the very components of customary international law. Frederic L Kirgis, 'Custom on a Sliding Scale' (1987) 81 *American Journal of International Law* 146; John Tasioulas, 'In Defence of Relative Normativity: Communitarian Values and the Nicaragua Case' (1996) 16(1) *Oxford Journal of Legal Studies* 85; Anthea Elizabeth Roberts, 'Traditional and Modern Approaches to Customary International Law: A Reconciliation' (2001) 95 *American Journal of International Law* 757.

[27] Simma (n 10).

[28] Akehurst (n 26), 20. This is not always the case. See for example the ICRC Compilation of the Customary International Laws of War, which by many is regarded as an authoritative text on the state of custom. Jean-Marie Henckaerts and Louise Doswald-Beck, *Customary International Humanitarian Law* (Cambridge: Cambridge University Press 2005).

an international or domestic court has not officially confirmed the customary norm.[29]

A much-debated issue within the standard account of the authority of international law has been the status of *pacta sunt servanda* and *ius cogens* norms and whether these norms require the consent of a state to be binding, or whether they are international laws that do not require the consent of states to wield authority.[30] The standard view's response to these questions is to suggest that the tools of tacit and general consent can address these problems. Ius cogens norms are not norms that are completely outside the consensual paradigm of international law.[31] The difficulty in illustrating the binding quality of ius cogens norms is akin to difficulties encountered with customary international law. Similar to custom, one has to show a level of acceptance of an ius cogens norm. In addition, however, an ius cogens norm must be recognized as such by the community of states. Only then can it have the unique power to restrict the scope of future consensual relations between states, alongside having authority over domestic legal orders. Once the acceptance and recognition of an ius cogens norm is ascertained, consensual relations that are in violation of it are treated as null and void.[32] This is not a contradiction as the basis of ius cogens to override ordinary norms is viewed to be consensual in the international system. The kind of authority that an ius cogens norm has in the domestic order is no different from the authority of any other norm of international law as far as the relationship between international law and domestic legal orders is concerned. In addition to having this authority, however, ius cogens norms have additional constraining effects on the law-making powers of states in the international system. They bind states horizontally as well as vertically into the future.

Under the standard account, the binding quality of international court judgments is also ultimately tied to the consent of states. If a treaty confers a binding quality on court judgments, the court judgments make authoritative demands on states. International institutions, such as the United Nations

[29] *North Sea Continental Shelf Cases (Germany v Denmark; Germany v Netherlands)* [1969] ICJ Rep 3 (*North Sea Continental Shelf*).

[30] Prosper Weil, 'Towards Relative Normativity in International Law?' (1983) 77(3) *American Journal of International Law* 413; Karol Wolfke, *Custom in Present International Law* (2nd rev edn, Dordrecht: Martinus Nijhoff 1993) 87.

[31] Jan Klabbers, 'International Legal Positivism and Constitutionalism' in Kammeroffer and Asperamont (eds) *International Legal Positivism in a Post-Modern World* (Oxford: Oxford University Press 2014) 273; Erika de Wet, 'The Prohibition of Torture as an International Norm of jus cogens and Its Implications for National and Customary Law' (2004) 15(1) *European Journal of International Law* 97; Alexander Orakhelashvili, *Peremptory Norms in International Law* (Oxford: Oxford University Press 2006).

[32] VCLT 1969 art 53.

human rights treaty monitoring bodies, that deliver non-binding views are, in the final analysis, not binding pieces of international law and do not make binding authoritative claims. The standard view places them as only having persuasive authoritative claims on domestic legal orders.

## Authority as an Either/Or Concept (With a Twist)

Whilst the relationship between the standard view and consent is well known, an under-explored feature of the standard view is its conception of authority. Under the standard account, an international law is either binding or it is not. Viewing the authority of international law through its binding quality forces authority to be an either/or concept. A piece of international law cannot be a little bit binding or very binding. If international law has authority when it is shown to be binding, then this too is an absolute concept. Again, it cannot have too little or too much authority.

Whilst any piece of international law that can be tied to the consent of states has authority, a core doctrine that accompanies the standard view is the freedom of states to discharge their international law obligations in the ways they deem most appropriate within their domestic systems.[33] The standard view regards the authority of international law as a separate issue from that of the modes of enforcement of international law domestically. International law cannot micromanage how states respect its authority domestically. This does not, however, change the presumption that states are ultimately under the obligation to respect the authority of international law.

The either/or view of the authority of international law in the standard account on the one hand, and the separate treatment of the authority of international law from the enforcement of international law on the other, presents us with two conceptual shortcomings.

First, there is a clear legal policy danger in recognizing the freedom of states to give effect to international law domestically. Such freedom can easily collapse into the failure to treat international law as authoritative. In other words, if domestic authorities are unwilling to respect the authority of international law, they may choose to under-comply with the authoritative norms.[34]

Second, the strict formulation of the authority of international law does not, on first analysis, seem to offer any defence of necessity to domestic

[33] Robert Jennings and Arthur Watts (eds), *Oppenheim's International Law*, vol 1 (9th edn, Harlow: Longman 1992) 82–3.

[34] A classic example of this is the enforcement of the *Abdulaziz, Cabales, and Balkandali v United Kingdom* case by the domestic authorities in the UK. The European Court of Human

authorities. Can it never be the case that a domestic authority may be in the position of being unable to respect the authority of international law?

This issue has also been raised by the proponents of the standard account.[35] This we may call the 'incapacity to obey or respect problem'. The response has been to argue that any incapacity to obey or respect international law is not a problem of the authority of international law as such, but rather a problem of giving effect to the authority of international law in domestic legal systems. The standard view, therefore, does not question the fact that a domestic legal order, with its own sphere of authority and with the capacity to devise different ways of respecting the authority of international law is in place. However, the standard view also requires that the fact that domestic legal orders enjoy a claim to authority in their own sphere does not impinge upon the claim to authority international law has over its areas of regulation through consensual international law-making. A state that makes a domestic defence of necessity argument in order not to fulfil duties imposed by international law may be acting in accordance with domestic law, but will nevertheless be regarded as acting in violation of international law.[36] This is also echoed in the case law of international courts and, ultimately, in the Vienna Convention on the Law of Treaties (VCLT). The Permanent Court of International Justice in the case of *Greek and Bulgarian Communities*, for example, stated that it was 'a generally accepted principle of international law that in relations between powers who are contracting powers to a treaty the provisions of municipal law cannot prevail over that treaty'.[37] This view has also been reflected in Article 27 of the VCLT. Article 27 states that 'A party may not invoke the provisions of its internal law as justification for its failure to perform a treaty'.[38]

Since the VCLT came into force this provision has been repeated in most textbooks, often as evidence for the argument that the authority of international law over domestic systems is given. Article 27 of the VCLT is indeed a measure to keep the authority of international law intact vis-à-vis domestic legal orders, preventing states from flouting international law by hiding

Rights in this case ruled that treating male and female migrant workers differently by allowing male migrants to bring their families to the UK, but not allowing female workers to do the same was in violation of art 8 (right to respect for family life) of the European Convention on Human Rights together with art 14 (non-discrimination). In order to enforce the judgment, the UK then revoked the male workers' right to bring their wives into the UK as well. *Abdulaziz, Cabales, and Balkandali v United Kingdom* (1985) 7 EHRR 471.

[35] Dionisio Anzilotti, *Cours de Droit International* (Sirey 1929) 57, quoted in Brownlie (n 2) 34.

[36] Brownlie (n 2) 35.

[37] *Greek and Bulgarian Communities (Advisory Opinion)* PCIJ Rep Series B No 17.

[38] VCLT 1969 art 27.

behind their domestic ones. The historical background of this doctrine, however, shows that it was initially developed with the assumption that subject matters regulated by international law are distinct from those regulated by domestic law.[39]

The analysis above shows that the either/or view of the authority of international law is sustained through decoupling the authority of international law from enforcement and insisting that domestic law is irrelevant for making counter-claims concerning authority. Both of these moves come with important costs. Granting full freedom of action to states domestically to give effect to the authority of international law sends the wrong signal about international laws that do not allow for any freedom of action domestically. Insisting that all international laws enjoy primacy as a matter of Article 27 also overlooks the fact that domains of regulation between international law and domestic law are no longer clear-cut. The drafters of the VCLT were not thinking of an international legal context where international laws and domestic constitutional norms were routinely overlapping and intersecting.

## Formal Neutrality and the Standard View

The standard view strives to offer a normatively neutral understanding of the authority of international law. In particular it seeks to remain neutral in relation to the competing visions of the relationship between the international legal system and domestic legal systems. The standard view neither tries to advocate for the unity of international and domestic legal systems (à la monism) nor for a thesis where these systems are separate (à la dualism).[40] Instead, it aims to steer a middle way by both advocating for the authority of binding international law alongside the possibility of domestic legal systems giving effect to international law through a variety of domestic measures. For example, whether a state is self-styled as monist or dualist by way of its constitutional design does not have any consequences for the standard view of the authority of international law. Just as it is up to the state to choose the means it uses to respect the authority of international law, it is also up to the state to declare itself as either a monist or dualist state. Whilst monism signals that states allow domestic courts a more active role in respecting the authority of international law, dualism assigns the primary duty for respecting international law to executives and parliaments. From the perspective of

[39] Ian Brownlie, *Principles of Public International Law* (7th edn, Oxford: Oxford University Press 2008) 31.

[40] For a fuller discussion of these see Chapter 4.

international law, these are simply two different ways, even perhaps styles, of respecting international legal authority.

Any solution that ties the authority of international law to its binding nature and defends the authority of international law over domestic law, not as a matter of primacy, or hierarchy, but as a matter of consent, is best conceived as a formal theory.[41] This approach is formal in the sense that it does not rest on a pre-defined value system, but merely on the ascertainment of the binding qualities of law based on consent.[42] For example, the standard view is neutral when it comes to questions such as whether international law's main concern is inter-state peace and security, some notion of the common good, or broadly conceived concerns about rights or justice. Nor does the standard theory pass judgment on the depth of co-operation or integration amongst states. For example, the view does not discuss whether the international system is one of anarchy, co-operation, or solidarity.[43] Nor does it discuss whether values such as human rights underpin the authority of a special set of norms.[44]

The implication is that consent-based standards of legitimacy for the authority of international law should hold regardless of what kinds of thicker views one has about the nature of the international legal system and the level of interdependence and normative integration in that very system. If, for example, one argues that the contemporary international system is based on an ingrained principle of co-operation, the standard view would see this reflected in the substantive norms to which states show consent. There is, therefore, no need to formulate a further legitimate basis for the authority of international law over domestic legal orders.[45] The same observation would hold for other types of conceptions of the international legal order. The standard view is compatible with each without demanding a particular characterization of the international legal order. It merely starts from

[41] On formalism in international law see Jean d'Aspremont, *Formalism and the Sources of International Law: A Theory of the Ascertainment of the Legal Rules* (Oxford: Oxford University Press 2011).

[42] Ibid. 13.

[43] Hedley Bull, *The Anarchical Society: A Study of Order in World Politics* (Basingstoke: Macmillan 1977); Nicholas J Wheeler, *Saving Strangers: Humanitarian Intervention in International Society* (Oxford: Oxford University Press 2000).

[44] Matthias Kumm, 'The Legitimacy of International Law: A Constitutionalist Framework of Analysis' (2004) 15(5) *European Journal of International Law* 907.

[45] This argument has also been put forward in the case of the European Union. See Bruno De Witte, 'The European Union as an international legal experiment' in Gráinne de Búrca and Joseph H H Weiler (eds), *The Worlds of European Constitutionalism* (Cambridge: Cambridge University Press 2011) 19.

the assumption that the consent-based binding quality of international law assigns authority to it.

The neutral and, by implication, formal nature of the standard view shields its proponents from having to provide any kind of normative justification (other than the consent of states to international law) for why international law should enjoy practical authority over and above state institutions and officials. In this way, the standard view steers clear away from discussing the moral basis of the authority of international law.

The formal neutrality of the standard view has a number of advantages when analysed from the perspective of legal policy and doctrinal guidance. In a world in which, in effect, states do not always respect the authority of international laws to which they have expressly provided consent, it is problematic to adopt a position that ties the authority of international law to deeper values, rather than simply to its binding quality through consent. Such values are often contested or may amount to pointing to the values of a particular group of states as the source of the authority of international law.[46] Inherent in such a move is the erosion of the distinction between authority and coercion.[47] To claim that international law has authority over states is to suggest that international law offers a distinct reason for action on the part of state authorities. If international law imposes a set of values over states, there is no longer an authority relationship between international law and states. It becomes one of coercion in which states are acting in a particular way because they do not have any other option. The formal approach to the authority of international law bypasses the problem of collapsing the authority of international law into such a relationship. This view also allows for a defence of the independence of international law from its makers—states. Whilst states are the creators of international law, once international law is created, it forms an authority relationship with the states that have consented to it.

Aside from the advantage of allowing international lawyers to make clear demands for the authority of international law, however, the standard view falls short of offering a comprehensive defence of the authority of international law over domestic legal systems. The standard account does not openly discuss the pitfalls of the relationship between the authority of international law and the doctrine of the freedom of means to discharge

[46] Benedict Kingsbury, 'Legal Positivism as Normative Politics: International Society, Balance of Power and Lassa Oppenheim's Positive International Law' (2002) 13 *European Journal of International Law* 401 at 426; Jason Beckett, 'Behind Relative Normativity: Rules and Process as a Prerequisite of Law' (2001) 12 *European Journal of International Law* 627.

[47] A conceptual mark of authority, on the other hand, is its distinctiveness from coercion. Richard E Flathman, *The Practice of Political Authority: Authority and the Authoritative* (Chicago: The University of Chicago Press 1980).

one's duties towards international law. In an international world, in which international law regulates a diverse range of issue areas, most of which go beyond the co-ordination of inter-state diplomatic relations, how convincing is this formal view of authority based on the primacy of international law and the freedom to choose the means through which to respect that authority? Should the authority of international law be conceived as an either/or concept? Should international law remain oblivious to the domestic capacities of states to respect it, or their arguments in favour of not respecting it? The downside of the lack of a systematic discussion of these questions is that the standard view becomes an axiomatic defence of the authority of international law, rather than a fully developed account with explicit conceptual underpinnings.

I now turn to debates that go beyond the formalistic and value-neutral standard view of the authority of international law to investigate whether the thicker constitutionalist and pluralist conceptions of the international legal order can offer answers to some of these questions.

## Constitutionalist and Pluralist Conceptions of the Authority of International Law

Discussions surrounding constitutionalist and pluralist conceptions of the authority of international law have proliferated in recent years, particularly in response to current developments in international law. On the one hand, European Union law brought theoretical challenges to international lawyers and asked whether a sui generis inter-state entity with constitutional features could move us beyond authority as being binding law in international law. On the other hand, the debate on the fragmentation of international law under current conditions of globalization spearheaded soul searching about norm conflicts and the authoritative demands of international law.[48] Constitutionalism and pluralism have, to a large extent, developed to make

[48] Both constitutionalism and pluralism are ideas with a much longer intellectual tradition. The classic text in the German tradition is often identified as A Verdross, *Die Verfassung der Völkerrechtsgemeinschaft* (1926). In English, see T Opsahl, 'An "International Constitutional Law"?' (1961) 10 *International & Comparative Law Quarterly* 760; C Tomuschat 'International Law: Ensuring the Survival of Mankind on the Eve of a new century' (Hague Academy of International Law, General Course on Public International Law) (1999) 281 *Recueil des Cours* pp 9–438. On theoretical foundations of pluralism see, John Griffiths, 'What is legal pluralism?' (1986) 24(1) *Journal of Legal Pluralism* 2; Peter Fitzpatrick, *The Mythology of Modern Law* (London: Routledge 1992); Chris Fuller, 'Legal Anthropology, Legal Pluralism and Legal Thought' (1994) 10(3) *Anthropology Today* 9; Boaventura de Sousa Santos, *Towards a New Common Sense*

sense of these current developments. These two frameworks are not pointed conceptual debates about international legal authority. Rather, they are part of larger attempts to make sense of the structure of the contemporary international legal order. They both have important implications for the standard view.

Unlike the formal attributes of the standard view, the pluralist and constitutionalist approaches rely on and develop normative views beyond state consent. They operate by making a priori observations or assumptions about the nature and characteristics of the international legal order. In light of these, adjustments to different aspects of the standard view become necessary. These a priori characterizations of the international legal order are either presented descriptively, with reference to new legal developments illustrating how the basic assumptions concerning the international legal order have changed, or interpretively as the most fitting ways of explaining the nature of the international legal order. In both constitutionalist and pluralist accounts, however, the empirically descriptive and constructive dimensions of the analysis are often intertwined. As I will discuss later in this chapter, observers who are unimpressed with the characterization of the legal order by constitutionalists or pluralists have branded this scholarship too Euro-centric at best.[49] At worst it is seen as too removed from reality to claim to be an accurate description of general international law.[50]

In order to understand why constitutionalist and pluralist approaches to the authority of international law have become prevalent, it is necessary to consider two current developments: the challenges that the European Union and the proliferation of international legal regimes pose to international legal theory. Let me consider these in turn.

## EU Law and Fragmentation as Challenges to the Standard Account

Although the European Union is a creation of international law, the debate about whether the EU is a 'strong case' for moving beyond the standard view of authority in general international law is long standing.[51] If European Union law aims to integrate 28 states more deeply, does this mean its authority

(London: Routledge 1995); Sally Engle Merry, *Colonising Hawai'i: The Cultural Power of Law* (Princeton: Princeton University Press 2000).

[49] Guzman (n 3). [50] Posner (n 3).

[51] Daniel Halberstam 'Constitutionalism and Pluralism in Marbury and Van Gend' in Miguel Poiares Maduro and Loïc Azoulai (eds), *The Past and Future of EU Law: Revisiting the Classics on the 50th Anniversary of the Rome Treaty* (Oxford: Hart Publishing 2008); de Búrca (n 45).

should be understood in ways that match the normative intentions of its creators? Are European Union member states under a more profound duty to respect the authority of European Union law? Does European Union law have authority on grounds other than the binding nature of the treaty? In other words, does it attract obedience for reasons beyond the standard account?

These questions have prompted European Union lawyers to look beyond the bindingness of international law paradigm of authority when trying to make sense of the relationship between domestic legal orders and the EU.[52] This has led to approaches that define the authority of the European Union in constitutionalist, pluralist, and more recently, in constitutional pluralist terms.[53] European Union lawyers have found themselves divided between seeing the European legal order either as a thick political community with top down constitutional principles or as a heterogeneous political community with multiple authorities co-existing side-by-side that make strong, but incommensurate claims to authority simultaneously.[54]

In European Union law literature, constitutionalism has a number of meanings. There are two uses of the term in particular. One is the acceptance of other (constitutive) grounds for the legitimacy of EU law beyond mere state consent. The second is the assumption that higher constitutive rules exist (rules emanating from EU law itself) which would resolve authority competitions between domestic legal orders and the EU.[55] Pluralism, on the other hand, claims that there are competing claims to authority in the European Union, and these cannot simply be resolved by reference to a priori EU constitutional norms.[56] The outcomes of authority competition have to reflect the plurality of authorities.

Whilst these approaches have developed in response to the *sui generis* problems of political and legal integration within the EU, they have also attracted

[52] Joseph H H Weiler, 'A Constitution for Europe? Some Hard Choices' (2002) 40(4) *Journal of Common Market Studies* 563; de Wet (n 9) 52–3; Martin Louhglin and Neil Walker (eds), *The Paradox of Constitutionalism: Constituent Power and Constitutional Form* (Oxford: Oxford University Press 2007).

[53] I must enter a caveat here when discussing these two debates. The analyses move—often frequently—between descriptive and normative discussions of the state of international law. I will distinguish, as far as possible, between the descriptive and the normative versions in the following discussion.

[54] Neil Walker, 'Beyond boundary disputes and basic grids: Mapping the global disorder of normative orders' (2008) 6 *International Journal of Constitutional Law* 373.

[55] I am wary of making definitions of constitutionalism and pluralism here as there is a lively debate on what these terms mean. See eg Weiner and others 'Why a new journal on global constitutionalism? Global Constitutionalism—Human Rights, Democracy, and the Rule of Law' (2012) 1(1) *Global Constitutionalism* 1.

[56] Krisch (n 3).

significant theoretical currency amongst general international lawyers. It is safe to state that constitutionalism and pluralism have become the broad conceptual frameworks for approaching the authority of international law.[57]

The second significant development which has made international lawyers turn to the language of constitutionalism and pluralism is what has been framed as the debate on the 'fragmentation of international law'.[58] This debate holds that the proliferation of international law since 1945 has brought unique challenges to understanding the authority of international law. This both from the perspective of domestic legal orders and the perspective of horizontally situated international legal regimes.[59] There are now a number of multilateral treaty regimes that regulate overlapping issues. For example, many states have signed up to both multilateral human rights treaties regulating economic and social rights and bilateral investment treaties granting concessions or immunities to multinational corporations. These treaties send conflicting authority signals to states, such that if a state accepts the authority of one treaty, it may be disrespecting another.[60] The treaties also send conflicting signals to international interpretive authorities. Article 31(3) of the Vienna Convention on the Law of the Treaties requires state parties to take 'any relevant rules of international law applicable in the relations between the parties' into account.[61] This means that an international interpretive authority must decide the extent to which another body of international law is relevant to the interpretation of a treaty for which it is responsible.[62]

In these situations, the standard view's axiom that each binding commitment has authority over domestic systems seems less helpful. An argument is still needed for why one of the commitments has more authority than another. One is forced to offer reasons other than the binding nature of the treaty for the acceptance or non-acceptance of the authority of these treaties. The literature on the 'fragmentation of international law' has therefore

[57] Kumm, (n 45); Klabbers et. al (n 3); Krisch (n 3).

[58] The International law Commission in 2002 established a Study Group on 'Fragmentation of International Law: Difficulties arising from the Diversification and Expansion of International Law', and presented a Report to the UN General Assembly in 2006: GE.06-62863. See indicatively Martii Koskenniemi and Paivi Leino 'Fragmentation of International Law? Postmodern Anxieties' (2002) 15(3) *Leiden Journal of International Law* 553.

[59] Matthew Craven, 'Unity, Diversity and the Fragmentation of International Law' (2005) 14 *Finnish Yearbook of International Law* 3.

[60] *Sawhoyamaxa Indigenous Community v Paraguay* Inter-American Court of Human Rights Series C No 146 (29 March 2006).

[61] Joost Pauwelyn, *Conflict of Norms in Public International Law: How WTO Law Relates to Other Rules of International Law* (Cambridge: Cambridge University Press 2003) 161–212.

[62] *Behrami v France*; *Saramati v France, Germany and Norway* (2007) 45 EHRR SE10 (GC joined cases); Case C-402/04, *P Kadi and Al Barakaat International Foundation v Council* [2008] ECR I-6351, Opinion of AG Maduro.

prompted international lawyers to consider whether some treaties have a stronger claim to authority than others (say because of its constitutional features), and on what grounds they may enjoy such authority.[63] The constitutionalism and pluralism debates offer significant—if opposing—solutions also to the fragmentation debate.

## Constitutionalist Conceptions of the Authority of International Law

A constitutionalist analysis of the authority of international law requires a view of the international legal system as one in which some constitutional values, laws, and practices are present and action-guiding both as means for marking out the boundaries of legitimate forms of politics and as a means of resolving conflicting or overlapping claims by multiple actors. There is often a tension between descriptive and normative constitutional projects of international law.[64] Descriptive constitutionalists might argue that, in descriptive terms, certain treaties or principles already operate like constitutional principles and that there is no need for a world state or a world court for an international consensus on such principles.[65] There are also those who view constitutionalism as a realistic utopia, in the sense that it is the most normatively compelling project which one should strive to achieve in practice.[66] These tensions aside, constitutionalism, in its most general sense, evokes an understanding of the international legal system as an order in which certain norms have authority over domestic officials regardless of state consent.[67] The assumption of the system as an order (rather than, for example, a temporary juxtaposition of norms and actors) made up of constitutive elements has implications for the conceptual underpinnings of authority.

[63] Christoph Schreuer and Ursula Kriebaum, 'From Individual to Community Intertest in International Investment Law' in Ulrich Fastenrath and others (eds), *From Bilateralism to Community Interest: Essays in Honour of Bruno Simma* (Oxford: Oxford University Press 2011); Erika de Wet and Jure Vidmar, *Hierarchy in International Law: The Place for Human Rights?* (Oxford: Oxford University Press 2012).

[64] T Giegerich, 'The *Is* and *Ought* of International Constitutionalism: How Far Have We Come on Habermas's Road to a "Well Considered Constitutionalization of International Law"?' (2009) 10(1) *German Law Journal* 31, 38.

[65] I would place Kumm's discussion in this category. See Kumm (n 45).

[66] Jürgen Habermas, 'The Crisis of the European Union in the Light of a Constitutionalisation of International Law' (2012) 23(2) *European Journal of International Law* 335.

[67] Joseph Weiler, 'Prologue: Global and Pluralist Constitutionalism: Some Doubts' in Gráinne de Búrca and Joseph H H Weiler (eds), *The Worlds of European Constitutionalism* (Cambridge: Cambridge University Press 2011) 8, 12.

The constitutional norms of the international system enjoy authority not because they acquire the legally binding status of law (although in most cases they would also fulfil that), but because of their transcendental constitutional quality. Constitutionalist approaches, therefore, accept that there must be a hierarchy of norms in the totality of the universe of international and domestic legal systems in the sense that some norms that are firmly located in the international legal system take priority over other norms or considerations in the domestic legal system.

This conceptualization has implications for a number of features of the standard view. Firstly, it challenges the distinction between states undertaking one type of business internationally and another domestically. If a norm is said to have a constitutional character as a matter of universal law,[68] it breaks down the barrier between domestic and international law and makes action-guiding claims on any *actor* in a position to address that norm. The ambivalence of the standard view towards the relationship between domestic and international orders can no longer hold under constitutional approaches. Secondly, constitutionalism gives extra force to the claim of international law that domestic laws do not constitute an obstacle to the performance of obligations under an international law, when such obligations have constitutive character. This implies that some international norms have to have more authority—independent of state consent—in domestic legal orders than other norms. Thirdly, constitutionalism differentiates between international laws that are subject to the ongoing consent of states and those that have a legitimate authority according to other values, such as original consent or moral foundation. The authority of some norms cannot therefore be questionned by domestic legal orders.

A central debate within constitutionalist approaches is the attempt to show which bodies of international law have constitutional qualities and, therefore, are able to impose duties on all actors in the constitutional system—encompassing both the domestic and international legal orders. Mattias Kumm calls these norms the foundational blocks of 'global public law' thus collapsing the distinction between domestic and international law and creating direct duties for domestic officials under international constitutional law.[69]

Constitutionalists often distinguish between structural and fundamental constitutional norms.[70] Structural constitutional norms are those that

[68] Mattias Kumm, 'The Cosmopolitan Turn in Constitutionalism: An Integrated Conception of Public Law' (2013) 20(2) *Indiana Journal of Global Legal Studies* 605.

[69] Mattias Kumm, 'Constitutionalism and the Cosmopolitan State' (2013) *NYU Public Law and Legal Theory Research Paper Series* Working Paper No 13–68.

[70] Alfred Verdross, 'Droit international public et droit interne' (1954) 32(3) *Revue de Droit International de Sciences Diplomatiques et Politiques* 219, 221.

constitute the international system proper. They operate as Kelsen's *grundnorm* and condition the remaining international laws.[71] Structural international norms, for example, explain why international norms are binding in the first place.[72] The authority of international law, therefore, flows from the constitutional quality of these norms, not from the immediate consensual qualities a particular norm has. Fundamental constitutional norms, on the other hand, are those that would trump other norms when they are in conflict. Scholars, for example, have proposed the ban on the use of force, ius cogens norms, or human rights provisions as fundamental constitutional norms.[73]

Which norms should have constitutional quality and on what grounds is, however, subject to dispute. A well-known proposal by Verdross was to derive substantive constitutional norms from the UN Charter.[74] Verdross put forward two reasons for this: first, that almost all states have ratified the Charter, pointing to solid collective consent,[75] and second, that Article 103 of the UN Charter explicitly provides for the Charter to trump any other international treaty with which it may come into conflict. This offers both a consensual backing and a substantive backing to the norms embodied in the Charter.

Others, most notably Kumm, argue that constitutional norms are in effect a distinct set of principles that generate different kinds of duties of obedience in domestic legal orders.[76] He proposes that these principles are: the formal principle of international legality, the jurisdictional principles of subsidiarity, the procedural principle of adequate participation and accountability, and the substantive principle of respect for fundamental rights.[77] In Kumm's version, each of these principles has a corresponding justification for its constitutional quality, which is not directly wedded to state consent.

[71] Hans Kelsen, *Principles of International Law* (New York: Rinehart, 1952); also Verdross (n 70).

[72] Verdross explains this as 'Wir nennen den allgemeinen Teil des Völkerrechtes die "Verfassung der Völkerrechtsgemeinschaft" um dadurch zum Ausdruck zu bringen, daß auch das Völkerrecht keine bloße Sammlung von einzelnen Bruchstücken ist, die keinen inneren Zusammenhang aufweisen, sondern eine harmonische Ordnung von Normen bildet, die in einer einheitlichen Grundordnung verankert sind' in Alfred Verdross, *Die Einheit des rechtlichen Weltbildes auf Grundlage der Völkerrechtsverfassung* (The Unity of the Legal Order on the Basis of the International Constitution) (Tübingen 1923) 59.

[73] Andreas L Paulus, '*Jus Cogens* in a Time of Hegemony and Fragmentation—An Attempt at a Re-appraisal' (2005) 74 *Nordic Journal of International Law* 297.

[74] Thomas Kleinlein 'Alfred Verdross as a Founding Father of International Constitutionalism?' (2012) 4(2) *Goettingen Journal of International Law* 385.

[75] Ibid. [76] Kumm (n 3). [77] Kumm (n 45) 917.

How does constitutionalism alter and affect the standard account of the authority of international law? First, this approach is one that is foremost interested in identifying norms with constitutional qualities. Norms with constitutional qualities—by that very same virtue—would make strong authority claims on all state officials (or international officials for that matter). It makes the claim that, once the constitutional quality of an international norm is accepted, the basis of the authority of that norm is decoupled from the ongoing consent of states to that norm. The norm attracts duties of obedience and respect due to the constitutional qualities it possesses. The constitutionalist account also offers a space for consent as a basis of authority for ordinary norms of international law.[78]

## Pluralist Conceptions of the Authority of International Law

Pluralist approaches to the authority of international law tackle the same questions as the constitutionalists, but reach more cautious descriptive conclusions about the existence of constitutional values and arrive at more open-ended prescriptions about the either/or quality of the authority of international law. For pluralists, a central tenet of the legal world is the co-existence of distinct, yet overlapping legal systems. Systemic pluralists such as Walker conceive international law and domestic law as closed and autonomous systems. These systems cannot ultimately claim any authority over each other.[79] Institutional pluralists, on the other hand, think that legal systems—be they domestic or international—are semi-autonomous. Sometimes one has a legitimate claim to authority and sometimes the opposite may be true.[80]

What is central to the pluralist conception of the authority of international law is the rejection of a hierarchical ordering of the international legal system. This is one area in which pluralists distinguish themselves from constitutionalists. Whilst constitutionalists insist that there are some hierarchical relationships between international law and domestic legal orders, pluralists have an open-ended attitude towards how the authority competition between different types of authorities is ultimately resolved.[81] Krisch, in particular, argues that the open-ended and indeterminate nature of the authority competition between international and domestic orders is also a normative virtue. He argues that pluralism is accurate descriptively, but also

[78] See in particular, Kumm's discussion of this. Kumm (n 69).

[79] Walker (n 54).

[80] Nico Krisch, 'The Case for Pluralism in Post National Law' in Gráinne de Búrca and Joseph H H Weiler (eds), *The Worlds of European Constitutionalism* (Cambridge:Cambridge University Press 2011) 203, 227–38.

[81] As Krich puts it 'Pluralsim promises to relax (formal) ties, to allow for adaptation to new circumstances in a more rapid and less formalised way: by leaving the legal relationships between subordinates undetermined, it keeps them open to political redefinition over time' Ibid. 228.

has strong normative appeal as the guardian of diversity in the international system.[82]

Pluralist conceptions of the authority of international law differ from the standard view in at least four ways. First, the pluralist account downplays the significance of consent in generating authority. It emphasizes dialogue between different kinds of authorities as a way of generating authoritative outcomes. Secondly, pluralism is not concerned with maintaining the formal position of the standard view. Instead, the conception of authority is informal, open to constant definition. Thirdly, pluralism abandons any claim to the primacy of international law as a matter of principle. As Krisch puts it 'it is a matter of political judgment' whether international law triumphs or not.[83]

There has been much debate about how much difference there is between constitutionalism and pluralism when conceiving authority relationships between international law and domestic legal orders.[84] The biggest difference between these frameworks would appear to be their disagreement on the description of the very nature of the international legal order. Whilst constitutionalist conceptions assume that it is possible to indicate stable points of international constitutional authority, pluralism contests this view. Constitutionalists, however, do not contest the view that the authority of ordinary international laws may be debated.[85] Neither do pluralists deny that a constitutionalist consensus could emerge amongst competing authorities.[86] As Weiler puts it, most of those who participate in the debate seem to concede that there are constitutionalist and pluralist dimensions to understanding the authority of international law.[87]

Two significant differences remain between the constitutionalist and the pluralist conceptions of authority and the standard conception of authority in international law. Firstly, the concept of constitutionalism allows for the assertion that some international laws have (or ought to have) a much stronger claim to authority than other international laws. This differs from the standard view that all international claims make the same claim to authority as long as they are shown to be binding. The constitutionalist account (at least some versions of it) also sits better with the higher authority of *ius cogens* norms over domestic legal orders than the standard view. Secondly, the

[82] Ibid. 229. [83] Krisch (n 3) 69.

[84] Alec Stone Sweet, 'Constitutionalism, Legal Pluralism, and International Regimes' (2009) 16(2) *Indiana Journal of Global Legal Studies* 633; Gráinne de Búrca, 'The European Court of Justice and the International Legal Order After Kadi' (2010) 51(1) *Harvard International Law Journal* 1; Neil Walker 'Postnational Constitutionalism and Postnational Public Law: A Tale of Two Neologisms' (2012) 3 *Transnational Legal Theory* 61.

[85] Kumm (n 3). [86] Krisch (n 3) 242. [87] Weiler (n 68) 18.

concept of pluralism introduces the idea of an ongoing rebuttal to understanding the authority of international law. This idea is rejected by the standard view and its interpretation of Article 27 of the Vienna Convention on the Law of Treaties.

## Self-Interest and the Authority of International Law

Constitutionalism and pluralism often justify the soundness of their approaches through the need to develop theories for changing times. The fundamental changes that have taken place in Europe with the establishment of the European Union and the European Court of Human Rights in the 1950s makes this a descriptively forceful perspective. Perspectives from international law scholarship in the US, however, fundamentally differ from theoretical approaches advanced in Europe.[88] The most prominent attacks on the standard view in US legal scholarship do not focus on whether international law embeds constitutional values or how values then create competition and conflicts of authority in a pluralist legal order. The focus is more fundamental. They ask whether legally binding documents at an international level can have any authority over domestic legal systems at all.[89]

Goldsmith and Posner have posed the most direct challenges.[90] The key conceptual challenge to the standard view of the authority of international law they make is to suggest that international law is not capable of claiming authority *proper* in relation to state authorities. Having authority *proper* has a very particular meaning here. Posner holds that the relationship between state authority and international law is not prima facie a case of an authority relationship. This has a dual dimension. First, international law does not possess the qualities of authority *proper*. Second, the state is not an institution that can be subject to external authority.

[88] Indeed, US international lawyers protest the dominance of the European Union in discussions on general international law. For example, Guzman states that '[the] extensive use of European examples strikes me as having little persuasive value when illustrating a general point about co-operation among states', Guzman (n 3) 14.

[89] Such an attach on the authority of international law is not new, and may be better conceived as the legacy of Hobbes, who viewed self-interest as the only source of stability internationally. On the relationship between Hobbes and contemporary rational choice scholarship, see, M Hollis and S Smith, *Explaining and Understanding International Relations* (Oxford: Clarendon Press 1990).

[90] Jack Goldsmith and Eric A Posner, *The Limits of International Law* (Oxford: Oxford University Press 2005); Posner (n 3).

It could be argued that this challenge is out-dated. It is not dissimilar to discussions that took place in the early nineteenth century about whether international law was *really* law.[91] If international law is not really law, then its claim to authority is suspect. Goldsmith and Posner do not take their challenge this far. They agree that international law is law. It is, however, a kind of sui generis law whose authority is both subject and content dependent. Their challenge has both descriptive and normative dimensions. In its descriptive dimension, Goldsmith and Posner start with a basic observation about international law: that it is not self-enforcing and is dependent on the co-operation of states to enforce it. They then make a key assumption about state actors, holding that states only enforce international laws that coincide with their self-interests. This assumption dovetails with explanatory political scientific approaches to international law, which regard compliance predominantly as an outcome of the opportunity structures and leverage powers of actors in the domestic context.[92] Putting these two observations together, Goldsmith and Posner argue that the standard view of authority in international law is simply a bad theory. It distorts the basic operation of international law, or how international law 'really' works.

By closely associating binding legal obligations under custom and treaty law with a rightful claim to authority over domestic actors, the standard view overlooks the fact that, whilst they do wish to co-operate with other states to advance their common interests, states do not co-operate in ways that would undermine their own interests. In other words, the principle of *pacta sunt servanda* does not impose a perfect obligation on states. It imposes an imperfect one on them. It is not theoretically or practically sound to assume that states would prioritize a legal obligation above and beyond the self-interest of that state as defined by domestic political actors. Some international laws would enjoy 'authority' as understood by the standard account, others would not. Whether international laws enjoy authority or not depends on whether states are in full agreement about how to co-ordinate their actions at a given time.[93] For example, a state may sign up to a human rights treaty because such a gesture is a cheap way of signalling to states with worse human rights records to do the same. This does not, however, mean that the same state would agree with the interpretation of freedom of expression advanced by

[91] John Austin, *The Province of Jurisprudence Determined* (ed W Rumble, 1995), Lecture 1.

[92] Xinyuan Dai, *International Institutions and National Processes* (Cambridge: Cambridge University Press 2007); Beth A Simmons, *Mobilizing for Human Rights: International Law in Domestic Politics* (Cambridge: Cambridge University Press 2009).

[93] Guzman (n 3) 28.

the body set up to monitor that same treaty. The true intention of the state in singing up to the treaty was not to fully submit itself to its authority.

In the self-interest version of authority, therefore, the authority of international law is not given. It is subject to content-dependent considerations by the subject of authority. The self-interest view demands that the conceptual understanding of the authority of international law be more closely associated with that of the political scientist. The reason that political science has a sceptical view of compliance with international law[94] (especially when compared to international lawyers)[95] is not because political scientists do not appreciate the authority pull of international law. It is because they insist that, conceptually speaking, this authority pull is subject to an initial screening by state interests.

## Democratic Legitimacy and International Law

The interest in the authority of international law amongst political philosophers is motivated by a different concern: that of the legitimacy of international law as a system of rules when pitted against the standards that make the state and its institutions legitimate.[96] In political theory, concerns for the legitimacy of institutions are ultimately tied to how the authority of an institution can be justified over individuals. This implies the need to focus on the individual as the ultimate subject of authority for any institution whose legitimacy is to be defended.[97] It is not that political philosophers share an aversion to international law, or are necessarily committed to the democratic state as the only legitimate authority.[98] Their concern is that international law lacks the qualities of a legitimate authority, thereby making the state, in particular the democratic state, the only game in town in terms of making claims

[94] George W Downs, David M Rocke, & Peter N Barsoom, 'Is the Good News About Compliance Good News About Cooperation?' (1996) 50 *International Organization* 379; James D Fearon, 'Bargaining, Enforcement, and International Cooperation' (1998) 52 *International Organization* 269; Oona A Hathaway, 'Why Do Countries Commit to Human Rights Treaties?' (2007) 51 *Journal of Conflict Resolution* 588; Jana Von Stein, 'Do Treaties Constrain or Screen? Selection Bias and Treaty Compliance' (2005) 99 *American Political Science Review* 611.

[95] Louis Henkin, *International Law: Politics, Values, and Functions* (1989) 216 *RCADI* 45; Abram Chayes and Antonia Chayes, *The New Sovereignty: Compliance with International Regulatory Agreements* (Cambridge: Harvard University Press 1998).

[96] Allen Buchanan, 'The Legitimacy of International Law' in Samantha Besson and John Tasioulas (eds), *The Philosophy of International Law* (Oxford: Oxford University Press 2010) 79.

[97] Samanth Besson, 'The Authority of International Law—Lifting the State Veil' (2009) 31 *Sydney Law Review* 342.

[98] Allen Buchanan and Robert Keohane, 'The Legitimacy of Global Governance Institutions' (2006) 20 *Ethics and International Affairs* 405.

to authority.[99] A key feature of the writings on the authority of international law by political theorists is their concern about how rules identified or interpreted by unaccountable bodies in seemingly far away places can impose obligations on democratically sanctioned parliaments or governments.[100]

Political philosophers have two types of objections to the standard view of authority in international law. Firstly, they find the standard view conceptually unsound. Secondly, they find it normatively indefensible. The conceptual objection to the standard of authority in international law stems from scepticism about the ability of international law to demand strict obedience from individuals. Political theory treats the political obligation to obey as a standard that is difficult to obtain even in the domestic case.[101] That international law can be capable of demanding obedience from individuals that also asks them to set aside their respect for domestic laws seem far-fetched from a political theory perspective. In other words, where standards for political obedience are high in the domestic context, what reasons are there for having no standards in the international context? The suggestion that binding international law has a claim to authority sits oddly with these questions. For this reason, political philosophers have even proposed abandoning the term 'authority' in the international context, and using 'legitimacy' instead.[102]

A further objection to the authority of international law is that it lacks democratic legitimacy. There is significant consensus amongst political philosophers that democracy is the most legitimate framework through which to measure the authority of domestic rule. What follows on from this consensus is a concern about the lack of meaningful democratic rule at an international level from the perspective of the citizens involved. This has led to democratic deficit criticisms being levied against international law, not only by political theorists[103] but also by international lawyers[104] and domestic constitutionalists.[105] From the perspective of the proponents of democratic legitimacy, the standard

[99] Hessler (n 8).

[100] Richard Bellamy, 'Political Constitutionalism and the Human Rights Act' (2011) 9 *International Journal of Constitutional Law* 86.

[101] Cf A John Simmons, *Moral Principles and Political Obligations* (Princeton: Princeton University Press 1979).

[102] Allen Buchanan and Robert O Keohane, 'The Legitimacy of Global Governance Institutions' (2006) 20(4) *Ethics and International Affairs* 405.

[103] Thomas Christiano, 'Democratic Legitimacy and International Institutions' in Samantha Besson and John Tasioulas (eds), *The Philosophy of International Law* (Oxford: Oxford University Press 2010) 119.

[104] Steven Wheatley, *The Democratic Legitimacy of International Law* (Oxford: Hart Publishing 2010).

[105] Armin von Bogdandy and Ingo Venzke, 'In Whose Name? An Investigation of International Courts' Public Authority and Its Democratic Justification' (2012) 23(1) *European Journal of International Law* 7.

view of the authority of international law is insensitive to the importance of democratic governance in backing up domestic constitutional regimes and offering authority to law. When a perfectly democratic rule comes into conflict with an international treaty, this inevitably leads to reactions from proponents of legitimacy that the latter lacks any democratic quality, hence full-blown pre-emptive authority. This is afterall why Mr Davis filed his motion in the UK Parliament.[106]

## The Authority of International Law: The Need for Appraisal

The standard international law assumption—that international laws enjoy authority because of the legally binding nature of international obligations—has been subject to revisionist international law theories. It has also come under attack from a diverse range of intellectual traditions informed by the neighbouring disciplines of political science and political theory.

Constitutionalist and the pluralist conceptualizations of authority have both called for differentiation concerning the level of authority international laws have over domestic legal orders. A by-product of this is the deconstruction of the formalistic and neutral qualities of the standard view of authority. Both constitutionalism and pluralism call for a normative turn in the conceptualization of the standard view of the authority of international law. They insist that arguing for the same degree of authority for all international laws based on variations of state consent theory is normatively impoverished. What we need is to make the normative values that underpin the authority claims of international law more explicit. It is time for domestic state officials to 'take sides' as to what values they believe are safeguarded by international law in order to decide when international law trumps domestic law.

The self-interest-based accounts of authority have called for a deeper questioning of the conceptual underpinnings of the standard view, by insisting that there are strong reasons for viewing the authority of international law as a fluid and ultimately content-dependent concept. International law has a claim to authority only in cases where the underlying background preferences for inter-state co-ordination are similar across states. In such cases, international law can enjoy de facto authority. Normative claims to authority by international law, however, is ultimately suspect.

106 Cf Chapter 1.

Democracy-based accounts of authority, too, view the demands on authority made by international law as lacking strong normative foundations. They claim that we have much more stringent expectations from domestic institutions when they demand obedience from citizens. International law is unable to meet these expectations and, therefore, to make a genuine claim to authority. When there are disagreements on the authority of international law, what matters is which forum is ultimately more justified to resolve such disagreements. For democracy-based accounts of authority, democratic states, and their parliaments in particular, are best placed to resolve such disputes. This is not only because democracy offers the best procedure, but also because domestic democratic procedures are the best way of showing concern for the political equality of individuals.[107] Respect for the political equality of individuals has to be the ultimate arbiter of whether some distant international law obligation trumps substantive rules and procedures validated by democratic governance.

So far, the proponents of the standard view of the authority of international law have not addressed these challenges in any systematic way. It may even be argued that the ongoing attacks on the authority of international law are, in part, the doing of international lawyers themselves. Mainstream international law has offered a theoretically impoverished account of its authority. Whilst this defensive account may work before an audience of public international law students or before friends of international law, it remains open to attack from disciplines and approaches that are inherently sceptical of the authority of international law and its ability to generate obligations in non-piecemeal ways. The plain account of the authority of international law renders it subject to attack. Proponents of the authority of international law can easily be regarded as naïve crusaders, unable to counter the anti-democratic, imperialist, and counter-domestic rule of law challenges.[108] Furthermore, the claim to authority of international law is too easily depicted as a straw man by sceptics concerned about democratic legitimacy or the demise of sovereignty or domestic constitutionalism.

Is seeing the authority of international law as a relational concept a fundamental move away from the standard view of the authority of international law? Do we need to subscribe to thick normative visions of either

[107] Richard Bellamy, 'Democracy as Public Law' (2013) 14(8) *German Law Journal* 1017.

[108] Posner, for example, calls those who defend the authority of international law over domestic orders 'global legalists'. Eric Posner, *The Perils of Global Legalism* (Chicago: Chicago University Press 2009).

constitutionalism or pluralism to advance our understanding of the conceptual underpinnings of the authority of international law? On what basis, if any, should we revisit the authority of international law as international lawyers? How far can international law go to accommodate the content-dependent views or democratic rebuttals of its authority? We now turn to these questions and argue for a reconstruction of the standard view of the authority of international law.

# 2

# The Authority of International Law: A Doctrinal Account

'One of the various thorny problems that international law has to face is the relative impermeability of national systems to international legal imperatives'[1]

## Introduction

The previous chapter showed that international lawyers, political scientists and political philosophers have different ways of discussing the authority of international law. Their discussions diverge not only in terms of the normative or social theories of authority, but also with respect to the conceptual underpinnings of authority when applied to international law. There are, for example, disagreements as to how international law acquires its authority, whether international law has pre-emptive authority, and whether international law allows for disobedience.

This chapter lays the groundwork for an alternative conceptual account of the authority of international law. This account is committed to the aspiration of value neutrality of the standard account, but it also revises the core argument that international laws make identical claims to authority in relation to domestic orders.

As highlighted in the introduction, I approach the conceptual account as a commitment to focus on what is important and essential about the authority of international law. I primarily seek to understand which conceptual scheme should be applied in order to acknowledge the authority due to international law over domestic legal systems. In so doing, I am aware of the fine line

[1] Antonio Cassese, 'Towards a Moderate Monism: Could International Rules Eventually Acquire the Force to Invalidate Inconsistent National Laws?' in *Realising Utopia: The Future of International Law* (Oxford: Oxford University Press 2012) 187–8.

between conceptual analysis and normative analysis. I acknowledge that any conceptual analysis of law is not free of normativity.[2] I do hold, however, that normativity in a conceptual account is distinct in that a conceptual approach to the authority of international law seeks to stand on its own without becoming a larger normative programme. I do not, therefore, seek to develop a thick normative theory. My goal is a thin, conceptual theory that may nevertheless stand compatible with diverse normative theories of international law.

The starting point for the alternative account I develop in this chapter is that international law is in need of its own disciplinary account of its authority. With all its imperfections, the standard account has represented the operational international law point of view for a significant amount of time. One of the central features of the standard account is its thin value-structure. It posits that maintaining neutrality over a decidedly value-driven agenda is the most viable way for international law to make general authoritative claims over the full diversity of legal and political systems across the world. This basic concern for applicability over diverse domestic systems is clearly a disciplinary mark of international law that distinguishes it from political theory or political science. Any account that seeks to develop an account of the authority of international law has to be sensitive to this basic concern. As will become clear here, however, this is where my agreement with the standard account ends. I question both the centrality of consent as the necessary and sufficient source of authority in international law and the either/or image supported by the standard view.

My argument has three parts.

First, I go back to the drawing board and discuss the concept of legal authority to show that the justification of state law over individuals has been the key preoccupation of theorists of authority. They have asked what key attributes should be attached to law in order for it to have a rightful claim to authority over individuals. As we will see below through my discussion of Austin, Hart, and Raz, theorists of domestic law have conceptualized the basic attributes of law in order to claim authority in fundamentally different ways. What brings them together, however, is the presence of heavy 'conceptual baggage' when we turn to the matter of the authority of international law over state institutions. This baggage is heavy because discussions here are often over-shadowed by debates on the authority of law over individuals and the significant reliance on domestic analogy. In order to achieve conceptual clarity on the authority of international law, it is crucial that we free it from questions about the authority of domestic law. This involves a careful

[2] See also Nicola Lacey, 'Analytical Jurisprudence versus Descriptive Sociology Revisited' (2006) 84(4) *Texas Law Review* 945.

deconstruction of our expectations from the authority of law *qua* domestic legal authority. It also requires us to review what features of the authority of law are also essential components of international legal authority.

Second, I hold that as soon as we release authority from competition with individual autonomy, the need to evaluate the role of consent in assigning authority to international law becomes clear. What is more, it becomes possible to see that consent, albeit important, is not an all inclusive route through which to claim authority for international law. It is not necessary at all times, just most of the time. Consent—when needed—however is also not sufficient. The authority of international law depends to a significant degree on what a specific international law demands from state authorities. Consent in and of itself cannot explain such demands.

Third, I argue that a general disposition to take international law into account does not equate to a general, pre-emptive, and exclusionary duty to obey all international laws. The authority of a particular international law *depends* on the capacity of particular international laws to impose duties or confer powers on state authorities. International laws do not always impose the same kind of duties, and sometimes they do not impose duties at all, but instead confer powers. Therefore, I discuss the authority of international law as a function of the different duties that it imposes on states and the types of power it confers. This allows me to argue that, in discussing the authority of a specific international law, that a piece of international law is binding is not a sufficient condition for assessing the authority of that international law. What matters is what kinds of duties particular international laws generate for domestic authorities and what kinds of powers it confers on them. This requires an assessment of the kind of duty or power engaged by any particular piece of international law as a necessary condition to assess its authority claims.

## The Conceptual Baggage of Domestic Law

Literature on the authority of law offers important starting points for conceptualizing the authority of international law.[3] There is also some significant conceptual baggage. On the positive side, there are three important

[3] Richard B Friedman, 'On the Concept of Authority in Political Philosophy' in Richard E Flathman (ed), *Concepts in Social and Political Philosophy* (New York: Macmillan 1973); Leslie Green 'Law and Obligations' in Jules Coleman and Scott Shapiro (eds), *The Oxford Handbook of Jurisprudence and Philosophy of Law* (Oxford: Clarendon Press 2002).

observations about the concept of authority as applied to law. First, there is the common intuition that law is generally understood as having a claim to authority.[4] As Hart puts it, 'all speculation about the nature of law begins from the assumption that its existence at least makes certain conduct obligatory'.[5] Second, the authority of law is authority over certain conduct.[6] Law demands that those who are subject to it conduct themselves in ways it directs. What law asks of its subjects, however, varies significantly. It may, for example, ask subjects not to carry out a range of conducts (prohibitive authority) or it may exclude one type of conduct, but leave subjects free to choose beyond this. As Hart has also pointed out, law does not only impose duties, it can also confer powers on its subjects.[7] This suggests that the authority of law also operates by assigning status, enabling certain subjects to carry out certain types of conduct, and requiring bystanders to respect this. Third, law is understood to offer a special reason for action to its subjects. Law, once enacted, confers legal obligations on subjects, which may exist alongside personal choices or preferences to act in certain ways, as well as the interests of powerful groups in obtaining certain outcomes. Law, as a special and independent reason for action, is important in order to separate legal authority from personal ethics and brute power.[8] The authority of law makes an autonomous claim on its subjects, asking them to conduct themselves in certain ways. It can overlap with personal interests or moral demands. It can also conflict with them.

All of these core features apply to international law. As the standard account says, both treaty-made law and custom make an authority claim over domestic legal orders and state officials. The authority of international law is best understood as authority over conduct both in terms of imposing duties to act and on conferring powers to act. International law also covers a rich range of conduct. It claims authority over prohibitive, permissible, mandatory, as well as programmatic conduct. The UN Charter, for instance, prohibits the individual use of force except in situations of self-defence.[9] This is both prohibitive and permissible conduct. The Statute of the International Criminal Court permits domestic courts to prosecute a full range of war crimes alongside more serious breaches of the laws of war, crimes against humanity, and genocide.[10] This is

[4] Joesph Raz, *The Authority of Law* (Oxford: Clarendon Press 1979) 116–20

[5] HLA Hart, *The Concept of Law* (2nd edn, Oxford: Clarendon Press 1994) 217.

[6] Friedman (n 3). [7] Hart (n 5).

[8] Max Weber, *On Law in Economy and Society* (Max Rhinstein ed, Edward A Shils trans) (Cambridge: Harvard University Press 1954).

[9] Charter of the United Nations (adopted 26 June 1945, entered into force 24 October 1945) 892 UNTS 119 (UN Charter) art 2(4).

[10] Rome Statute of the International Criminal Court (adopted 17 July 1998, entered into force 1 July 2002) 2187 UNTS 90 (ICC Statute).

both mandatory conduct and permissible conduct. The Agreement concerning the Conservation and Management of Straddling Fish Stocks and Highly Migratory Fish Stocks sets its objective as the 'long-term conservation and sustainable use of straddling fish stocks and highly migratory fish stocks'.[11] The treaty does this by setting out programmatic, prohibitive, and permissible forms of conduct.

Finally, international law's claim to authority is also distinct from directing conduct based on principles of morality or on global power dynamics. It overlaps with both at times. It conflicts with both at other times. The Genocide Convention is a paradigmatic example of the overlap between the legal and moral authority of international law. To suggest that the Genocide Convention only has legal authority is not convincing: the prohibition of genocide also has moral authority. Subjects of international law, we would think, are moved by both the moral and legal authority of the prohibition on genocide. The Genocide Convention, however, can be argued to impose a complex range of specific legal duties on states and other actors compared to the moral duties stemming from prohibition.[12]

Legal authority and de facto authority, too, overlap. The fact that the UN Security Council is an authoritative organ of the UN in the domain of international peace and security as directed by Article 24 of the UN Charter exists side-by-side with the fact that any act it takes is a convergence of the preferences of its five permanent members and the fact that these five have significant military, economic, and political power.[13] Article 24 of the Charter makes a legal claim to authority alongside the political claim to authority made by the world's most powerful nations. Not all international laws, however, enjoy the backing of universal moral authority or the backing of unanimous power in the same degree. Not all moral or political norms are legalized in the international law domain.

The commonalities between the authority of law and the authority of international law do not, however, extend to other important and central debates

[11] United Nations Agreement for the Implementation of the Provisions of the United Nations Convention on the Law of the Sea of 10 December 1982 relating to the Conservation and Management of Straddling Fish Stocks and Highly Migratory Fish Stocks (adopted 4 August 1995, entered into force 11 December 2001) 2167 UNTS 88 (Straddling Fish Stocks Agreement) available at: https://www.un.org/Depts/los/convention_agreements/texts/fish_stocks_agreement/CONF164_37.htm.

[12] Cf *Application of the Convention on the Prevention and the Punishment of the Crime of Genocide (Bosnia Herzegovina v Serbia and Montenegro)* (Judgment) (2007) ICJ Rep 266 (Genocide Convention).

[13] Antonios Tzanakopoulos, *Disobeying the Security Council Countermeasures against Wrongful Sanctions* (Oxford: Oxford University Press 2011).

about the nature of the authority of law. Here I identify four types of conceptual baggage that may come with approaching legal authority in domestic terms. The first two, the Austinian claim that legal authority depends on the threat of sanctions, and Hart's claim that the authority of law depends on the existence of secondary rules, are well-known and have been debated exhaustively. The second two, made popular by Raz's theory of legal authority, are equally prevalent, albeit less exposed. The first of these is a problem that undercuts most thinking about the authority of law: the claim that law gives *conclusive reasons* for action. The second is Raz's important juxtaposition that the authority of law can only be obtained if it does not conflict with the value of individual autonomy.

All of these theoretical advancements on legal authority in the domestic sphere, I argue, obscure any conceptual analysis of the authority of international law rather than clarify it. It is, however, the latter two that offer the biggest challenge to any clear-headed conceptual analysis of the legal authority of international law.

## Authority as Commands

John Austin is the best known proponent of reliance on conceptual baggage. Austin not only believed that, for it to hold over individuals, the authority of law needed to be backed by sanctions. He also conceptualized authority as operating by way of command. In Austin's words, 'command, duty and sanction are inseparably connected'.[14] Law enjoys authority by virtue of delivering commands given by a superior body capable of imposing such sanctions. Austin's theory espoused a fundamental view about human nature: individuals are self-interested and self-preserving agents who will only give up claims to autonomy under threat of sanction.

The theoretical consequences of Austin's theory of law for international law are well known and have been rebutted by generations of international lawyers.[15] Under his theory international law cannot enjoy the status of

[14] John Austin, *The Province of Jurisprudence Determined* (ed W Rumble) (Cambridge: Cambridge University Press 1995) 17.

[15] Leading theoretical and doctrinal studies of international law tackled with this question. See, notably Hans Kelsen, *Principles of International Law* (New York: Rinehart 1952); Gerald G Fitzmaurice, 'The Foundations and the Authority of International Law and the Problem of Enforcement' (1956) 19 *Modern Law Review* 1; James Leslie Brierly, *The Basis of Obligation in International Law* (Oxford: Clarendon Press 1958); Hart,(n 5). Most recently, Thomas M Franck, *Fairness in International Law and Institutions* (Oxford: Clarendon Press 1995); Jack Goldsmith and Eric A Posner, *The Limits of International Law* (New York: Oxford University Press 2005).

law, let alone enjoy any authority over domestic legal systems. The authority of international law does not belong to the concept of authority developed by Austin at all. In contemporary theories of international law, the self-interest-based rationalist school continues to follow Austin's conception of legal authority. In so doing, they transfer notions about the self-interested account of the individual in the domestic realm into the international realm for the purpose of characterizing states. Given that there are no consistent and credible forms of sanctions on states, the rational school finds debates about the authority of international law superfluous.[16] There are no special reasons to consider the authority of international law. International law, therefore, is best understood as a tool of co-ordination, into which states may or may not opt, depending on their assessments of self-interest.

## Authority as Existence of Secondary Rules

It is sometimes suggested that Hart did not really develop a theory of the authority of law. He assumed that if something was law it was authoritative.[17] Hart was more preoccupied with debunking Austin's command theory than with questioning what made law claim authority over individuals. One of his central contributions to understanding the authority of law has been to underline that law's subjects often understand themselves to be acting for reasons other than coercion and that there are a diversity of laws, both duty imposing and power conferring, which do not fit into the command model. In so doing, Hart turned to the qualities of a society's social structure (as opposed to threats of sanctions) in order to define what law is and how it claims authority. His answer is the basis for the rule-based approach to the authority of law. Law enjoys authority *qua* law only when the legal system of the society is developed enough to have secondary rules alongside primary ones. Secondary rules are, for the most part, rules that tell us how to authoritatively determine the existence of primary rules. They also tell us the method of introduction, amendment, and violation of these primary rules.[18] Secondary rules therefore confer authority to law and justify its authoritative claims. A legal system prima facie is a system made up of primary and secondary rules. This may be why Hart spoke of a legal system exhibiting a 'mark' of authority.[19]

[16] Cf Chapter 2.

[17] Candace J Groudine, 'Authority: H.L.A. Hart and the Problem with Legal Positivism' (1980) 4(3) *Journal of Libertarian Studies* 217.

[18] Hart (n 5) 12–13. [19] Ibid.

Hart's view poses difficulties when one turns to conceptualizing the authority of international law, because he did not regard international law as a fully developed legal system. That is, he did not consider international law to have settled secondary rules that authoritatively resolve disputes about primary rules.[20] This is despite the fact that he recognized the existence of primary rules in international law. What made international law non-authoritative was not its lack of sanctions, as Austin would have it, but the lack of a legal system made up of secondary rules to authoritatively resolve disputes about primary rules. The conceptual baggage we inherit from Hart is that primary international laws are laws in the sense that participants in the international system are compelled to follow them for reasons other than the threat of sanction. In cases of disagreement about the scope of primary laws, or conflict between different sets of primary laws, however, the legal system (the backbone of which is the existence of secondary rules recognized by all) is unable to impose the final word. Conceiving international law's authority as a matter of the final word, however, sets the bar too high. We may go a step further and suggest that although they theorized legal authority in fundamentally distinct ways, Austin and Hart have both set standards that international law—by its very nature—is unable to meet.

## Conclusive Reasons for Action

Most lawyers then agree that all law creates special reasons for conduct. The sticking point in the literature about the authority of law is about *what exactly* is meant by 'special reasons'. Of particular importance is whether law creates pre-emptive and/or exclusionary reasons for action or inaction, and whether such reasons are so central to the conception of the authority of law that when they are absent we can no longer claim that law has authority. The theme of conclusive reasons for action is present in the works of most theorists. Austin, for example, sees the notions of law and commands as being closely linked.[21] Hart endorses this view, stating that 'when there is law human conduct is in some sense made non-optional or obligatory'.[22] Raz, however, is the most influential theorist who explicitly states that conclusive reason for action is a necessary condition for legal authority to obtain. This is his pre-emption thesis.[23]

[20] Hart (n 5). See also Mehrdad Payandeh, 'The Concept of International Law in the Jurisprudence of H.L.A Hart' (2010) 21(4) *European Journal of International Law* 967.

[21] Austin (n 14), Lecture 1. [22] Hart (n 5) 82.

[23] Raz (n 4). Raz's theory of authority, of course, is not made up solely of the pre-emption thesis. Pre-emption is part of his other two thesis, namely, the dependence thesis and the normal justification thesis. Joseph Raz, *The Morality of Freedom* (Oxford: Oxford University Press 1986) 53.

The pre-emption thesis holds that law functions to replace reasons that apply to individuals *qua* individuals through the provision of second-order reasons in the form of legal norms. Second order reasons are pre-emptive. They pre-empt other reasons that individuals have for conducting or not conducting themselves in certain ways. When law claims authority it, in effect, claims to make a practical difference in the deliberation of its subjects by a pre-empting appeal to the first-order reasons that individuals may have for their conduct.[24] This suggests that when a law asks A to do X, A has to do X no matter what other reasons may apply.

I leave aside the question of whether the conclusive reason approach is the right one to help us understand the authority of law over individuals.[25] For international law, however, this is yet another very demanding test—one, indeed, that most international laws are bound to fail. This can be illustrated using a well-known example that involves a prohibitive norm of international law. There is a long-standing debate about the authority of the prohibition of torture as part of customary international law.[26] Assuming, for the sake of argument, that we are interested only in the most widely accepted dimensions of the prohibition of torture, that of the absolute prohibition of torture by public officials with the aim of extracting information.[27] When we say that the prohibition of torture under customary international law claims authority over domestic legal systems, we are in effect saying that all domestic actors—be they parliaments, domestic courts, or law enforcement officers—have special reasons to act in accordance with international law. Even for the law enforcement officer (the state official with the most direct duty to respect the international legal prohibition on torture), international legal authority is not prima facie pre-emptive. The duty that the law enforcement official has towards international law depends on whether an overlapping norm prohibiting torture also exists in domestic law. If domestic law

[24] There is a tension between the pre-emption thesis and Raz's second thesis: normal justification. Whilst the pre-emption thesis requires a pre-commitment to authority, the normal justification thesis relies on a case-by-case assessment of the bindingness of norms. On this tension, see Margaret Martin, 'Raz's *Morality of Freedom*: Two Models of Authority' (2010) 1 *Jurisprudence* 1.

[25] Scott Hershovitz, 'The Role of Authority' (2011) 11(7) *Philosophers Imprint* 1.

[26] Rosalyn Higgins, *Problems and Process: International Law and How We Use It* (Oxford: Clarendon Press 1994); Erika de Wet, 'The Prohibition of Torture as an International Norm of jus cogens and Its Implications for National and Customary Law' (2004) 15(1) *European Journal of International Law* 97.

[27] This is the definition of the Convention Against Torture and Other Cruel, Inhuman, or Degrading Treatment or Punishment (adopted 10 December 1984, entered into force 26 June 1987) 1465 UNTS 112 (Convention Against Torture or UNCAT).

already prohibits torture—even under a different name—the authority of international law is such that it brings an *additional* weight to the prohibitive authority of domestic law. If domestic law neither prohibits nor allows torture (a likely scenario in countries where criminal codes do not define torture), the international prohibition would operate to exclude one reason for action in favour of another reason for action. It is only when a domestic law openly permits torture that the authority of international law offers reasons that look more pre-emptive to the law enforcement officer. They must set aside a law that sanctions torture and act on the international legal prohibition.

The pre-emption thesis also does not apply neatly to other public officers who are under the authority of the prohibition of torture under international law. International law in this case demands that judiciaries prosecute torturers. The judiciary, however, may have other reasons to prosecute—based on provisions of manslaughter, for example. Parliaments may have a range of other important reasons to criminalize torture, such as achieving the reconciliation of state and society. To push international legal authority into the frame of pre-emptive reasons, therefore, does an injustice to our understanding of the particularities of how the authority of international law operates over diverse sets of domestic authorities. International legal authority fundamentally operates by boosting, changing, or framing the reasons that domestic authorities have for action, not by solely demanding obedience to a norm.

## Individual Autonomy

The problem of individual autonomy in domestic conceptions of authority is the fourth piece of conceptual baggage I will focus on. The theoretical foundations of the authority of law are principally discussed with an attention on individuals and their relationship to the law.[28] The literature on legal authority tends to concentrate on how law can make a claim to have authority over individuals. Under what conditions should individuals defer to the commands of law? What justifies law's authority over individuals? Why should individuals abandon their autonomy in favour of authority?

The key obstacle for those who take individual autonomy seriously is how to reconcile individual autonomy with legal authority. Raz's work on legal authority is an important departure from both Austin and Hart here. For Raz a major problem is the tension between individual autonomy and legal

[28] Raz (n 23) at 72; Samantha Besson, 'The Authority of International Law-Lifting the State Veil' (2009) 31(3) *Sydney Law Review* 343.

authority. As he puts it: '[T]he duty to obey conveys an abdication of autonomy, that is of the right and duty to be responsible for one's action and to conduct oneself in the best light of reason.'[29] The task, then, for Raz is to demonstrate that legal authority can be consistent with acting 'in the light of best reason'. Raz takes up the challenge laid down by anarchists, of the inflexible opposition between the individual and the state, to be a real challenge for any claim to the authority of law. Wolf's challenge to authority is well known. As he puts it, the 'defining mark of the state is authority, the right to rule' while the 'primary obligation of man is autonomy, the refusal to be ruled'.[30] Raz seeks to overcome this problem by arguing that law has authority precisely because it is able to act more successfully on reasons that *already* apply to individuals.[31] Conversely, when individuals disagree on a specific instance that they will do better by not conforming to law, the law loses its foundational basis for authority. For Raz, therefore, legal authority is always qualified and piecemeal. It can only seek to be compatible with, not override, individual autonomy.

The concern to make authority compatible with autonomy also leads to what Raz calls the 'paradox of just law'.[32] For the authority to be *authentic*, individuals must conform to a reason to which they would not have otherwise conformed. For the authority to obtain authenticity, it must show individuals that reasons offered by law will help them do better than reasons they already have. This is what Raz calls the normal justification thesis for the authority of law.[33] The paradox of just law, therefore, is that 'the more just and valuable the law is, the more reason one has to conform to it, and the less to obey it'.[34]

The individual autonomy concern—if transferred to the international realm as a concern for the individual autonomy of states as a representative of the individual autonomy of citizens residing in those states—poses a range of difficulties for conceptualizing the authority of international law as an autonomous claim apart from the individual preferences of states.

First, the search for *authentic* authority (rather than authority-disguising individual preferences) does have a tendency to set the bar too high in terms of proof that an authoritative relationship is in place. If a state has good, self-interested reasons for conforming with a piece of international law, then

[29] Jospeh Raz, 'Introduction' in Joseph Raz ed, *Authority* (New York: New York University Press, 1990) 4.

[30] Robert Paul Wolff, *In Defense of Anarchism* (Berkley: University of California Press 1998) 29.

[31] Raz (n 23) 67.

[32] Joseph Raz, 'The Obligation to Obey: Revision and Tradition' (1984) 1 *Notre Dame Journal of Law Ethics & Public Policy* 139, 141–2.

[33] Raz (n 23) 53. [34] Raz (n 32) 141–2.

it is more appropriate to hold that a state's preferences coincide with international law rather than that international law has authority over a state. There are many empirical examples of this. For example, the United States is known to be a good complier with international laws that it has actively exported from its own domestic laws.[35] In such cases, compliance with legal authority and conforming to individual state preferences is one and the same. Goldsmith and Posner are quick to point out that this is how effective international law works. If international law is not effective, it is because a claim to authority does just not do the trick. There must be an overlap between reasons that already apply to an individual state and the regulation international law promotes.

Second, and conversely, it is too easy for states to opt out of international legal authority. For example, a state could claim that following international law would be contrary to following the best reason to advance some important self-interest of the state. In such cases, international law would be incompatible with the individual autonomy of the state and therefore would not enjoy any authority. As we have seen in the previous chapter, rational choice theorists are also happy with this instrumental view of law. For them, law cannot penetrate the autonomy of a state's internal decision-making processes, it can only survive when it is compatible with them.

One might propose overcoming the individual autonomy difficulty by suggesting that 'confirming to best reason' is not a free-flowing concept, but subjects the arbitrary rebuttal of authority to scrutiny. Scholars who criticize international legal authority from a democratic legitimacy perspective, for example, are able to concede this.[36] Bellamy argues that there is no conflict between a democratic state bowing to international legal authority if that authority protects the citizens of a democratic state from negative externalities in the international system.[37] One could, therefore, develop an account of what constitutes best reason for a democratic political entity in order to further specify the scope of international legal authority. This research agenda, however, comes with a trade-off. Focussing on the legitimacy of

[35] A good example of this is the Protocol to Prevent, Suppress, and Punish Trafficking in Persons, Especially Women and Children (adopted 15 November 2000, entered into force 25 December 2003) 2237 UNTS 319 (Palermo Protocol), which is modeled on US domestic anti-trafficking legislation.

[36] Richard Bellamy, 'The Democratic Legitimacy of International Human Rights Conventions: Political Constitutionalism and the Hirst Case' in Andreas Føllesdal, Karlsson Schaffer, and Geir Ulfstein (eds), *The Legitimacy of International Human Rights Regimes: Legal, Political and Philosophical Perspectives* (Cambridge: Cambridge University Press 2013) 243–71.

[37] Bellamy (n 36).

states avoids the question of what kinds of claims to authority international law makes on states.[38] It rather asks the question of what is a legitimate state and how a legitimate state should behave in the international system.[39] The broad answer to this is that states respect international law's authority to the extent that such authority is compatible with political equality. Such a view does not allow us to develop the authority of international law *qua* all states in the international legal system and with respect to all obligations to which states commit. The theory also does not allow us to discuss the authority of international laws that concern the rights and obligations of non-citizens[40] or extra-territorial rights and obligations,[41] even if states undertake such obligations as a matter of positive law.

## Escaping the Conceptual Baggage of Domestic Law

What does it mean to free the conception of authority from the baggage of domestic law? Each of these essential characteristics of domestic legal authority sets the bar too high in conceptualizing the authority of international law. Under normal circumstances, international law does not operate with the threat of sanction. It does not operate under a vertical legal system with firm and clear secondary rules. Particular international laws do not offer conclusive reasons for action. To confirm the authority of international law by turning it into a subjective assessment of state officials in the light of best reasons feels too tentative a conceptualization of the authority of international law.

It is no wonder, therefore, that the standard account of the authority of international law adheres so strongly to the notion of consent and the binding nature of international laws over domestic orders through consent as a closed and complete account. Focussing on obligation acquired through consent appears to remove the obstacles presented by individual autonomy, lack of sanction, and offers a conclusive reason for action to those that have consented. However, consent in and of itself is unable to ground the authority of all international laws *tout court*. At times it is unable to be a necessary

[38] Samantha Besson, 'Sovereignty, International Law and Democracy' (2011) 22(2) *European Journal of International Law* 37, 380.

[39] This has been a common critique of political philosophical accounts of international law by international lawyers, that is that their interest is not in the *actual* international laws.

[40] For example the Convention relating to the Status of Refugees (adopted 28 July 1951, entered into force 22 April 1954) 189 UNTS 150 (1951 Geneva Refugee Convention).

[41] For example the United Nations Convention on the Law of the Sea (adopted 10 December 1982, entered into force 16 November 1994) 1833 UNTS 3 (UNCLOS) art 136.

condition for authority, and, more importantly, it does not operate as a sufficient condition.[42]

Why consent is not at all times a necessary condition for international laws to enjoy authority has been discussed by international lawyers and legal philosophers, be they natural lawyers, interpretivists,[43] or positivists.[44] For natural lawyers and interpetivists the problems of consent are deep seated and go to the heart of the separation thesis between law and morality. To hold objective truths that bear on all human beings to the requirement of consent denies the important place of morals in international law.

From the perspective of legal postivisits, some international laws, either due to an incoherency argument or self-standing as a widely accepted social fact, do not require consent. Pacta sunt servanda and the prohibition of genocide are standard examples. With regard to pacta sunt servanda international lawyers are aware of the problems of circularity: if states are required to have consented to the norm of pacta sunt servanda then they would also need to have consented to consenting to pacta sunt servanda and the problem continues.[45] The contestation of the prohibition of genocide on the other hand is unthinkable as it is a well-established part of the imagination of the social convention.[46]

A closer look at customary international law further shows that what makes customary norms to assume authority is not consent, but collective participatory processes of state actors over time in forming a norm of international law. Such participation is inclusive of all organs of state, from the legislative, to the executive, and the judiciary.[47] The evidentariay basis of custom does not allow states to be taken as unitary actors consenting to international laws. Equally, states are not conceived as being capable of withdrawing consent from custom in a one-off fashion. The undermining or evolution of custom remains to be a matter of making sense of states'

[42] For a fuller discussion, see Başak Çali, 'On Interpretivism and International Law' (2009) 20(3) *European Journal of International Law* 805; Emmanuel Voyiakis, 'Customary International Law and the Place of Normative Considerations' (2010) 55(1) *American Journal of Jurisprudence* 163.

[43] Ronald Dworkin, 'A New Philosophy for International Law' (2013) 41(1) *Philosophy and Public Affairs* 2.

[44] Jan Klabbers, 'International Legal Positivism and Constitutionalism' in Kammeroffer and Asperamont (eds), *International Legal Positivism in a Post-Modern World* (Cambridge: Cambridge University Press 2014) 273; Duncan B Hollis (ed), *Oxford Handbook on Treaties* (Oxford: Oxford University Press 2012) 2.

[45] Hollis (n 44).

[46] *Application of the Convention on the Prevention and the Punishment of the Crime of Genocide (Bosnia Herzegovina v Serbia and Montenegro)* Judgment (2007) ICJ Reports 227, para 427.

[47] International Law Commission, Formation and Evidence of Customary International Law—Elements in the previous work of the International Law Commission that could be particularly relevant to the topic (2012) (A.CN.4/659).

collective participation in norm change over time.[48] When a single executive changes its own practice, for example, it is not also granted that the judiciary will follow suit.[49] The ambivalence of the legislator to a customary norm also does not necessarily imply the ambivalence of the judges to the same norm.[50]

In contemporary international law the pressing question, however, is not whether strictly non-consensual forms of law can exist. It is rather what the boundary between consensual and non-consensual international law is and how much consent we seek for which international norms we have. This is partly because for every claim of non-consensual law, the central question remains whether these are truths recognisable by our social convention and whether they are power in disguise. Whilst, for the non-ideal political circumstances under which international law exists, consent serves as an important value to offset power being camoflaged as universal truths, for certain norms, most international lawyers, including positivist lawyers, concede that the demands of consent are simply not identical and do not carry the same force.[51]

Consent, more importantly for our analysis, is also not sufficient for the authority of international laws to have a pre-emptive force in domestic law. The standard view associates the authority of international law too closely with having the necessity of having conclusive reasons for action. The assertion that international law is either binding or non-binding is insensitive to the different ways international law creates duties for state officials. As discussed above, international law can operate by making a domestic law more weighty, by creating an additional source of authority where there is a gap in domestic law or by presenting state officials with a conflict between pieces of domestic and international law. International legal authority, therefore, operates differently. By its very nature it makes a different claim in degree of influence over the conduct of state officials. The binding/non-binding understanding does not encompass this variety adequately.

In sum, the standard view does not escape the conceptual baggage that comes with domestic analogies of the authority of law. The standard view holds on to consent in order to respond to the individual autonomy concern. It also operates with a demanding criterion of authority focussing on

[48] Michael P Scharf, *Customary International Law in Times of Fundamental Change Recognizing Grotian Moments* (Cambridge: Cambridge University Press 2013).

[49] See for example the Hong Kong Court's finding of the customary principle of non refoulemont despite lack of executive state practice. *FB v Director of Immigration* [2009] HKEC 581 (CFI); Daly, 'Effective Judicial Review: Necessary because of Bad Governance' in C Forsyth et al (eds), *Effective Judicial Review: A Cornerstone of Good Governance* (Oxford: Oxford University Press 2010) 413–15.

[50] Italian Constitutional Court, judgment no 238/2014.

[51] Klabbers (n 44).

conclusive reasons. Once we free international law from these concerns, we may also be able to come closer to a more practical understanding of the authority of the current corpus of international law.

## Re-Defining the Authority of International Law

At this point I hope to have convinced the reader of two things. The first is that transferring the conceptual starting points of domestic legal authority to the international realm is not straightforward and is often an exercise of setting the bar too high for international law to claim any degree of authority over domestic legal and political systems. Most of the critiques of the standard view of the authority of international law laid out in Chapter 2 employ conceptions driven by domestic legal authority. This, I believe, is being too harsh on international law and the authority relationships it establishes with domestic legal and political orders. My second point is that the peculiar characteristics of international law demand that we think of its claim to authority in the light of those characteristics and not *at their expense.*

In particular, there are two unique features of international law for which a pratice-oriented conceptual account of authority has to cater. First, the contemporary corpus of international law almost always makes authority claims over state officials alongwith domestic laws. It augments the explicit provisions present in domestic laws, offers a framework for interpreting domestic law, provides new reasons for re-considering the interpretations of domestic laws, it offers a foundation on which domestic authorities build laws, and it asks states to set aside their existing laws. It also fills gaps in domestic law or demands that domestic laws are repealed or re-drafted. This means that state officials have to engage in a deliberative exercise, comparing and contrasting the authority of domestic law and international law when responding to authority claims made by international law. A common principle in international human rights law, for example, is that if a domestic law gives higher protection to a norm also protected by international law, the domestic law should be given priority.[52] For this principle to hold, however, state officials first have to compare the two laws. The authority of international law,

[52] See the Convention for the Protection of Human Rights and Fundamental Freedoms (European Convention on Human Rights, as amended) (ECHR) art 53 which states 'Nothing in this Convention shall be construed as limiting or derogating from any of the human rights and fundamental freedoms which may be ensured under the laws of any High Contracting Party or under any other agreement to which it is a party.'

therefore, emerges following a process of constant comparison and deliberation rather than an automatic fact.

Secondly state officials to whom we are usually seeking to justify the authority of international law do not have inherent (moral) interests.[53] More significantly, as Waldron claims, 'it [the state] does not have an interest in being unconstrained by law, in the way that the individual does'.[54] We could go a step further and say that if a state could have any interest as a legal person, it ought to be an interest in being constrained by law. The legal and political science behaviourist views that hold that states can withdraw their consent from international laws from one day to another often overlook the fact that this view ultimately encourages state officials not to respect the principle of legality. This is at odds with a basic principle that state actions need regulation.

The standard account of authority does not do justice to either of these insights. It is too one dimensional to be able to chart the waters of multiple authority relationships between different international laws, domestic systems, and the deliberative process that needs to be followed when respecting the authority of international law on the one hand and between different kinds of state officials and international law on the other. The over-reliance on consent to ground the authority of international law leaves a large number of questions under-developed and unanswered when we turn to the actual practice of international law.

In what follows, I take a practical view on the existence of international law. By doing so, I assume that a corpus of international law exists through consensual treaty obligations and quasi-consensual processes of custom formation. I also do recognize that some norms of the international legal system are constitutive and, by that very virtue, cannot depend on consent. Pacta sunt servanda and the prohibition of genocide are such rules. I also recognize that states have taken on varying degrees of obligations through consensual arrangements. Building on this practical view, I develop a two part argument in order to re-conceptualize the authority of the existing corpus of international law. This conception demands acceptance of the first part in order to move on to the second. I first propose that we return to the drawing board and characterize the initial social situation that underpins the operation of international law in the current international legal system. By the social situation I do not mean what individual states do or do not think international law represents in particular instances. It refers to 'social' in the

[53] I do not rule out the fact that at times we also seek to justify the authority of international laws over individuals or non-state actors, such as international organizations.

[54] Jeremy Waldron, 'The Rule of International Law' (2006) 30(1) *Harvard Journal of Law and Public Policy* 15, 18.

sense that Durkheim uses the term.[55] The initial social situation is a social reality *sui generis*.[56] The setting out of the initial social situation is necessary for an understanding of the circumstances of authority in international law.[57] This is also necessary in order to make an *explicit* effort not to fall back on a domestic theory of authority. Circumstances of authority in international law are such that state officials can neither follow international law in full isolation from other obligations they may have in the domestic order, nor can they claim full ignorance of international law.

In the light of the initial situation set out, I then propose that the best conceptualization of the authority of international law is that of a *relational notion* of authority. International laws do not impose the same strength of duties on all state officials. There are weaker and stronger duties that international law can impose on state officials. Conversely, state officials sometimes violate both strong and weak duties. The duties that international laws impose range from the stronger duty to obey to the duty to respect and the duty to rebut.

## Stage I: Back to the Drawing Board: The Initial Situation

The initial situation is a useful heuristic tool for setting out the circumstances in which a conceptual account is relevant.[58] Given my argument that conceptions based on domestic legal authority are inadequate for the authority of international law, there is a need to spell out the initial situation in which we might appropriately make sense of the conceptual structure of the authority of international law.

[55] Emile Durkheim, *The Rules of Sociological Method* (edited with an Introduction by Steven Lukes, translated by W D Halls) (New York: The Free Press 1982) 50–60.

[56] There is much alignment between this approach and the constructive scholarship on international law and order. For the latter, too, the constitutive elements of the international system are sui generis and not reducible to the wills, desires, and interests of individual states. The international system constitutes and imposes limits on the individual states. See, generally, Vincent Poulliot, 'The Essence of Constructivism' (2004) 7 *Journal of International Relations and Development* 319.

[57] I am inspired by the 'circumstances of politics' described by Waldon when emphasizing that the circumstances of the authority of international law need more attention from international lawyers. Waldron refers back to Rawls's idea of 'circumstances of justice' when discussing this. Waldron defines 'circumstances of politics' as 'the felt need among the members of a certain group for a common framework or decision or some course of action on some matter, even in the face of disagreement about what that framework, decision or action should be'. Jeremy Waldron, *Law and Disagreement* (Oxford: Oxford University Press 1999) 102.

[58] On initial situations, see John Rawls, *Lectures on the History of Political Philosophy* (Samuel Freeman ed, Cambridge: Harvard University Press 2007) 16–20.

The initial situation in this case is foremost a description of the central characteristics of the contemporary international legal system. In particular, I am only concerned with those characteristics that most accurately depict the state of international law today. Below, I identify four characteristics of the initial situation. I regard these as non-controversial for any international lawyer practising today, regardless of their commitments to normative visions of international law.

## International Law and Common Social Risks

*The first* characteristic of the initial situation is a description of the existing social conditions underlying the international legal system. How are state authorities situated vis-à-vis the international system? How deep and extensive is the interaction between state authorities and international law? I submit that the social conditions underlying the international legal system are marked by an interdependence of individuals, peoples, and states in the world and the existence of the shared risks they face. These risks include, but are not limited to, international and internal armed conflict, mass displacement of populations, harmful weapons, environmental degradation, climate change, food crisis, health epidemics, and the depletion of natural resources.

Since the end of the Second World War, international law makers have also started to address these common social risks through the medium of international law. This notion played an important role in the creation of modern international law. The creation of the international human rights law regime in the aftermath of the Second World War, for example, justifies this regime based on the risks of genocide, deadly conflict, and political oppression.[59] International law is an 'institution', as Brierly calls it, that is collectively endorsed and maintained to fight these common risks and minimize threats to the lives of individuals living in separate states.

This depiction of social conditions that inform the current corpus of international law as we understand them today are different from earlier, more historical depictions of the underlying social conditions of international law. In the nineteenth and early twentieth centuries it was commonplace to think about social conditions as background rules sustaining the co-existence of states.[60] Following the UN Charter, international lawyers argued for a shift

[59] From an international relations perspective, see also Andrew Moravcsik's lock-in argument, 'The Origins of Human Rights Regimes: Democratic Delegation in Postwar Europe' (2000) 54(2) *International Organization* 217.

[60] Wolfgang Friedman, *The Changing Structure of International Law* (New York: Columbia University Press 1964).

in the understanding of the social fabric of international law.[61] In the contemporary social setting, the existence of separate states in the international system is coupled with increasing levels of interdependence between these states, as well as a conception of states not as 'autonomous' agents, but as agents from whom individuals living in these states have legitimate expectations to address the common risks that we face as members of single political communities.[62] State officials, therefore, have responsibilities to regulate domestically as well as internationally in co-operation with others.

A central quality of international law is its ability to set common standards for conduct. This in turn serves the purpose of protecting the common interests of individuals and peoples who face common vulnerabilities and who either do not have much choice but to address these vulnerabilities internationally,[63] or are better off addressing them both domestically and internationally.[64] The proliferation of regional and sub-regional organizations that seek to set common fine-grained standards of conduct in the fields of human rights, trade, environmental protection, international crimes, or refugee protection is evidence of this more inter-dependent view of the social conditions of the current international legal system.[65]

Granted, some states still argue that concern for the human rights of their citizens or the degradation of their environment is an interference in their internal affairs. It is, however, widely accepted that these are mostly rhetorical political tools or reactions to particular interventions. They do not add up to an identification of the social background conditions of international law as being characterized by a minimum level of interaction between isolated or

[61] Ibid. See also Bruno Simma, 'From Bilateralism to Community Interest in International Law' (1994) 250 *Recueil des Cours* 217.

[62] Dworkin (n 43).

[63] Douglas Hurd, *The Search for Peace* (London: Little, Brown 1997) 6.

[64] In areas where purposes of domestic law and international law overlap, the latter operates as an insurance mechanism rather than full regulation.

[65] See generally, African Charter on Human and Peoples' Rights (adopted 27 June 1981, entered into force 21 October 1986) (1982) 21 *International Legal Materials* 58 (Banjul Charter); American Convention on Human Rights (adopted 21 November 1969, entered into force 18 July 1978) 1144 UNTS 123 (Pacta of San Jose); European Convention on Human Rights; Convention governing the Specific Aspects of Refugee Problems in Africa (adopted 10 September 1969, entered into force 20 June 1974) 1001 UNTS 45 (1969 Convention); African Convention on the Conservation of Nature and Natural Resources (adopted 15 September 1968, entered into force 16 June 1969) 1001 UNTS 3; Convention on Political Asylum 1933, OAS Treaty Series No 34; Inter-American Convention on Transparency in Conventional Weapons Acquisitions (adopted 7 June 1999, entered into force 21 November 2002); Bamako Convention on the Ban of the Import into Africa and the Control of Transboundary Movement and Management of Hazardous Waste within Africa (adopted 30 January 1991, entered into force 22 April 1998) 30 *International Legal Materials* 773; European Agreement on the Abolition of Visas for Refugees (adopted 20 April 1959, entered into force 4 September 1960) 376 UNTS 85.

closed political communities. It is also difficult to interpret most key texts of international law with the presumption of isolationism. Rather, we should look at co-operation and creating standards that mirror or support standards that domestically inform international law making in most areas. In some regimes (such as international human rights law, international criminal law, and international environmental law) the mirroring and supporting aspects are strongly pronounced. This depiction of the social conditions does not mean that international law as an institution operates effectively to offset these risks. It means rather that these are the conditions under which we can recognize the authority claims that international law makes over domestic legal orders.

## A General Disposition for Taking International Law into Account

*Secondly*, I hold that, given the common risks that all political communities face, the need to co-ordinate action and specify common standards for action is genuine and a shared common purpose for all domestic communities and legal orders. All state officials, at the very least, share a *general disposition* to participate in international law making and to subsequently take that international law into account in their legal and political actions. I should highlight that this is an expectation that we have from state officials in their public roles as state officials of domestic polities. It is important to state what a general disposition to take international law is not about before arguing the case for it.

The general disposition to take international law into account is neither a duty to obey nor a duty not to interfere with international law. Rather it is a *general attitude* towards the *corpus* of international law. The attitude to have a disposition towards international law is based on the genuine and common purpose of all state officials to ensure co-ordination between and amongst separate political authorities. This general disposition is a fundamental attitude for approaching the full range of duties and powers imposed or assigned by international law through consent or otherwise. In this respect, it is necessary for a state official to declare that their office has a strong duty to obey a particular piece of international law or a duty not to interfere with international law. The disposition to take international law into account is a *general attitude* of principled engagement with it. The principled engagement foremost means that there has to be consistency in engaging with international law. State officials ought not view international law as policy options, but as a body of law that has a purpose of imposing varying degrees of obligations on states for the very benefit of individuals living in them. This means that whether deference to a particular international law takes place or not is not determined by having a general duty to take international law into account. This attitude therefore assumes a minimalist understanding of deference. The authority of a particular international law would require more than a general attitude to take international law into account.[66]

The general disposition to take international law into account is not about taking a structurally monist stance towards the relationship between domestic law and international law and suggesting a strict and a hierarchical unity between international law and domestic law.[67] I will discuss the long standing debate between monism and dualism in greater detail in Chapter 5. It must also be said here, however, that the general duty to take international law into account is a more abstract duty of state officials irrespective of their monist or dualist constitutional set ups. This signifies that there is no principled reason for state officials to approach international law as an authority that they should not take into account, regardless of debates about the extent to which they should respect the authority of a particular international law. This argument applies to politicians as well as judges. In the case of the latter, it also applies to those who regard themselves as explicitly constrained by dualist constitutional structures or common law precedent.[68] The general disposition to take international law into account does not equate to a stronger obligation to follow the letter of a particular international law.

The general disposition to take international law into account is not an empirical argument. The empirics of international law look at whether a state complies or not with particular international laws, and which factors influence particular compliance decisions. In order to approach something like a general disposition empirically, one would have to read the minds of each and every state official in the world. This is neither feasible nor necessary: the general disposition to take international law into account is a priorty given that the alternatives are not convincing.

This is both logical and historical. It is logical because it would be nonsensical to assume that states participate in the international legal system

[66] A general disposition of deferral to international law is also an important view to understand the relationship between states and quasi-judicial international institutions whose decisions are not legally binding. On the application of this view to United Nations Human Rights Committees, see Başak Çalı, 'The Legitimacy of International Interpretive Authorities for Human Rights Treaties: An Indirect-Instrumentalist Defence' in Føllesdal (n 36).

[67] By structural monism I refer to the place of international law as structurally shown in a state's constitution.

[68] The evidence from dualist states also support the view that even under dualist constitutional conditions, judiciaries are willing to take international law that has been ratified, but not yet incorporated into domestic law into account. See, for example, the Judgment of the High Court of Australia in *Dietrich v The Queen* (1992) 177 CLR 292.

with the purpose of disregarding that very system or make international legal commitments with the intention of violating them. International law for the most part concerns either areas where inter-state co-operation is necessary (such as areas of international peace and security) for state officials to pursue their domestic aims or areas where states have set common standards of treatment, policy, or action because co-ordination improves the regulation of issues that are of common concern to all (such as the environment, human rights protections, prosecution and punishment of international crimes). At the very minimum this indicates a general attitude amongst domestic state officials to respect international law in good faith. The presumption is also historical, in the sense that there is no credible evidence to show that a clear intention not to respect international law is prevalent amongst nations. As most commentators point out, states often provide excuses (however incoherent) for why they do not follow a certain international law, rather than expressing an outright rejection of the authority of the totality of international law.[69] In addition, the rise in treaty making attests that using international law to co-operate is widespread and prevalent.[70]

The general duty to take international law into account takes a strong view on the so-called Lotus principle. This principle takes the lack of a prohibition to suggest permissibility. Judge Simma notes this is an 'excessively deferential approach'[71] to make sense of the initial situation of international law and it does not match the conditions of international law at least since the end of the Second World War. He further asserts that 'under this approach, everything which is not expressly prohibited carries with it the same colour of legality; it ignores the possible degrees of non-prohibition, ranging from 'tolerated' to 'permissible' to 'desirable'.[72] In my defence of the general duty to take international law into account, just as legality has shades, the authority of international law also has shades when imposing duties on domestic legal orders. The initial duty to engage with international law does not prejudge the degree of authority it has over domestic legal orders.

[69] For a classical discussion of this see Higgins (n 26).

[70] The United Nations gives the number of multilateral treaties deposited with the Secretary General of the United Nations as more than 500. This number does not include treaties deposited with governments or other international organizations. http://www.un.org/en/globalissues/internationallaw/.

[71] Declaration of Judge Bruno Simma in *Accordance with International Law of the Unilateral Declaration of Independence in Respect of Kosovo (Advisory Opinion)* [2010] ICJ Rep 403 (Kosovo), 480, para 8.

[72] Ibid.

## Authority Competition

*The third* feature of the initial social situation is that the authority competition is a prevalent feature of the relationship between international law and domestic orders. In the international system, there is no final authority, but often multiple overlapping authorities with different sources of validation.[73] This feature is prevalent, but not fundamental. Domestic political institutions have no overlapping authority with international law when it comes to acts that are strictly forbidden by international law, such as, for example, acts of genocide or aggression. No national parliament has a claim on supreme or overlapping authority to legislate on matters that concern humanity as a whole. Equally, if the same crimes exist in domestic law, the presumption of deference to international law as an interpretive authority is undoubtedly strict. It would be problematic for domestic judges to interpret an international crime primarily based on the intentions of its own domestic legislatures. These situations aside, the presumption of authority competition is also a reasonable one both because there is no central legislative, interpretive, or enforcement authority in international law, and because there are limited explicit prohibitive rules for which the large input of the domestic legislative or judicial actors in interpreting and enforcing such rules would be an anathema to the existence of the rule in the first place.

What I mean by the prevalence of competition here, however, is not that domestic orders and international law are always in a position to offer their own versions of international law—a claim often made by normative pluralists.[74] It simply means that there is—in most cases—more than one forum that has the authority to make pronouncements on international law. The presumption of authority competition is therefore aligned with descriptive pluralism.[75] Authority competition may take place between two states, between an international organization and a state, between an international interpretive body and the legislature, or between an international interpretive body and the judiciary. I also do not rule out the existence of competition between domestic legislatures and domestic judiciaries with regard to deciding which obligations must be discharged in order to honour international law in good faith.

[73] Armin von Bogdandy 'Pluralism, Direct Effect and the Ultimate Say: On the Relationship between International and Domestic Constitutional Law' (2008) 6 *International Journal of Constitutional Law* 397.

[74] Cf Chapter 2 and also Paul Schiff Berman, *Global Legal Pluralism: A Jurisprudence of Law Beyond Borders* (Cambridge: Cambridge University Press 2012).

[75] I must, however, note that the existence of authority competition is unlikely to be challenged by any descriptive or normative account of the international legal order.

## Disaggregating the Duties of State Officials Towards International Law

*The fourth* component of the initial situation is that different domestic authorities (ie political organs of states and the judicial organs of states), whilst constrained by a general attitude towards taking international law into account, do not share the *same reasoning structures* for obeying or respecting the authority of particular international laws. This suggests that the fabric of the authority relationships between international law and domestic courts are not identical to authority relationships between international law and parliaments. The differences between these domestic institutions stem from differences in the nature of their decision-making powers. Whilst political organs participate in the making of international law, domestic judges have to interpret them alongside domestic laws under specific circumstances. The judicial duty to interpret law may, in some circumstances, bring domestic judges and domestic politicians into conflict as to the appropriate form through which to respect the authority of international law. Chapters 3 and 4 focus in greater detail on the differences in the authority relationships between political and judicial state officials and international law. For now, it should suffice to say that international law operates in distinct ways to augment, challenge, or exclude the authority of domestic political and judicial officials. In particular, judicial and political state officials are not furnished with similar powers and face different constraints on their decision-making authority. For example, whilst domestic legislative authorities have a power to change existing legislation, judicial authorities are under a duty to consider whether that new legislation is compatible with the existing obligations of the state as a whole.

I submit that none of the four components of the initial social situation set out above is controversial. That is, I am putting forward the initial social situation as a matter of a descriptive account of the place of international law in domestic systems. The four components are reasonable descriptions of the attitude towards international law in most of the world's legal systems. Even in very strongly monist countries where international law is above all law—the standard example here is the Netherlands—one can talk about authority competition.[76] Even in dualist states with strong traditions of following only the law of the land, judges may use reasons other than parliament in their decisions to follow a particular international law.

[76] A recent example of this discussion is Giuseppe Martinico, 'Is the European Convention Going to Be "Supreme"? A Comparative-Constitutional Overview of ECHR and EU Law before National Courts' (2012) 23 *European Journal of International Law* 401.

## Stage II: A Relational Notion of Authority

In the light of these basic characteristics of the initial situation, I hold that the *conceptual structure* of the authority of international law is a matter of degree. That is, international law exerts different degrees of authority upon state officials, and not all binding international law (treaty law or custom) enjoys the same degree of authority in relation to domestic legal systems.

The conceptual decoupling of the binding qualities of international laws (as opposed to non-legally binding international laws) and the authority claims of international laws offer us analytical leverage and clarity on a number of levels. First, we no longer need to insist that each international law makes an identical claim to authority over domestic legal orders. The assertion that international law gets its authoritative quality from its binding nature obscures the variable degree of the authority of particular international laws. Some make stronger claims to authority than others. Second, we do not need to assert that international law has any legitimate claim to authority *solely* due to individual or collective consent giving processes. Consent facilitates authoritative claims of international law, but it does not define them. As I have laid out in my description of the initial social situation of international law, a general disposition to take into account international law is not rooted in states' consent to international law, but in a more fundamental *attitude* that is necessary for international law to be a meaningful institution.

International law is not an accidental excess of inter-state relations or a secondary by-product of co-operation. It is a purposive social practice that only makes sense if actors participating in social practice have a general disposition towards it. What follows from this general attitude, however, is not blind obedience to each and every rule in international law. There are some international laws that leave no space for deliberation or discretion to the subjects of authority. The most notable example of this is the prohibition of the act of genocide. There are, however, also areas where the authority of international law is more negotiable and subject to argument. GATT Article XX concerning general exceptions to free trade exemplifies this.[77]

Holding that international law has relational authority is different from stating that in the real world international law is sometimes obeyed and sometimes ignored (or, as Henkin has stated, 'obeyed most of the time by most

[77] Thomas Cottier, Petros C Mavroidis, and Patrick Blatter (eds), *Regulatory Barriers and the Principle of Non-Discrimination in World Trade Law: Past, Present and Future* (Ann Arbor: Michigan University Press 2000).

of the states').[78] A combination of factors, such as lack of knowledge or capacity, self-interest, or prudence, explain why international laws are not always complied with in everyday practice.[79] What the relational authority denotes is not the motivations of the compliers, but the authoritative weight of the international norms themselves. This conception of authority is inescapably normative, also for this very reason. Whilst actor-focussed conceptions of authority, such as those that ask why A obeys B, have to make central assumptions about the identities, incentives and motivations of actors, norm-focussed conceptions of authority make assumptions about the nature of the norms, the kinds of demands they make, and under what conditions they *request* compliance.

This shift in focus for understanding the authority of international law sets it apart from other approaches I discussed in Chapter 1. On the one hand relational authority characterization departs from theories that depict international law as absolute authority (*à la* Kelsen)[80] and those theories that hold that the authority of international law is at best suspect (*à la* Posner and Goldstein).[81] On the other hand, the focus on the relational authority of norms, rather than on the reasons of compliers, sets this view apart from Razian theories of authority. As discussed earlier, the latter is overtly concerned with preserving individual autonomy and therefore, the reasons individuals may reasonably have to submit to authority. In the case of international law, however, this concern has no central place. International law does not command authority over individuals. It commands authority over artificial political entities in order to enable them to work towards protecting individuals from common risks better. International law does this either by imposing strong duties on states or by offering them a framework in which there is a wide space to manoeuvre in order to find solutions to common problems. In short, international laws make different types of authoritative claims on state officials.

If the conceptual structure of international legal authority is relational, it must follow that there are ways of distinguishing between the different degrees of authority imposed by particular international laws as a matter of legal doctrine. I submit that the degrees of the authority of international law can be distinguished by classifying the kinds of duties international

[78] Louis Henkin, *How Nations Behave: Law and Foreign Policy* (New York: Frederick A Praeger 1968).

[79] Political science is foremost interested in identifying which compliance factors matter for which states for which areas of law and under what kinds of conditions. See Beth Simmons, 'Treaty Compliance and Violation' (2010) 13(1) *Annual Review of Political Science* 273.

[80] Hans Kelsen, *General Theory of Law and State* (New York: Russell & Russell 1961).

[81] Goldsmith (n 15).

laws impose and the kinds of powers international laws confer on domestic authorities.

## Strong, Weak, and Rebuttable Duties

The distinction between strong, weak, and rebuttable duties imposed by international law is central to understanding the diversity of international laws that exist in the international system today and the different kinds of authority relationships that exist between international law and state officials. Strong duties are those that leave no discretionary space to state authorities. An international law with a strong duty structure will ask State A to do X. State A must do X or refrain from doing what X says to the letter. Weak duties are duties that grant state authorities room for discretion when taking action to respond to the authority claims of international law. When an international law with a weak duty structure tells State A to do X, State A is free to assess and deliberate about how to do X before it takes any action *towards* fulfilling its obligations. A rebuttable duty is a duty where there is a case for the duty to be balanced against another important duty that exists in either international or domestic law to the extent that, after deliberation, the rebuttable duty may be set aside in particular instances.

### Strong Duties

Consider Article 6(5) of the International Covenant on Civil and Political Rights (ICCPR). 'The sentence of death shall not be imposed for crimes committed by persons below eighteen years of age and shall not be carried out on pregnant women.'

This leaves no space for discretion to state authorities, judicial, executive, or legislative, in defining the persons upon whom the death penalty cannot be imposed. The article, for example, does not only prohibit the use of the death penalty against children per se, but also offers an international legal definition of children. State authorities may dispute when a woman can be considered to be 'pregnant', but the scope for this is very narrow. This particular rule of international law imposes a strict and prohibitive duty on all state officials that have ratified the ICCPR. Commentators, including UN human rights bodies, have further pointed out that the prohibition of the death penalty for juveniles and pregnant women has also been hardened into customary international law.[82]

[82] United Nations Economic and Social Council Resolution, 'Safeguards Guaranteeing the Protection of the Rights of Those Facing the Death Penalty', ESC Res 1984/50, UN Doc

The strong duties imposed here by international law make a powerful authoritative claim on state officials that does not solely take its power from the consent of the state to the treaty. These duties engage an obligation akin to the obligation to obey in the conceptual paradigm of domestic law. The obligation to obey in this case, however, does not stem from a prima facie obligation to obey international law. Rather it is a piecemeal obligation rooted in the fact that the authority structure of the international legal norm leaves no choice but to act or not to act in a specific way. All bodies of international law incorporate the imposition of some strong duties.

Whilst treaty law-making may be viewed as a better way of imposing strong duties, this is not always the case. In the field of the international law of state immunity, for example, the rule that no state can bring a civil case against another state in its domestic courts with respect to criminal acts is a strong duty that makes a strong authoritative claim on all state officials.[83] International laws that impose strong duties on state officials may emerge from any branch or under any accepted source of international law. In the case of state immunity, we also particularly see that actions of individual states do not and cannot undermine the authority of the particular international law. Italian and Greek courts consenting to allow individuals to bring civil cases against Germany in their courts does not undermine the authority of the principle of state immunity from civil suits with respect to past crimes.

The prevalence of strong duties in international law is a function of a number of things. First, the common risks laid out in the initial situation change in nature and scope over time. Some moral stances (such as the limited prohibition of the death penalty with regard to pregnant women and juveniles) may also get legalized over time within the framework of common risks to all peoples living under the jurisdiction of any state. Strong duties emerge when the inter-state community reaches consensus, either in the form of drafting a provision to a multilateral treaty or in the form of state practice, such that states (and their political and judicial institutions) do not enjoy any political or judicial discretion in managing such risks. Admittedly, this is a social approach to understanding emerging strong duties in international law. It

E/1984/84, 1984; United Nations Commission on Human Rights Resolution, 'Rights of the Child', E/CN.4/Res/2004/48; Commission on Human Rights Resolution, 'Human rights in the administration of justice, in particular juvenile justice', E/CN.4/Res/2004/43; United Nations General Assembly Resolution, 'Human Rights in the Administration of Justice', A/Res/56/161, 22 February 2002.

[83] *Jurisdictional Immunities of the State (Germany v Italy: Greece Intervening)* [2012] ICJ Rep 99 (*Jurisdictional Immunities*).

exists independently to arguments that hold that there may be strong moral duties that bind state officials.

Secondly, there are some regulatory fields of international law for which leaving a discretionary space to state officials in performing their duties under international law is anathema to the very purpose of the regulation. The prohibition of genocide is one such strong duty. Other specific prohibitive norms of international law, such as the prohibition of certain weapons,[84] also come under this. Prohibiting a particular conduct is so central to fending off common risks that such prohibitions impose strong duties and leave no space for deliberation. In the case of the prohibition of nuclear weapons, the International Court of Justice follows a similar logic, despite the fact that its rejection of the argument that the prohibition of nuclear weapons imposed a strong duty.[85]

Thirdly, strong duties are imposed by international laws that have the character of power conferring or power disabling. This is because power conferring and power disabling international laws operate by way of creating a new legal fact, which the state authorities respond to by way of recognizing it. In other words, power conferring or power disabling international laws exert authority over domestic orders by asking them to exercise authority or to refrain from exercising authority. For example, in the case of the law of the sea, international law confers powers to the flag state with regard to navigation on the high seas. This is reflected in Article 92 of the LOS Convention, the relevant parts of which reads:

'Ships shall sail under the flag of one State only and shall be subject to its exclusive jurisdiction on the high seas'.[86]

This provision exerts the authority of international law over domestic legal orders by explicitly conferring powers to it. The state obeys the authority of international law by accepting the power conferred upon it. A similar logic operates in the case of power-disabling international laws. A state is bound by

[84] In particular the absolute prohibition of chemical weapons and biological weapons. Cf The Protocol for the Prohibition of the Use in War of Asphyxiating, Poisonous or Other Gases, and of Bacteriological Methods of Warfare (adopted 17 June 1925, entered into force 8 February 1928) 94 UNTS 65; Convention on the Prohibition of the Development, Production and Stockpiling of Bacteriological (Biological) and Toxin Weapons and on Their Destruction (adopted 10 April 1972, entered into force 26 March 1975) 1015 UNTS 163; Convention on Prohibitions or Restrictions on the Use of Certain Conventional Weapons Which May Be Deemed to Be Excessively Injurious or to Have Indiscriminate Effects (adopted 10 October 1980, entered into force 2 December 1983) 1342 UNTS 137.

[85] *Legality of the Threat or Use of Nuclear Weapons (Advisory Opinion)* [1996] ICJ Rep 226 (*Nuclear Weapons*).

[86] UNCLOS art 2.

the authority of international law and must set aside its own domestic powers to respect it. The recognition of the prisoner of war status of combatants in the international law of armed conflict is a power disabling type of international law. Domestic state authorities are under an obligation to set aside their domestic criminal law when dealing with enemy combatants. What is more, these combatants must be governed by a legal regime exclusively defined by international law.[87]

## Weak Duties

Weak duties operate under a different logic from strong duties. Let us now consider Article 2(3) of the United Nations Charter:

> 'All Members shall settle their international disputes by peaceful means in such a manner that international peace and security, and justice, are not endangered.'

According to the distinction between weak and strong duty structures, Article 2(3) has a weak duty structure. It *guides* states (most notably the executives) to settle their disputes in peaceful ways. It further qualifies peaceful ways and requires such ways not to endanger international peace, security, and justice. Within this broad and general direction, however, states are free to choose a diverse range of peaceful means. The article neither condones nor lists any such means. These might include, for example, submitting disputes to judicial settlement or arbitration; seeking diplomatic methods, such as negotiation, mediation, good offices, inquiry, or conciliation; seeking settlement by the UN or regional organizations; or inviting in international or regional peacekeeping forces. The authority of international law in this specific instance operates by guiding states towards a general purpose without specifying the means of fulfilling that object. State authorities continue to have a wide range of discretion.

Weak duties imposed by international law attract duties of respect. The duty to respect requires state officials to take international law into account and decide and deliberate on the most adequate option/means/measures to discharge their international law obligations. The authoritative claim that international law makes in the case of weak duties is a claim for changing the original normative situations of state officials. Weak duties place state officials in a new normative framework and create special reasons for action for those same officials. By being part of an international legal framework,

[87] Convention Relative to the Treatment of Prisoners of War (adopted 12 August 1949, entered into force 21 October 1950) 75 UNTS 135 (Third Geneva Convention) is the key governing authority for this.

state officials accept that they will conduct their actions in the light of the broader purposes of that regulatory framework. They may, for example, have to enact new legislation, or empower their judges to adjudicate matters in a different way. As executives, they may have to carry out new plans of action, or revise old ways of carrying out public policy. Again, all branches of international law impose such weaker duties. A well-known example in international human rights law is the International Covenant on Economic, Social, and Cultural Rights (ICESCR).[88] For a long time, critics of economic and social rights in general dismissed this treaty as not creating *real* legal obligations and creating *merely* recommendations for policy.[89] Whilst this is an inaccurate description of the range of obligations included in the treaty,[90] it also underplays the prevalence of weak duty imposing obligations in all bodies of international law.

## Rebuttable Duties

The third way in which the authority of international law operates is by imposing rebuttable duties on states. Rebuttable duties are those duties that state authorities can set aside when they are able to show that another equally important duty is preventing them from performing it. On first analysis, rebuttable duties may sound like the apologist's paradise. They allow states to provide reasons for not obeying or respecting the authority of international law. They may also appear to be playing into the hands of the rational school of international law. This school argues that all international law is composed of rebuttable duties. When faced with contrary self-interest, the rational school holds that states ought to follow self-interest (a paramount duty) at the expense of international law.

I hold that rebuttable duties need not be hostage to these criticisms. First, as is also the case for strong and weak duties, rebuttable duties are an observation about the conceptual features of fundamental international law. Contrary to what the rational choice school holds, not all duties of international law have a rebuttable structure. For a duty to have a rebuttable structure there has to be a clear competition between two competing and equally important values in the specific circumstances, and state authorities have to

[88] International Covenant on Economic, Social, and Cultural Rights (adopted 16 December 1966, entered into force 3 January 1976) 993 UNTS 5 (ICESCR).

[89] For exposition of these views, see Kitty Arambulo, *Strengthening the Supervision of the International Covenant on Economic, Social and Cultural Rights: Theoretical and Prodecural Aspects* (Oxford: Intersentia 1999) 17, 66–88.

[90] ICESCR art 13(2)(a), for example requires all states to make elementary education free and compulsory, leaving no space of discretion to state officials.

show that the competition is tangible. Rebuttable duties, therefore, allow states to set aside the authoritative influence of a norm of international law on a case-by-case basis, only when it would be impossible to discharge another equally important duty.

Rebuttable duties come in two forms. First are the rebuttable duties that explicitly make reference to an equally important duty in their conceptual structures. Second are those which do not explicitly indicate the range of other values in competition with the duty imposed by international law. The best known rebuttable duty in international law is the prohibition on the unilateral use of force under the United Nations Charter. Article 2(4) bans the unilateral use of force, but explicitly writes that states have an inherent right to self-defence under Article 51. Each time a state employs unilateral force, it has to show that an equally important interest—that of self-defence—was at stake.[91]

The law of the sea and the law of international trade also incorporate similar rebuttable duty structures. GATT Article XX incorporates social clauses that allow states to carry out protection measures which make the general duty of enabling free trade rebuttable.[92] The balance between navigational freedom and coastal state jurisdiction in matters protecting the environment in exclusive economic zones also brings with it rebuttable duties vis-à-vis the duty of coastal states to protect the environment.

Rebuttable duties that do not explicitly point to an equally important interest are also present in the corpus of international law. These often include provisions of international law over which there are important disputes regarding scope. Respect for the right to self-determination is one such disputed rebuttable duty. Whilst international law recognizes the right to internal and external self-determination,[93] the duty to respect peoples' right to self-determination can be subject to rebuttal due to the interests of international peace and security.[94]

In areas of international law in which the normative content of the law is under-determined, the rebuttal of international law obligations by state

[91] There is, of course, a long-standing debate in international law about whether the conditions of the rebuttablity of the ban on the use of force also include humanitarian intervention. For a review of these debates, see Niger Rodley and Başak Çalı, 'Kosovo Revisited: Humanitarian Intervention on the Fault Lines of International Law' (2007) 7(2) *Human Rights Law Review* 275.

[92] WTO, *United States: EC Measures Concerning Meat and Meat Products (Hormones), Complaint by Canada—Report of the Panel* (13 February 1998) WT/DS26/R as modified by the Appellate Body Report WT/DS48/R.

[93] UN Charter; common art 2 of ICESCR and International Covenant on Civil and Political Rights (adopted 16 December 1966, entered into force 23 March 1976) 999 UNTS 171 (ICCPR).

[94] For a critical assessment of this, see Steven Wheatley, 'The Security Council, Democratic Legitimacy and Regime Change in Iraq' (2006) 17(3) *European Journal of International Law* 531.

authorities may come across as international law being used purely as political rhetoric.[95] In fields of international law in which a third party adjudicatory mechanism is present, on the other hand, rebuttals can become more disciplined.[96] In the case of a mature adjudication culture, such as that of the European Court of Human Rights, rebuttable duties have also given way to a legal doctrine: margin of appreciation. Although this is a disputed doctrine[97] and the European Court of Human Rights recognizes that, for most of the rights protected by the Convention, the scope of rebuttal is either non-existent[98] or incredibly narrow,[99] the doctrine of margin of appreciation is a recognition that the authority of international law can be set aside in some specific instance.

The argument that some states are prone to rebut the authority of international law in most instances, or that rebuttals may be an insincere engagement with the authority of international law, are observations about the empirical operations of rebuttals in particular instances. Conceptually, what is distinct about rebuttable duties is that state authorities have to engage in a reason-giving exercise in order to set aside the authority of a particular law. Rebuttable duties are not a form of state disobedience to international law, as states are not moral entities and *do not* have an inherent right to disobey laws. Rebuttable duties are an important mechanism, on the other hand, to iron out the tension between democratic governance within states and international governance across states. A state characterized by high levels of deliberative democratic consciousness to protect the environment, for example, benefits from the rebuttable duty of free trade.

Whether the authority of international law is strong, weak, or rebuttable is not static and is subject to changes both through customary international law and the interpretative practices of existing treaty obligations. This is easily observed in the field of the international law of armed conflict. Whilst for

[95] Critical legal scholars maintain that the employment of the authority or lack of political authority of international law is political rhetoric *all the way*. For a now classic exposition of this see Koskeniemmi, *From Apology to Utopia: The Structure of International Legal Argument* (Cambridge: Cambridge University Press 2006).

[96] Although it is often highlighted that where there is a court, states are compelled to offer a long list of reasons for their rebuttal of the authority of international law, allowing the courts to identify the relevant reasons. See in particular, the defence of the United States in the *Case Concerning the Military and Paramilitary Activities In and Against Nicaragua (Nicaragua v United States of America)* [1986] ICJ Rep 14 (*Nicaragua*).

[97] H C Yourow, *The Margin of Appreciation Doctrine in the Dynamics of European Human Rights Jurisprudence* (The Hague: Kluwer Law International 1996); Yutaka Arai, *The Margin of Appreciation Doctrine and the Principle of Proportionality in the Jurisprudence of the ECHR* (Antwerp: Intersentia 2002).

[98] *Saadi v Italy* (2009) 49 EHRR 30 [GC].

[99] *Goodwin v UK* (1996) 22 EHRR 123 [GC].

significant periods of time the range of weapons used in armed conflict was subject to a rebuttal between the principle of military necessity and the principle of humanity, consensus and new treaties have significantly increased the number of prohibited weapons, graduating the duties of states from rebuttable duties to strong duties.[100]

## Ius Cogens and the Authority of International Law

How does the conceptual ranking of authoritative claims made by international law over domestic orders relate to the category of ius cogens norms of international law? The category of ius cogens norms with two distinct, well-known features.[101] Firstly, they are non-derogable. Secondly, when there is a conflict between an ius cogens norm and another norm, so long as the latter norm is not an ius cogens norm itself, the ius cogens norm should prevail.[102] The conceptual category of an ius cogens norm, therefore, allows us to distinguish between international laws that have a stronger normative claim than other international norms. Does this also mean that ius cogens norms have a stronger authoritative claim than other international norms?

Under the relative account of the authority of international law, the answer to this question depends on the very normative content of the norm itself. That is, if we cannot assume that all international norms do not have absolute authority over domestic systems, we must also hold that not all ius cogens norms have absolute authority over the very same systems. Not all norms that are regarded as ius cogens norms make a strong claim to authority even though we can safely assume that most norms that do have ius cogens status will be placing strong duties on strong authorities. The most well-known example of an ius cogens norm in contemporary international law is the prohibition of torture. The prohibition of torture is a norm (regardless of its ius cogens status) that sets out an absolute obligation on state authorities not to torture and, if torture happens, to prosecute its perpetrators.[103] Even without its jus cogens nature, the prohibition of torture makes a strong claim to authority over domestic legal orders. What the ius cogens characterization of the norm does is to offer additional normative assurances concerning the resilience of the prohibition of torture. It does so by indicating that states cannot choose to derogate from this norm and cannot override this norm with lex posterior.

[100] Christopher Greenwood, 'Law of Weaponry at the Start of the New Millennium' in Michael N Schmitt and Leslie C Green (eds), *The Law of Armed Conflict: Into the Next Millennium* (Newport: Naval War College 1998).

[101] Cf Vienna Convention on the Law of Treaties 1969 (VCLT) art 53.

[102] Cf VCLT 1969 art 64.

[103] de Wet (n 26).

Despite the close relationship between ius cogens norms and strong normative claims to authority, however, there may also be ius cogens norms that make a weaker claim to authority or even a rebuttable claim to authority. The right to self-determination of peoples is one such potential norm. The East Timor case before the International Court of Justice squarely declared the right to self-determination as an erga omnes norm.[104] Some have interprerted this as implied support for the ius cogens character of the norm.[105] The controversy over whether this is indeed the case aside, this declaration does not solve problems associated with the range of duties owed by domestic authorities that are attached to the right of self-determination.[106] In particular, there is uncertainty with regard to when a group is identified as a people, when a state representing a people loses the right to exercise self-determination on behalf of that people, and the means through which respect for the right to self-determination of other peoples must be exercised by states.

Consequently, the relative conceptualization of the authority of international law breaks the strong association made implicitly between ius cogens norms and strong or absolute binding authority. Ius cogens claims make a particular normative claim about a given international law by placing it in a category distinct from international law. The authoritative claims that *any* international law makes in domestic legal orders, however, depends on how the international law supports, replaces, or qualifies domestic norms.

## Violations of Strong, Weak, and Rebuttable Duties

The distinction between rebuttable duty imposing, weak duty imposing, and strong duty imposing international laws does not suggest that there is a difference in kind in terms of the failure of state authorities to discharge these duties. Put another way, state authorities do not violate international law *less* when they violate a weak duty or fail to adequately rebut. In the case of all duties, the consequence of non-performance is a violation of international law. The violation of any duty imposed by international law upsets the overall respect for the international rule of law as an institution that helps states to manage common risks to humanity. All formulations of duties are

[104] *Case Concerning East Timor (Portugal v Australia)* [1995] ICJ Rep 4 *(East Timor)* 102.

[105] John Crawford, *The Creation of States in International Law* (2nd edn, Oxford: Oxford University Press 2006) 101; Alexander Orakhelashvili, *Peremptory Norms in International Law* (Oxford: Oxford University Press 2006) 51.

[106] Antonio Cassese, *Self-Determination of Peoples: A Legal Reappraisal* (Cambridge: Cambridge University Press 1995).

culminations of years of co-operation, either through treaty drafting processes or long and consistent state practice around converging normative expectations. None of these duties emerge as arbitrary impositions on states, but are rather outcomes of painstaking processes.

Whether an actor is able to seek accountability for disregarding the authority of international law also does not depend on whether the authority of international law is strong, weak, or rebuttable. Rather, accountability for violations of international law is a matter of the strength of the institutional accountability systems in place. For example, the WTO offers a solid forum for providing accountability both for violations of free trade and for rebuttals of respecting the principle of free trade. No similar institution exists in the case of the use of force and its exception of self-defence or for the prohibition of genocide, given that ICJ jurisdiction is not compulsory for UN member states. Prohibition of torture, a strong duty imposed by international law, however, enjoys a good level of accountability, in particular because most domestic courts in the world have jurisdiction to try violators and regional human rights courts have a wide net to cast. The existence of accountability mechanisms certainly contributes to the perceived social authority of international law. The fact that an international law does not come with a particularly established and institutionalized judicial accountability and enforcement mechanism, however, does not alter international law's legal claim to authority.

Having said this, the authority of international laws is more effectively enforced judicially and has more traction politically when those international laws concern strong duties. In most legal systems, it is easier to adjudicate on strong duties than weak or rebuttable ones. Courts are also more approachable when a violation concerns a prohibition rather than a permission or a process of reason-giving concerning international laws. In the case of rebuttable duties, domestic courts may also shy away from adjudication by viewing international laws as not justiciable and more as a domain of the prerogative of the executive. This is often the case, for example, with the domestic protection of economic and social rights under the International Covenant on Economic Social and Cultural Rights.[107] Domestic courts view the 'duties to progressively realise' economic, social, and cultural rights as not attracting any accountability before domestic courts.

Strong duties in international law make their way more easily to domestic law as there is a better chance of them having an overlapping character

[107] For contrary evidence, see Varun Gauri and Daneil M Brinks (eds), *Courting Social Justice: Judicial Enforcement of Economic and Social Rights in the Developing World* (Cambridge: Cambridge University Press 2010).

with domestic norms. The violation of strong duties, therefore, may put other states in the better position of being able to take action in response to the violation itself. Such actions can be taken by foreign parliaments, judiciaries, or executives. The prosecution of foreign nationals for the crime of torture in foreign countries in domestic national courts is one example of this.[108] In the case of weak duties imposed by international law, violations lend themselves to judicial remedies, but there may be fewer incentives to trigger inter-state counter-measures. For states to be accused of violating weaker duties, it must often be shown that they are arbitrarily ignoring the normative framework of action imposed by international law. If adjudicated against, states may also have resort to various forms of defence to show that they were in the process of taking a duty into account, but that this process was taking time. This is often the case when states are required by international law to regulate a particular field in their domestic law.

## Conclusion

This chapter argued that the authority of international law is a function of the duties imposed and powers conferred by particular international laws. Whilst international law as a legal system enjoys a general duty of presumption of deference from domestic legal systems, this does not equate to a duty of blind obedience to each and every international law. Instead, the authority of international law attracts different kinds of duties ranging from strong to weak and from weak to rebuttable.

These are arguments with regard to the conceptual structure of the authority of international law. That being the case, they do not prejudice shifts in the content of international laws over time. By looking at the corpus of *existing* international law we can reasonably indicate which international laws impose strong, weak, and rebuttable duties. The allocation of international laws into these different duty structures can, however, change, alter, and evolve over time.

[108] See the seminal case of *Filartiga v Pena-Irala* 630 F 2d 876 (2nd Cir 1980), US Court of Appeals for the Second Circuit, 30 June 1980; as well as the Pinochet cases: *R v Bow Street Metropolitan Stipendiary Magistrate, ex p Pinochet Ugarte (No 1)* [1998] 3 WLR 1456 (HL); *affd* sub nom *(No 2)* [1999] 2 WLR 272 (HL); *affd* sub nom *(No 3)* [1999] 2 WLR 827 (HL).

# 3

# Minimal Deference and Domestic Political Authority

'If you believe in international law you've just got to take it on the chin, really.'[1]

## Introduction

The central aim in this chapter is to assess whether a minimal level of deference to international law and, in turn, the duty to act in accordance with the differentiated duties imposed by international law hold when pitted against the traditional and contemporary critiques of the standard view of the authority of international law. Are political authorities under a duty to adopt an attitude of deference towards international law at all times? Is the duty to defer to international law too demanding a criterion for political authorities?

As discussed previously, one of the central weaknesses of the standard view of international law has been its brief and perhaps defensive stance with regard to asserting the authority of international law over domestic political organs through consent. This view has come under sustained attack from many corners due to the brief, but oft repeated assertion of the binding qualities of international law. Consent and critiques from multiple corners cannot answer all questions about the authority of international law. In Chapter 2 I argued that a revision of the standard view is needed to offer a deeper justification for a more complex account of the authority of international law. Such a justification does not rely on consent *tout court*, but on an account that is based on a general attitude of minimalist deference towards international law. I also argued that such an attitude of minimalist

[1] Interview, British Politician, Houses of Parliament, London, July 2008.

deference is just one part of the story. Only after accepting that deference are we able to inquire as to how international law claims authority over domestic systems. The minimalist deference I outline covers international law lex lata. It is owed towards the existing corpus of international law, which still comes about largely through consent due to the prominence of multilateral treaties in international law, but with the allowance that consent may be withheld for a special class of norms or relaxed when searching for customary international law.

If consent cannot be defended adequately, can we defend the paradigm of minimalist deference? The objections, even to a duty to minimalist deference, can be wide and varied. There may firstly be objections to the very general idea that there is a duty of minimalist deference to international law. Secondly, some hold that international law does not impose a scheme of differentiated duties in the form of strong, weak, and rebuttable duties. Thirdly, there are objections to the authority of interpretive organs of international law to decide on the category of duties imposed by international law. Whilst some of these may be received sympathetically if the authority of international law is viewed from an uncompromising either/or perspective, I shall show in this chapter that they are misplaced when the authority of international law is conceived as imposing different strengths of duties on political power.

## The Nature of Domestic Political Authority

Domestic political authority has the authority to enact, apply, enforce, and even interpret domestic law through its different branches. The power to enact is the exclusive domain of the legislative political authority.[2] The power to apply and enforce domestic law, in other words the concretization of law in application,[3] is the domain of the executive political authority. This authority also interprets domestic law in the process of application when a statute is not clear. It also, depending on the particular features of a legal system in question, shares powers of interpretation, application, and at times, enforcement with the judicial authority. In some systems, the actions and omissions

[2] Here we must also note that in some states the distinction between executive and legislative authority is not well demarcated. These include states where there is no legislature or states where the executives have powers to act like the legislature through means introduced into domestic public law.

[3] On the specification of law see Tushnet, 'The Relation Between Political Constitutionalism and Weak-Form Judicial Review' (2013) 14 *German Law Review* 2249.

of the domestic executive authority are subject to judicial review.[4] In others, the actions and omissions of the legislative authority are subject to judicial constitutional review.[5]

Domestic political authority then is made up of overlapping and fragmented branches of authority domestically. Whilst parliaments (where they exist) are the initial source of authority, the authority of determining the content and the scope of legislation is shared with the executive political authority as well as the judicial authority. The degree to which this authority fragments or overlaps, however, is determined by the political and legal framework in each and every domestic political and legal order. Whilst in some jurisdictions the power to enact, implement, and enforce laws is heavily concentrated in one body, in other jurisdictions the domestic political authority is carefully divided. The fate of domestic law, once enacted by a political authority is, therefore, determined from interactions between political authority and other domestic powers within any domestic legal and political system.[6]

It is a well-known fact of international law that there is no customary or other international legal rule that determines the scope of domestic political authority within each and every domestic system. International legal society recognizes a wide range of domestic political authority arrangements as states for the purposes of international law. How domestic political authority is organized is primarily a matter of domestic constitutional law.[7] International law does not require states to judicially review the proper application of international laws by their executives or legislative authorities.[8] There is also no international law that offers any comprehensive guidance or instructions with regard to how domestic political authorities should make domestic law.[9] The relationship between domestic political authorities and

[4] This is indeed a modern concept. Reginald Parker, 'The Historic Basis of Administrative Law: Separation of Powers, and Judicial Supremacy' (1957–8) 12 *Rutgers Law Review* 449.

[5] The power of courts to strike down incompatible legislation and administrative action is an innovation of the American constitutional order, but it has spread widely across the world's legal systems. Tom Ginsburg, 'The Global Spread of Constitutional Review' Gregory A Caldeira, R Daniel Kelemen, and Keith E Whittington (eds), *The Oxford Handbook of Law and Politics* (Oxford: Oxford University Press 2008). It has also attracted significant skeptics, Jeremy Waldron, 'The Core Case against Judicial Review' (2006) 115 *Yale Law Journal* 1346; Richard Bellamy, *Political Constitutionalism* (New York; Cambridge University Press 2007).

[6] Martin Loughlin, *Public Law and Political Theory* (Oxford: Clarendon Press 1992) 138.

[7] Robert Y Jennings and Arthur Watts (eds), *Oppenheim's International Law*, Vol I (1992) 82–3.

[8] An exception to this is the rise of the right to individual petition before constitutional or supreme courts that allows for judicial review of international human rights law conventions in Europe, Africa, and the Americas.

[9] An 'emerging right to democratic' governance has been on the agenda of international lawyers for some time now. See Tom Franck, 'The Emerging Right to Democratic Governance' (1992) 86 *American Journal of International Law* 46; Gregory Fox and Brad R Roth (eds), *Democratic*

international law is primarily a domain of argument rather than a formally prescribed relationship. In discussions on the authority of international law over domestic political authorities, there is often a disconnect between the approach of international lawyers and the approach of domestic and public constitutional lawyers or theorists of democracy. As our discussion of the standard account illustrates, whilst international law imposes obligations on an entity called a state, the internal organs of that very state often do not recognize any legal authority above and beyond its very own constitution. Put simply, it is common place for domestic lawyers to recognize international law when their constitutional law nods to the importance of the authority of international law.[10]

Here lies the crux of the problem between the authority of international law and the authority of domestic political authorities. In the absence of a specific and explicit rule or norm that hierarchically places international law above and beyond domestic political authorities, how do we set out an authority relationship between international law and domestic political authority? What reasons are there to accept that international law imposes strong, weak, and rebuttable duties on domestic political authorities so that they are under a general obligation to take international law into account?

Here I tackle this disconnect and show that there are multiple arguments to support the two core theses of this book that all domestic authorities, including political organs, are under a general duty to take international law into account and to act in accordance with the differentiated duty scheme international law imposes on them. The authority scheme previously developed is flexible enough to accommodate the sovereignty (the 'we the people') concerns of most constitutional lawyers and proponents of democratic theory.

The discussion and analysis in this chapter is intimately linked to, and also comes prior to analyzing the authority relationship of international law and domestic judicial authorities. How we theorize the authority relationship between domestic judicial authorities and international law for the most part turns to how we initially conceive the relationship between political authorities and international law. Without arguing about the scope and extent of international law's authority over the legislative and executive branches of

*Governance and International Law* (Cambridge: Cambridge University Press 2000); Susan Marks, 'What has become of the emerging right to democratic governance?' (2011) 22(2) *European Journal of International Law* 507.

[10] On domestic constitutional recognition of international law, see, *Murray v The Schooner Charming Betsy* (1804) 6 US (2 Cranch) 64, 118, 2 L Ed 208 ('[A]n act of congress ought never to be construed to violate the law of nations, if any other possible construction remains...' is the classic statement of this.)

the domestic order, we cannot proceed with the relationship between international law and domestic courts and the latter's authority relationship with international law. The relationship domestic judges have with the authority of international law depends on their understanding of the relationship between domestic political authority and international law. Whether judicial authorities are best conceived as being in a position of 'loyalty conflict'[11] between international law and domestic law primarily turns on our perception of whether domestic political authorities are able to trump international law either when there is a conflict between existing domestic law and international law or old international law and new domestic law. I develop this in the next chapter.

## Objections to the Authority of International Law

The task of delineating the authority relationship between international law and domestic political authorities runs into two types of objections. I call these 'preliminary objections' and 'qualified objections' to the authority of international law over the political organs of state.

Preliminary objections are rooted in a traditional variant of sovereignty literature. This refuses the existence of any law above and beyond the will of a domestic political authority.[12] For Hobbes, this was primarily due to the necessity of having a single sovereign imposing law on society. The alternative requires creating a new sovereign and it has long been settled that international law without the absence of a world state does not present a hierarchical sovereign order, but a horizontal scheme of co-existence and co-operation. The preliminary objections, therefore, query the very possibility of an authority relationship between a sovereign state and international law in however weak a form. This is the ultimate normative absolutism about the authority of the political organs of a state.

Qualified objections, on the other hand, are rooted in the sovereign prerogative to interpret international law. These objections are most pronounced in the restrictive interpretation canon of international law[13] and democratic

[11] Eyal Benevisti, 'Judicial Misgivings Regarding the Application of International Law: An Analysis of National Courts' (1993) 4 *European Journal of International Law* 159.

[12] T Hobbes, *Leviathan* (ed Richard Tuck) (Cambridge: Cambridge University Press 1991) p 169. Cf J Bodin, *The Six Bookes of a Commonweale* (R Knolles trans (1606), KD McRae (ed)) (Cambridge: Harvard University Press 1962).

[13] Gerald Fitzmaurice, '*Vae Victis* or Woe to the Negotiators? Your Treaty or Our Interpretation of It' (review essay), (1971) 65 *American Journal of International Law* 372.

sovereignty literature.[14] Qualified objections to the authority of international law do not query the plausibility of the authority of international law per se. They are based on the inescapable nature of statism in the interpretation of international law. In that sense the latter dispute the authority of international law in cases when non-sovereign interpretations of international law conflict with domestic political authority.[15] It is here that we see Mr Davis's objections to the implications of the *Hirst* judgment for British legislation.

## Preliminary Objections: Traditional Sovereignty with Normative Absolutism

Normative absolutism is deeply sceptical about the authority of international law over domestic political organs. According to normative absolutism, international law is an antithesis to the political sovereignty doctrine. This has two important consequences. First, domestic political power cannot be dominated through fixed external arrangements. Second, international laws cannot have an independent existence at the level of the domestic legal order as it is governed by domestic law whose ultimate source of authority is the single domestic political authority of that order. Normative absolutism, therefore, relies on the core assumption that international law as a matter of a category of law cannot impose any duties on domestic political power. It does not possess the quality of authoritativeness because it lacks one essential element—validation from a single political source. Law's authority stems from the enactment of laws by the single and final domestic political authority. International law, made by a collection of political sovereign authorities, does not attain the necessary conditions of authority. As international law does not (and cannot) possess the authoritative qualities of a sovereign, it only exists in a different sphere of relationships offering mere guidance to orderly and co-operative interactions amongst sovereign nation states.

As international relations theorists have long reminded us, guidance provided by international law may be helpful, but it does not offer exclusionary reasons to explain how states decide on particular courses of conduct.[16] International

[14] See in particular, Chapter 2, pp 44–6.

[15] This is in parallel with what some scholars call the dynamic international law as opposed to static international law. See generally, von Bogdandy and Venzke, 'In Whose Name? An Investigation of International Courts' Public Authority and Its Democratic Justification' 23 *European Journal of International Law* (2012) 7–41. p 22; Jan Klabbers, 'On Rationalism in Politics: Interpretation of Treaties and the World Trade Organisation' (2005) 74 *Nordic Journal of International Law* 405.

[16] JJ Mearsheimer 'The False Promise of International Institutions' (1994) 19(3) *International Security* 5–49.

relations realism seeks to protect domestic political authority by maintaining that international law has relevance (but not authority) to the extent intended by the domestic political power. It, therefore, assigns a temporary and instrumental role to international law. It holds relevance for domestic political organs so long as that international law is useful for a political authority. The realist assigns value to international law up to the point that the value serves the self-interest of states.[17] When the self-interest of a state coincides with international law, the political authority may seem, for an external observer, to be bowing to the authority of international law. This is merely an overlap of content-dependent reasons that a sovereign power already has with the directives of international law. International law ought, therefore, to be viewed by decision-makers as fluid and subject to revision based on the continual calculations made between self-interest and authority.

The centrality of the actors in the system and not the demands of law has been a popular approach elsewhere. Rawls in 'The Law of Peoples' indicated that he was writing for a liberal political sovereign and how it ought to act in a world of states with diverse internal justice arrangements.[18] Despite the suggestion of his title, Rawls does not treat international law as an independent authority over domestic political power. Instead, he seeks to speak to an enlightened and domestically liberal political power with the aim of informing its conduct in a world liberal people share with people who are either well-ordered or outlawed.[19]

Normative absolutism sits oddly with the conceptual scheme of authority I introduced in Chapter 2. This is because the very idea of international law as an institution that imposes a variety of duties on a political sovereign power cannot be accommodated within this worldview. Normative absolutism cannot concede ground to a general attitude that asks for international law to be taken into account as a starting point of analysis, as even that general attitude cannot be reconciled with the sovereign power being absolute. Normative absolutism also cannot accept rebuttable duties on sovereign political powers as a right of rebuttal comes with duties to offer public reasons to the rest of the international community as to why a sovereign power has to rebut an undertaking it has already accepted in specific circumstances.

As a normative outlook on the authority of international law, normative absolutism can hold domestic politicians in a hefty grip. In the everyday practice of domestic politics, normative absolutism manifests itself when

[17] Jack Donnely, *Realism and International Relations* (Cambridge: Cambridge University Press 2000).

[18] Rawls, *The Law of Peoples* (Cambridge: Harvard University Press 1999).

[19] Ibid.

a political authority discusses or assesses a matter with sole regard for the domestic law regulating it, despite overlapping identical international law commitments. Normative absolutism also manifests itself when states legislate contrary to their international law obligations.[20] The proponents of normative absolutism do exist and do exercise political power.

The uptake of normative absolutism by politicians in everyday politics, however, does not tell us anything about the coherency of this view. There are four fundamental weaknesses in subscribing to a normative absolutist view when it comes to the authority of international law.

First is the well-known and well-exposed weakness of the outdated nature of this view. As observers have long suggested, normative absolutism fits better in earlier periods of international law and relations. A world of increasing interdependence between sovereign states means normative absolutism is an odd view to hold on the relationship between international law and sovereign political power. It is hard, if not impossible to find proponents that suggest that international law and domestic law exist in full isolation from one another in most jurisdictions.[21] Simply, there are too many treaties, too many international organizations and regimes in the international system to allow the suggestion that sovereign power recognizes no authority but itself. This is largely due to the proliferation and diversification of international law and institutions since 1945 and the increasing range of international law treaties that regulate areas that overlap with domestic law in areas ranging from human rights, trade, criminal law, environment, and investment.[22] The duties imposed by international law on domestic legal and political orders simply cannot be contained by a logic of peaceful co-existence between separate legal orders which all insist on the finality of their political power.[23]

Second, there is a deeper conceptual weakness to normative absolutism. It does not address what we may label as the authority of international law to

[20] Dualist normative dispositions, however, are not the only reasons for domestic political authorities ignoring international law. Chayes and Chayes, for example, carefully put the point forward that lack of knowledge or capacity may also be the reason for not interacting with international law, A Chayes and AH Chayes, *The New Sovereignty: Compliance with International Regulatory Agreements* (Cambridge: Harvard University Press 1995).

[21] But see, Jens David Ohlin, *The Assault on International Law* (Oxford: Oxford University Press 2015).

[22] For an early forceful statement of this, see Bruno Simma, 'The International Community: Facing the Challenge of Globalisaton' (1998) 9 *European Journal of International Law* 266–77.

[23] For a recent survey of the proliferation of international law beyond co-existence, see, Ulrich Fastenrath, Rudolf Geiger, Daniel-Erasmus Khan, Andreas Paulus, Sabine von Schorlemer, and Christoph Vedder (eds), *From Bilateralism to Community Interest: Essay in Honour of Bruna Simma* (Oxford: Oxford University Press 2011).

define the 'jurisdictional disabilities' of domestic political orders.[24] Even if one may subscribe to the separateness thesis, what a domestic political authority cannot regulate is a matter primarily settled by international law. Even if one may hold a view about the internal finality of political power, that very same view cannot settle the finality of political power externally. To take a conventional example, single political authorities are not the authors of the law governing sovereign immunities. They depend on other states to enforce their sovereign immunity in their external relations. Domestic political authorities must defer to customary international law on sovereign immunities as collectively developed by nations. This is because no one state has the final say on their own sovereign immunity before the courts of other states or before an international court. This serves to illustrate that parts of domestic political authority are necessarily constituted and regulated by international law. Normative absoluteness cannot point to an adequate solution when it seeks to protect its political powers externally.

The third problem with normative absolutism is less exposed. Normative absolutists do not take issue with states consenting to agreements with other states when they choose to do so. Their view on consent, however is different from international law's standard view on consent. Consent for a normative absolutist is temporary. It can be withdrawn at any time that the sovereign prerogative requires it to be withdrawn. This insistence on the temporary character of consent as a matter of principle is incoherent with the first principles of the very idea of contract. Consent to a contract is not just a symbol of free will, but it is also an acceptance of rules that govern consent giving and consent accepting. Giving consent to a treaty requests the consent-giver to recognize that it has established legal relations with the parties with whom it is exchanging consent. At the very least, the withdrawal of consent must be subject to rules that are not determined by a single consent-giver. Once a normative absolutist accepts the canon of consensual relations with other states, they must, at the very least, accept that they are bound by the principle of pact sunt servanda and, as a matter of positive law, the provisions of the Vienna Convention on the Law of Treaties for withdrawing consent.[25] The freedom to give consent cannot be defined independently from the rules that govern it. This is also supported by our conceptual understanding that underpins any authority: authorities can only claim to be authoritative

[24] This is in spirit of Hohfeld. W Hohfeld, 'Some Fundamental Legal Conceptions as Applied in Judicial Reasoning' (1913) 23 *Yale Law Journal* 16. Also see Pavlos Eleftheriades, 'Parliamentary Sovereignty and the Constitution' (2009) Oxford Legal Research Paper Series Paper No 45/2009.

[25] VCLT arts 42–5, 54–6, 65–8, 70–1.

within their own jurisdictions[26]—not in relation to those with whom they interact through consensual relations.

The fourth and final issue is that there are weaknesses with regard to normative absolutism from the perspective of the scope of regulation of domestic political authorities. Normative absolutists have come to concede that there may be internal limits to the reach of the powers of political authorities. The development of public and private law canons offers a range of justifications for such internal limits. Whilst this is the case, it is not clear why external limits to political authority with regard to spheres of regulation that well surpass the domain of a single political authority could remain contested. No one would claim that a single domestic political authority may possess the sovereign right to regulate the high seas, the moon, or Mars. This suggests not only that any consensual relations need to be regulated by an authority different from the single sovereign power, but also that a single domestic political authority is dependent on other sovereign powers to exercise its political authority within the bounds of stable rules. This external dependency on others for one's own benefit undermines a deep skepticism towards the authority of international law.

This dependency argument may be rebutted by pointing to the option of political commitments that sovereigns make to one another in place of legal commitments.[27] But the very idea of political commitments carries with it the problems of transience and self-judging. If we do not think that political commitments are not transient or self-judging, the distinction between political and legal commitments collapses.[28] Sovereign political powers have the need to turn to some conception of the authority of international law to stabalize regulation.

## Qualified Objections to the Authority of International Law

Qualified objections to the authority of international law over political domestic authority are the most common. These objections do not reject

[26] As Raz puts it 'Success in improving compliance with reason is not, however, enough to establish the legitimacy of government. It also depends on meeting a negative condition: that its jurisdiction does not run to matters regarding which it is better that people decide for themselves, unguided by authority than that they improve their compliance with reason.' Joseph Raz, 'Liberty and Trust', in RP George (ed), *Natural Law, Liberalism and Morality* (Oxford: Oxford University Press 1996), 119–20.

[27] Kal Raustiala, 'Form and Substance in International Agreements' (2005) 99 *American Journal of International Law* 581, 613.

[28] Jan Klabbers, *The Concept of Treaty in International Law* (Netherlands: Martinus Nijhoff 1996) 72.

the view that there is an authority relationship between international law and domestic political authorities *tout court*. Indeed, most skeptical views on the authority of international law within contemporary scholarship can be classed as qualified objections.

In this account, international law's authority over domestic political orders cannot be taken for granted at all times. What determines whether domestic law enacted by a sovereign political power should cede to international law (enacted by the collective political will of states) is primarily determined by the circumstances of domestic politics in a specific domestic sovereign polity. Whilst the idea that international law merely guides a sovereign is rejected, those who have qualified objections hold that sovereign political authority must be believed to have unlimited access to all normative or prudential reasons to calibrate its relationship with the authority of international laws. This view holds that the presumption to take international law into account cannot be constant at all times and that presumption, too, must be qualified. Qualified objections to the authority of international law would demand that international law has authority so long as it respects sovereignty.

Any account of the authority of international law must then include the idea of political disobedience. This must be reserved in all cases regardless of whether the authority of international law is posited as being strong, weak, or rebuttable. In the conceptual framework outlined earlier, qualified objections to the authority of international law would then see the conceptual scheme of international law as falling under a range of potentially rebuttable duties generally, whilst carving out the limited number of strong duties seen as pre-requisites for all sovereign political existence—namely prohibitions of genocide, slavery, or aggression.[29]

Neither sovereign-friendly nor democratic-friendly theoretical approaches fully deny the authority of international law. For that reason they diverge from normative absolutism about domestic political authority. Both, however, inject skepticism into any acceptance of an independent conceptual scheme for marking international law's authority. This skepticism is organized around the theme of limiting the access of the political authority to the full range of reasons at its disposal as a political power. More specifically it contains the idea of the illegitimate imposition of external commands over the domestic political authority—an authority whose primary duty is to respect and reflect the will of its citizens. We may call this the 'imposition concern'.

[29] T Christiano, 'Democratic Legitimacy and International Institutions' in S Besson and J Tasioulas (eds), *The Philosophy of International Law* (Oxford: Oxford University Press 2010) 123.

Whether international law respects or imposes on sovereign political power is effectively two separate problems in one. The first issue is the quality of static international laws created by states. The second is the dynamic interpretation of international law by third parties.

Two strands of literature have done the conceptual heavy lifting in advocating for qualified objections to the authority of international law. First is democratic sovereignty literature. This has primarily developed in the neighbouring discipline of political philosophy and now has also made its way to more mainstream international law debates.[30] Second is the sovereignty-friendly interpretation of international law and the corresponding 'restrictive interpretation' of explicitly consented treaty obligations[31] canon. This holds that 'if the wording of a treaty provision is not clear, in choosing between several admissible interpretations, the one which involves the minimum of obligations for the Parties should be adopted'.[32] Despite different theoretical underpinnings, both are linked by assumptions positing that, when there is an authority conflict between international law and the exercise of political power, international law has a qualified authority claim before domestic political organs of a state.

## Qualified Objections to the Authority of Static International Laws

Two separate perspectives have discussed the authority of static international law over political organs of a state. The first is the now largely mute debate that took part during decolonization and in its aftermath.[33] The newly

[30] On democratic sovereignty, Neal Devins and Louis Fisher, *The Democratic Constitution* (New York: Oxford University Press 2004); on democratic legitimacy and international law, see Kristen Hessler, 'Resolving Interpretive Conflicts in International Human Rights Law' (2005) 13(1) *Journal of Political Philosophy* 29; Bellamy (n 5); Allen Buchanan and Russell Powell, 'Survey Article: Constitutional Democracy and the Rule of International Law: Are They Compatible?' (2008) 16(3) *Journal of Political Philosophy* 326; Andreas Føllesdal, 'The Legitimacy of International Human Rights Review: The Case of the European Court of Human Rights' (2009) 40(4) *Journal of Social Philosophy* 595; Christiano (n 29) 269; Armin von Bogdandy and Ingo Venzke, *In Whose Name? A Public Law Theory of International Adjudication* (Oxford: Oxford University Press 2014). Democratic authority views concerning the authority of international law are not a homogenous bloc, cf in the democratic authority literature, the views indeed are more heterogeneous than one may expect. See for example, Bellamy (n 5); Føllesdal and Bogdandy and Venzke.

[31] Luigi Crema, 'Disappearance and New Sightings of Restrictive Interpretation(s)' (2010) 21 *European Journal of International Law* 21, 681–700.

[32] *Interpretation of Article 3, Paragraph 2 of the Treaty of Lausanne (Advisory Opinion)* PCIJ Series B No 12.

[33] Matthew Craven, *Decolonisation of International Law: State Succession and the Law of Treaties* (Cambridge: Cambridge University Press 2007).

independent states—and young members of the United Nations—asked whether the old international law, in which they had not participated in making, could be binding on new states emerging from colonial injustices.[34] At the time western states argued that was important for the newly independent states to recognize the authority of existing laws, citing the centrality of the continuity of international laws for newcomers to sustain general international rule of law.[35] The newly independent states, on the other hand, emphasized the centrality of the right to self-determination, not only as a political objective, but also as a core principle of international law.[36] Static international laws could not impose authority on newly independent states that not only were not involved in their creation, but were also systematically abused by them. These states, post the Second World War, therefore pointed to the fairness requirements of international law to even merit a general duty of deference from domestic political organs.

The structural unfairness argument of colonial international law was negotiated between western colonial states and post-colonial states after 1945. The practices of the new states confirmed that they were not in effect holding normative absolutist views on the authority of international law, rather that they were aiming to rebel against the authority of existing norms, which they regarded as unfair.[37] The open-ended nature of the international law on state succession—leaving it to political judgment as to whether a continuity or a clean slate approach is to be used in this regard—to some extent addressed their concerns. That is, international law recognized at the time of decolonization that the circumstances for making authority claims were exceptional. Although the Vienna Convention on Succession of States in Respect of Treaties offered limited guidance, it asserted that the principle of *uti possidetis* and territorial regimes attracted strong duties even in cases of succession.[38]

It is now accepted in contemporary international law that problems of post-colonial states are no longer relevant to core arguments about the authority of international law over political units. However, despite this, many states today pose similar questions to those of the then newly-independent

[34] Sundhya Pahuja, *Decolonising International Law* (Cambridge: Cambridge University Press 2013).

[35] See, Craven (n 287). As the focus of this book is on the authority claims in contemporary international law, I will not deal with the objection to the authority of international law as a matter of systematic injustice before a group of states come to join the international legal system.

[36] *Western Sahara (Advisory Opinion)* [1975] ICJ Rep 12 (*Western Sahara*) 31.

[37] BS Chimni, 'The Past, Present and Future of International Law: A Critical World Approach' (2007) 8 *Melbourne Journal of International Law* 499.

[38] Cf the Vienna Convention on Succession of States in Respect of Treaties (adopted 23 August 1978, entered into force 6 November 1996) 1946 UNTS 3 (Vienna Convention on Succession Treaties) arts 11, 12. To this date, however, the convention has only 22 state parties.

post-colonial states. These can be distilled down to three main questions. First, can past international law bind today's democracies?[39] Second, can international law consented to by a dictator bind a democratic or a 'transition' state? Third, can past international law be binding if it has come about through negotiations detrimental to post-colonial, poor, or weak states?[40] These questions go to the heart of the authority of static international laws and political actors' demands for making an assessment of the authority of international law based on the circumstances of politics.

The question of whether past international law can bind today's democracies is a variant of the critique of the initial consent doctrine in international law.[41] The question raises a deeper normative concern about the authority of international law over democratically constituted political organs.[42] The chain of thinking that leads to the concern is thus; if we value domestic political organs because of their democratic qualities, and if we value democratic qualities because that is the best system for showing equal concern and respect for individuals, then consent given to international law by a political organ in the past runs the risk of not fully showing equal concern and respect for individuals living in a state today.[43] The requirement of 'ongoing consent' as opposed to initial consent may assist in surmounting some of these problems, and avoid conflict between international law and the doctrines of equal value and worth of individuals.

The problem tackled by the second question is similar. This time the concern is not with a lack of ongoing consent to static international laws, but the lack of meaningful consent from individuals who have emerged from living under past tyranny.[44] As the post-colonial states before them, newly democratic states also demand a clean slate approach to their relationships with international law and wish to ensure its authority is constituted through the consent of a contemporary, representative government.

The final question that I identify concerns the role that coercion plays in the presentation of consent. Coercion as blocking the binding nature of

[39] Jack Goldsmith and Eric Posner, *The Limits of International Law* (Oxford: Oxford University Press 2005); Steven Wheately, *The Democratic Legitimacy of International Law* (Oxford: Hart Publishing 2010).

[40] David Singh Grewal, *Network Power: The Social Dynamics of Globalization* (New Haven: Yale University Press 2008) argues that WTO's imposition of trade norms mean that a sovereign state that chooses to remain outside of the system may mean that it significantly curbs its chances of trade.

[41] Deborah Baumgold, *Contract Theory in Historical Context: Essays on Grotius, Hobbes and Locke* (Leiden: Brill Academic Publishers 2010).

[42] Allen Buchanan, *Justice, Legitimacy, and Self-Determination: Moral Foundations for International Law* (Oxford: Oxford University Press 2003), Christiano (n 29).

[43] Buchanan (n 42). [44] Ibid.

international law has long been recognized in general international law. The Vienna Convention on the Law of Treaties has an explicit provision on coercion as a ground for arguing the invalidity of a legal obligation.[45] The coercion that the Vienna Convention regulates, however, is direct—this is when a state uses direct military force on another in order to force it into commitments it would not otherwise make. Such coercion does not create legally binding obligations. The kind of coercion that has been put forward by political theorists, however, is different in nature. It is what some have called 'systematic coercion'[46] suggesting that the disparities of a system of international law as a whole produces coercion indirectly. Some states—and, indirectly, their political organs—have no choice but to expect international laws that are in effect to the detriment to the well-being of their political community due to the inherent systemic coercion underpinning the very system itself.

In sum, all three of these objections to international law's authority over political organs point to a qualified understanding of the authority of international law. The colonial critique insisted that newly liberated peoples must not bow to the past authority of international law created by their colonizers. The democratic concerns take issue with not distinguishing between different kinds of political authority domestically. Democratic states that respect the will of their citizens and other states are not to be placed on an equal footing when discussing the authority of international law. Only international law which is meaningfully consented to or that allows for mechanisms of refreshing consent can attract claims of authority. Lastly, those who hold that there are pockets of systematic coercion in the international legal system echo the developing world approaches to international law. They hold that laws that are underpinned by systematic coercion cannot be treated as authoritative.

## The Way Out: Consent as a Procedural Value of International Law

All of the concerns I identified above share a commonality: static international law trapping the political will of states and, indirectly, the rights of individuals to meaningfully take part in the decision-making process. The argument states that accepting that international law binds merely through an expression of initial consent undermines the ability and the right of a political power to be flexible and, as recent waves of writing suggest, a properly

[45] Cf VCLT 1969 art 52.

[46] Laura Valentini, 'Coercion and (Global) Justice' (2011) 105(1) *American Political Science Review* 205.

democratic political institution.[47] International law, therefore, unduly restricts the space in which domestic political organs, that first and foremost have the duty to be responsive to the needs of their citizens, can manoeuvre. The need to be flexible is even more so in cases when international law and domestic law regulate the same matter. For a polity (and in particular a democratic polity) to be forced to be bound by a law that does not meet its urgent needs is an anathema to having political power in the first place.[48]

How can a view that seeks to defend the attitude of minimalist deference to the authority of international law over domestic political organs counter those that hold qualified views on the authority of static international laws? My view of the authority of international law as a qualified authority as developed in Chapter 2 goes a long way towards addressing these concerns. This is because most duties imposed by international law under the authority scheme of strong, weak, or rebuttable duties provide a significant breathing space to governments, democratic and non-democratic alike, to respond to the authority claims of international law.

Static international law rarely traps the political will of citizens. In cases when international law imposes strong duties (the prohibition of genocide, the prohibition of slavery, the inviolability of diplomatic premises) we cannot meaningfully speak about trapping the will of a people as these domains do not concern the rightful political authority domain in the first place.[49] Most concerns about trapping the will of the people target either treaty or customary obligations that overlap with political authority. Proponents of the will of the people argue that even weak or rebuttable duties raise concerns about the domain of domestic political authority.

I submit that on balance we cannot do away with the initial consent doctrine grounding the general duty of deference on behalf of political authorities both on procedural grounds and on grounds of prudence. On procedural grounds, *pacta sunt servanda* does not merely trap the will of political authorities. It is a process through which a single political authority takes a number of public steps in locating itself in a web of international legal obligations. On prudential grounds, there is no other feasible alternative that caters for the critiques of *pacta sunt servanda*. Some political philosophers have proposed that international lawyers may consider treating the

[47] Buchanan (n 42).

[48] Martin Loughlin, 'Constitutional Pluralism: An Oxymoron?' (2014) 3(1) *Global Constitutionalism* 9.

[49] Lynn Dobson, 'Legitimacy, institutional power, and international human rights institutions: a conceptual enquiry' in Andreas Føllesdal, Karlsson Schaffer, and Geir Ulfstein (eds), *The Legitimacy of International Human Rights Regimes: Legal, Political and Philosophical Perspectives* (Cambridge: Cambridge University Press 2013).

consent of democratic states to international treaties in a qualitatively different manner from the consent of non-democratic states.[50] This, however, is not a practicable option for grounding the co-operation of all types of political communities within the international system. This is the international system we have and are likely to have for some time to come.[51] Whilst on political grounds it may send a signal to non-democratic polities to become more democratic to be included in the world of democratic states, it equally signals double standards and exclusion and overlooks the roots of democracy as a deeply historical process with close links to wealth accumulation linked to exploitation through colonial exploitation. However imperfect, a procedural commitment to pacta sunt servanda stands to offer a better aide for internal domestic reform than exclusion from the international law project altogether.

## Consent Giving as a Public Procedure

Whilst domestic political powers are final authorities domestically, they are interactional authorities on the international plane. Domestic political authorities, both through treaty law and customary international law participate in the interactional process of international law-making. There is, in the current system of international law, no other alternative vision for international law-making.[52] The idea that international law as a system of differentiated duties is 'external' to domestic political authority lacks a strong descriptive basis. International law as a system of procedural rules operates on the basis of participation. Political authorities participate in the making and unmaking of international law. There is a strong and continuous element of 'publicness' through procedures of international law-making. What is more, international law is not made behind closed doors and by experts. On the contrary, it is made by political actors through negotiation or signalling processes involving actions and reactions.[53]

[50] Buchanan (n 42).

[51] Luigi Condorelli and Antonio Cassese, 'Is Leviathan still holding sway in International Dealings' in Casesse (ed), *Realising Utopia: The Future of International Law* (Oxford: Oxford University Press 2012) 31.

[52] Importantly, a long tradition of philosophical thinking also agrees that other visions are worse than current practice, however imperfectly. See Immanuel Kant, *Perpetual Peace* (trans Lewis White Beck 1797) (Indianapolis: Bobbs-Merrill 1957) 31; John Rawls, 'The Law of Peoples' (1993) 20 *Critical Inquiry* 41.

[53] Jose E Alvarez, *International Organizations as Law-makers* (Oxford: Oxford University Press 2006).

We must, therefore, depart from the premise that domestic political authorities are law-makers internationally as much as they are domestically. Granted, modalities of law-making in international and domestic spheres differ greatly from one another. But this has more to do with the nature of the community and the differentiated purposes of domestic and international laws rather than the law-like qualities of domestic and international law. It is also for this reason that international laws made by political authorities have differentiated authority claims on domestic authorities. Not all international laws impose strong, strict duties. Most international laws allow political authorities to maintain their freedom to enact domestic legislation on a diverse range of issues.

The image of the dynamic will of political powers being 'trapped' by static international laws posits a contradiction between the distant and removed from the ground international law, and responsive and dynamic domestic political power to the needs of a domestic polity. The procedural rules that allow for the making and unmaking of international law, however, do not support this view.

Significantly, political authorities play a crucial role in the differentiation of duties imposed by international laws on themselves. In the previous chapter, I defined strong duties as duties that leave discretionary space to state authorities with regard to the performance or non-performance of a conduct. An international law with a strong duty structure will ask State A to do X. State A must do X or refrain from doing what X says to the letter. Such a strong duty as a matter of international law does not come from nowhere. It evolves through the negotiation of treaty texts and customary international law. Even rules that we regard as falling within the jurisdictional disability of single political organs lend support to this understanding. Whilst one may argue that the prohibition of genocide came around as a matter of morality, upholding it as a matter of international law nevertheless involves the participation and acquiescence of states. The idea of imposition, therefore, does not hold, even in the case of strong duties. The idea of imposition becomes harder to hold on to when it comes to duties of respect and duties of rebuttal. Both duties are dialogic and ask political authorities to engage with the duty to the extent that is appropriate and possible. What is more, shifting international law duties from one category of authority relationship to another also emerges through the participation of states in the international law-making processes leading up to the imposition of stricter or looser types of duty construction.

## Treaty Negotiation as a Public and Participatory Process

A central procedure that involves domestic political actors in international law is executive political powers of the state negotiating international treaties. International law allows for all executive actors—appointed by the state through domestic internal procedures—to participate in treaty negotiations in order to give conclusive form and content to international laws.

International treaty law negotiations are long-winded bargaining processes through which executive political actors engage in give and take exercises with other states. Treaty provisions are drafted and re-drafted over the course of decades.[54] Whilst members of civil society increasingly participate in treaty negotiations—more actively in some fields than others—executive political authorities retain the ultimate authority. Consensus building in the creation of particular international laws plays such an important role that what often comes out from treaty negotiations are watered down versions of more clear principles or the resulting treaty fails to regulate important areas of common interest. In long-winded treaty negotiations executive authorities act as purposive actors. They actively contribute to what kinds of duties are imposed by specific international laws. Whilst in some areas of international law, negotiations often end up with soft law documents that ultimately generate persuasive duties,[55] in other areas the formulation of strong duties, alongside weak and rebuttable duties is possible.

What emerges from this descriptive picture is that the participation and the inevitability of bargaining amongst political powers are a central feature of the emergence of treaty law. While heavily negotiated texts sometimes do not achieve effective international regulation, the meaningful participation of political powers and the emergence of texts that each state can accept with grace has a distinct value in and of itself, even though negotiated texts hamper the effectiveness or completeness of regulation.[56] It is for this reason that what ultimately emerges as international law must also enjoy a presumption of deference from the political masters of the treaties. The adopted texts that emerge through negotiations are texts that are acceptable to the executive powers of domestic communities.

[54] See for example, Fanny Benedetti, Karine Bonneau, and John Washburn, *Negotiating the International Criminal Court* (Leiden: Brill 2014).

[55] John J Kirtin and Michael J Trebilcock (eds), *Hard Choice, Soft Law: Voluntary Standards in Global Trade, Environment and Social Governance* (Farnham: Ashgate 2004).

[56] For example, consider the Vienna Convention on Succession Treaties (n 38).

That the initial consent to a negotiated text over decades could expire after four or so years of a democratic government seems to accord significance to both the interactionary character of political authority and the public processes through which the texts come about. Texts can, of course, be renegotiated by state parties over the lifetime of the treaty or they can be upgraded by way of additional or optional protocols.[57]

Democratic state sovereignty theorists find discomfort in the fact that treaties are negotiated between democratic states who, presumably, come to the negotiating table in full knowledge and responsibility of the peoples they represent, and non-democratic states, who may simply be representing the interest of one man or a small elite group. It could, therefore, be argued that treaty negotiation does not represent responsible participation by all states in the international system. Whilst this view has merit, it in effect criticizes the diversity of regime types in the international system rather than the procedures of international law that allow for voluntary participation in international legal systems. Whilst it is true that executive political authorities from democratic states are likely to be more responsive delegates to their citizens, this is in effect all the more reason to support a presumption of deference to texts produced by responsible executives. What is more, all states are able to create coalitions of states, protest the negotiation process, and opt out of negotiations at any time. The process of prior and informed involvement in international law by executives does not, therefore, support the imposition view.

The Vienna Convention on the Law of the Treaties only allows treaties to be signed by members of the executive with full powers.[58] This allows for feedback between the treaty negotiators from the executive political branch and those that have the political power to sign treaties. The executive branch with full powers is not obliged to sign a treaty which has been actively negotiated by its representatives. The United States, for example, was one of the major and active negotiators of the Statue of the International Criminal Court.[59] Despite this, the United States has not signed the treaty. This also suggests that international law has procedures to involve domestic powers in the making of international treaty law even though those states do not express any political commitment at the end of the negotiation process. When we see

[57] The upgrade of the international laws of armed conflict treaties between 1949 and 1977 is an important example of this.

[58] VCLT 1969 art 7.

[59] On the participation of the US in the negotiation process, see John Washburn, 'The Negotiation of the Rome Statute for the International Criminal Court and International Lawmaking in the 21st Century' (1999) 1 *Pace International Law Review* 361.

that that states are free to be part of multilateral negotiations with no duty to show any political commitment to what emerges from them, it becomes harder to sustain the view that international law is foreign and distant law imposed on political powers.

## The Ratification of Treaties

Domestic legislators scrutinizing negotiated treaty texts is what some may regard as the key objection to the imposition of international law over domestic political authorities. According to McNair, ratification is a 'definitive confirmation of a willingness to be bound' by a political authority.[60] When treaty texts come before parliaments, the domestic political authority in charge of making laws is given a genuine opportunity to consider whether to offer political consent to creating binding international law. The time between the signing of a treaty by the executive power and its ratification by the legislative does offer the political power space to deliberate whether the political powers that come after it should be bound by international law. The ratification of a treaty is different from passing ordinary legislation. When a parliament ratifies a treaty it rubber stamps a piece of international law and enables it to become both international and domestic law (or, in strictly dualist countries, international law that brings in obligations to respect the object and purpose).

Parliaments take on a dual role when they decide whether to ratify international treaties or not. First, all multilateral treaties require a certain number of ratifications for the treaty to come into force. In some, all parliaments must approve the treaty for the treaty to come into force.[61] In others, the number of requisite parliamentary approvals is also decided by the executive powers who negotiate the treaty.[62] This presents a collection of parliaments with a joint role in the making of international law. Some international laws,

[60] Draft Articles on Treaties concluded between States and International Organizations or between International Organizations (ILC) UN Doc A/37/10, 17 (1982), 19.

[61] Treaties negotiated under the auspices of the European Union for example require approval from all members of the EU.

[62] See for example, the high bar required for Amendment to Annex B of the Kyoto Protocol to the United Nations Framework Convention on Climate Change (Nairobi, 17 November 2006), art 20: '4. An amendment [to Annex B of the Protocol], shall enter into force for those Parties having accepted it on the ninetieth day after the date of receipt by the Depositary of an instrument of acceptance by at least three fourths of the Parties to this Protocol. 5. The Amendment shall enter into force for any other Party on the ninetieth day after the date on which that Party deposits with the Depositary its instrument of acceptance of the said Amendment.'

despite executive political support, are unable to become treaties in force because some element of the legislative political authorities does not think the treaty should attract legislative approval.

One objection to this law-making quality of political legislative authorities for a collection of states is the numbers game that is involved for a treaty to come into force. It may be argued that, as long as a treaty does not require all parliaments to approve it, international law may mask the domination of a critical number of states over the legislative political authority of others.[63] Is this a view that offers additional support to concerns about the imposition thesis?

Two arguments are pertinent here. The first lies in the ultimate freedom of an individual political authority to refuse to become party to an international treaty even if it actively participated in the negotiation and the adoption of said treaty. As highlighted already, this was the case when the United States chose not to ratify the Statute of the International Criminal Court. Furthermore, the US went on to conclude bilateral treaties with other states who ratified the ICC Statue to exclude any effects that its ratification may have on the presence of its armed forces in their territories.[64]

Would a state with weaker economic and political power be able to follow suit? It may be suggested that the treaty ratification process is truly participatory for some political authorities only. Only those with sufficient political and economic power are able to counter the effects of treaty-making that they see as running against their political will. We have to concede this as being a matter of *real politik* and turn to a second argument about participation in international law. Also, domestically, a critical number of legislators determine the faith of a proposed legislation. Those individual legislators who wholeheartedly and genuinely oppose domestic legislation often have to live with legislation that they find to be an anathema to their views on collective political life. In circumstances of domestic politics, unlike in a perfect democracy, who is represented in political decision-making is a matter of path dependence, political history, and specific configurations of electoral rules. Despite these real life constraints, however, we nevertheless support the legitimacy of the majority rule domestically.

Given that the current international system is made up of states with unequal political and economic power, we must also ask if the initial ground rules of participation in international treaty law-making allow us to make a

[63] Valentini (n 46).

[64] Diane Marie Amann & MNS Sellers, 'The United States of America and the International Criminal Court' (2002) 50 *American Journal of Comparative Law* 381.

prima facie argument that the outcome of treaties may be such that even the losers in negotiations may accept their loss with 'good grace'.[65] In this context, the relative bargaining powers of a collection of weaker states during treaty negotiation, and the political authorities' right to not ratify international law treaties even after negotiation and adoption may not be taken lightly. International law cannot be divorced from the power of states.[66] Domestic political authority cannot be divorced from the powers of domestic elites either. The rules of formal equality in the negotiation and adoption of treaties coupled with the subsequent powers of political authorities in entering reservations to treaties and their ultimate power to refuse to ratify them, offer important procedural opportunities for political authorities to counter the imposition of power of other states in international law treaty making. Even those that remain worried about deep power disparities in the international system may at least concede that international treaty making—negotiations which sometimes last over half a century[67] and at times fail[68]—does not present domestic political authorities with fait accompli decisions.

Those that worry about international treaty law being binding on political authorities often overlook the fact that political orders are able to denounce or withdraw from treaties by following the procedures laid out in international law.[69]

## Making Reservations, Interpretative Declarations, and Statements

The reservations regime to treaties is a further participatory step that allows for domestic executive powers (and, in some jurisdictions, also the legislative powers) to exclude the domestic effects of some international laws which they regard as

[65] Jeremy Waldron, *The Dignity of Legislation* (Cambridge: Cambridge University Press 1999).

[66] Martti Koskenniemi and Paivi Leino 'Fragmentation of International Law? Postmodern Anxieties' (2002) 15(3) *Leiden Journal of International Law* 553.

[67] The negotiation of the Statue of the International Criminal Court officially started in 1948 and was completed in 1999.

[68] The members of the World Trade Organization, for example failed to reach an agreement on the treaty text on trade facilitation (streamlining customs and other border procedures) in Bali in 2013.

[69] Withdrawals from international legal regimes that have been perceived as unfair are part and parcel of contemporary international law. This has been a notable trend in the field of international investment law. See J E Alvarez, 'The Once and Future Foreign Investment Regime' in MH Arsanjani et al (eds), *Looking to the Future: Essays in the Honour of W Michael Reisman* (Leiden: Nijhoff 2011) 607.

incompatible with the will of the domestic legislature. This allows states to enter into their treaty obligations, but also to guard and protect their own peculiarities as a domestic legal system.

When seen in this light, the reservations regime offers an extra layer of protection to the domestic political authority, and, in particular, to their particular legislative preferences at the time of concluding and ratifying an international law treaty. Reservations to treaties allow domestic political authorities time and space to deliberate on the kinds of legislative changes or innovations they need to make. It also allows for them to delay legislative changes as seen fit by domestic political authorities, but also to benefit from international rules that are brought in by international treaties. States are free to lift their interpretive statements or reservations to treaties whenever they see fit. International law that demands more than what current domestic law can offer, therefore, can be put on hold until domestic laws can be changed to meet the requirements of international law. The reservations regime to international treaties effectively respects what Waldron calls 'the dignity of legislation'.[70] Political authorities are not disadvantaged by participating in the making of international law because of the history of their previous domestic laws.

There is, of course, a long standing debate on the interpretation of Article 19 of the Vienna Convention on the Law of Treaties[71] and the framework within which we may determine which reservations are incompatible with the object and the purpose of the treaty.[72] Some may regard my positive interpretation on the reservations regime as a way of masking the fact that some international interpretive authorities are quick to dismiss the reservations of political authorities as incompatible with the object and the purpose of international treaties.[73] Indeed, international human rights law jurisprudence has

[70] Waldron (n 65).

[71] On this debate, see generally Catherine Redgewell, 'Universality or Integrity? Some Reflections on Reservations to General Multilateral Treaties' (1993) 64 *British Yearbook of International Law* 245–67; William Schabas, 'Invalid Reservations to the International Covenant on Civil and Political Rights: Is the United States Still a Party?' (1995) 21 *Brooklyn Journal of International Law* 277, 278; Alain Pellet, '1969 Vienna Convention, Article 19 Formulation of reservations', in Olivier Corten and Pierre Klein (eds) *The Vienna Convention on the Law of Treaties A Commentary* (Oxford: Oxford University Press 2011) Vol 1.

[72] Allain Pellet, 'The ILC Guide to Practice on Reservations to Treaties', A General Presentation by the Special Rapporteur, Jean Monnet Working Paper 15/12, The Jean Monnet Program, NYU, 2012; and also Seventeenth report on reservations to treaties, by Mr Alain Pellet, Special Rapporteur, A/CN.4/647, General Assembly International Law Commission Sixty-third Session, 26 May 2011.

[73] *Belilos v Switzerland* (1988) 10 EHRR 466. See UNHRC, 'Reservations to the Covenant or the Optional Protocols or Declarations under Article 41 of the Covenant' (1994) UN Doc CCPR/C/21/Rev1/Add6 and Responses of UK, US, and France.

been at the forefront of the 'severebility' thesis with regard to reservations entered into human rights treaties by domestic political authorities.[74] I will come back to this in the following section.

It is important to note, however, that the specific international law that is in effect on this matter is Article 19 of the Vienna Convention on the Law of Treaties. Article 19 regulates the permissibility of reservations. It states that reservations that are incompatible with the object and the purpose of a treaty will not be valid. In the authority scheme that I developed in Chapter 2, duties imposed by Article 19 fit within the scheme of a weak authority relationship between international law and domestic political authorities. In other words, whilst Article 19 sets out a general rule (ie the invalidity of reservations subject to an object and purpose test of a treaty), it does not specify what further specific tests need to be employed in order to determine such incompatibility. Political authorities are required to respect the authority of Article 19, but any specific duties that flow from this are insufficiently specified.

The International Law Commission in its final report on reservations to human rights treaties has made important progress in clarifying the powers of the domestic executive and legislative authorities to make reservations to treaties. In particular, the ILC report made two important observations. First, reservations to a treaty as a whole are likely to be incompatible with the object and the purpose of the treaty.[75] Second, reservations that are specific to a provision of a treaty, but subject the provision of general rules laid out within domestic law, such as a country's constitution, are likely to be not specific enough to meet the compatibility test.[76] Both of these guidelines do not support the view that international law seeks to take what it grants to domestic political authorities through the backdoor. It rather demands political authorities to exercise their duty to be responsible law-makers both internationally and domestically. A general or a vague reservation to a treaty makes the job state authorities have in determining the international legal obligations of states, be they parliaments, executives, or the judiciary an impossible task. The duty of the political authority to make good, clear, and

[74] Ryan Goodman, 'Human Rights Treaties, Invalid Reservations, and State Consent', (2002) 96 *American Journal of International Law* 531.

[75] Guideline 3.1.5.2 of Guide to Practice on Reservations to Treaties entitled 'Vague or general reservations' reads: 'A reservation shall be worded in such a way as to allow its meaning to be understood, in order to assess in particular its compatibility with the object and purpose of the treaty.' Guide to Practice on Reservations to Treaties, Adopted by the International Law Commission at its sixty-third session, (2011) Vol II Part 2 *Yearbook of International Law*.

[76] Ibid. Guideline 3.1.5.5.

clearly ascertainable law also extends to their right to enter reservations to international law treaties. Making clearly reasoned and accessible reservations, therefore, can be regarded as an extension of domestic political authorities to make clearly reasoned and accessible law in general.

## Customary International Law and the Participation of Political Organs

The authority of customary international law is a key concern for those that are concerned with political will becoming trapped. It may be argued that, even if treaty law may be offering some procedural assurances for sovereign states, customary international law cannot meet the expectations of meaningful participation by states to grant it a level of authority in domestic legal orders. How can unwritten international law make any claim of authority over written domestic law laid down by domestic political authorities? Why is it that customary international law, when it crystallizes, binds states that have not participated in its creation? What arguments, if any, are there for a state to unilaterally withdraw from custom?

Here we must recognize that there are a number of theories on the formation of customary international law. International lawyers continue to debate which norms of international law are customary in nature and in what form.[77] I will only seek to defend here the authority of what I call the 'conventional view' on customary international law as developed by the International Court of Justice in the North Sea Continental Shelf cases.[78] According to this case, custom emerges as a result of consistent state practice over time.[79] Consistent state practice amounts to states practicing a particular norm with accompanying legal motivation (*opinio juris*). Consistency excludes random, unconscious, or unintentional acts by political authorities. On the contrary, it looks for purposeful acts accompanied by legal motivation. That state practice must be over time offers an additional assurance to political authorities. A state that has acted in a way that supports the formation of custom has the freedom to change its course of action when confronted with a different but similar situation. Customary law formation is not about catching domestic authorities unguarded. It is about carefully tracing what obligation

[77] Cf Second report on identification of customary international law by Michael Wood, Special Rapporteur of 22 May 2014, International Law Commission Sixty-sixth session, A/CN.4/672.

[78] *North Sea Continental Shelf Cases (Germany v Denmark; Germany v Netherlands)* [1969] ICJ Rep 3 (North Sea Continental Shelf).

[79] Ibid.

their purposeful actions or omissions amount to as a matter of duties under international law.

In customary international law, how states react is as important as how they act. This is, in some respects, akin to processes of negotiation in treaty law-making. The importance of reaction means that a powerful state cannot create customary international law. Nor can a small group of states. A critical mass of countries needs to act and positively react for the formation of custom. The category of specially affected states, also introduced by North Sea Continental Shelf cases, offers an additional safeguard for political authorities not to be trapped in international rules that do not adequately reflect the prudential needs of a certain group of political authorities.[80]

Two objections may be raised about customary international law and its authoritative qualities over political authorities. First, once it is formed through consistent practice and over time, it binds all political authorities, regardless of whether they have actively participated in the formation of custom. This is called the universal application of customary international law and stands in contrast to the selective application of treaty law.[81] Customary international law does not require all political authorities to accept the rule that becomes part of custom. It upsets the one political authority one vote rule. What reason could there possibly be to defend the authoritative quality of an international law (regardless of the duties it imposes) if a state does not consent to be bound by it? Second, unlike exiting a treaty, a state cannot individually exit custom. Why must a state remain bound by a norm with which it no longer agrees?

In order to respond to this challenge, we must first highlight that the formation of a very specific rule that limits the breathing space of political authorities is a long, difficult, and public process. From no custom to emerging custom to existing custom, states have ample opportunities to communicate to persuade other states to act or not to act in particular ways in order to prevent the formation of custom. When it is finally accepted that a norm is custom, this often reflects a long process of consensus-building amongst political authorities. The consistency and the time requirements of

[80] *North Sea Continental Shelf (Judgment)* (1969) ICJ Reports 3, 42, para 73 ('With respect to the other elements usually regarded as necessary before a conventional rule can be considered to have become a general rule of international law, it might be that, even without the passage of any considerable period of time, a very widespread and representative participation in the convention might suffice of itself, provided it included that of States whose interests were specially affected'), 43, para 74.

[81] Jonathan Charney, 'Universal International Law' (1993) 87 *American Journal of International Law* 529.

custom, therefore, ask losers of custom formation to accept the new law with good grace.

That an individual state cannot simply exit custom is also part of respecting the public process of custom change. A state may encourage other states to exit custom and can seek to change the consensus on which a particular norm is based. If a state is asking for *less* than what the existing consensus accepts, this would involve violating a norm of international law to change it.[82] Political authorities may take this risk in a similar way to the risk citizens take in circumstances of political disobedience. Taking this risk involves providing the public with reasons as to why the customary international law in question has to change and why more and more political authorities must change their ways to consider the new law. If a state is asking for *more* than the existing law requires, a political authority does not need to violate existing customary norms to change it. On the contrary, it would need to act in ways that would require, for example, transforming a weak norm into a strong norm[83] and encourage other states to act in the same way.

In sum, the fact that customary international law-making happens in public and it treats political authorities as purposeful actors capable of interacting with each other consistently does not support the view that customary international law is an imposition of external laws over political authorities. Customary international law is not disrespectful to the political agency of states. On the contrary, it thrives on it.

## Taking Stock: The Duty of Political Authorities to Take International Law into Account

The participatory procedures of international law are not democratic. They are not directly based on the principle of equal concern and respect for individuals. The rules of participation in international law operate on the basis of international law-making powers being delegated to political authorities in the knowledge that political authorities will be able to use these powers jointly with other political authorities. The joint authorship of international law, through participation in treaty negotiation and ratification as well as through the accumulation of political and legislative will in certain issue

[82] R Higgins, *Problems and Process: International Law and How We Use It* (Oxford: Clarendon Press 1994) 22.

[83] Consider for example political authorities requiring an environmental impact assessment when involved in projects involving significant risk of harm. See *Case Concerning Pulp Mills on the River Uruguay (Argentina v Uruguay) (Judgment)* [2010] ICJ Rep 135 (*Pulp Mills*).

areas in the form of custom, is a political necessity of law formation in a horizontal international legal system. That political authorities participate in the making of international law through multiple channels make them take international law into account in their domestic legislative functions. The alternative is to support an erratic and internally inconsistent view of political power that has both an international and a domestic face.

Is there a plausible alternative to not valuing the initial consent of the states to static international laws through treaty-making and customary international law? Could we hold on to any other principle other than pacta sunt servanda if we deeply value the worth of individuals as the authors of the political will of states? Can pacta sunt servanda be a qualified principle in and of itself? From the perspective of international lawyers, the response to this is clear. International law cannot maintain any claim to rule of law across a diversity of political authorities without holding on to and defending the value of pacta sunt servanda. The qualification of pacta sunt servanda comes with a price tag that is too high to maintain the institution of international law. This point is also not mute from the perspective of a single political authority and its demand for domestic flexibility as there is an inherent trade-off between domestic flexibility and foreseeability of relations between states and the domestic political authority's concern to shape international legal regulation. The single political authority, therefore, has to make a choice between isolationist policies, ad hoc coalitions of willing partners, and international law.

I have not aimed to defend why we need to commit to the institution of international law here. How I explain the initial situation of international law assumes that very commitment. The goal has been to show that a general commitment to international law as a scheme of co-operation for all states underpins the value of initial consent for the authority of international law on a balance of reasons assessment and the everyday operation of international law.

## Dynamic International Law and the Risk of Overriding the Authority of Political Organs

Dynamic international law raises a unique cluster of challenges between the authority of international law and the authority of domestic political organs. Skeptics of the authority of international law over domestic political authority assert that authority claims of international law are not confined to static international treaty law or long-standing customary principles, but rather the dynamic application of these laws by delegated organs created by states themselves. Even if one makes a concession to the principle of deference to static laws, such a concession cannot be extended to dynamic international law *tout court*, that is, international law as interpreted by third parties.

The proliferation of international courts and tribunals over the past forty or so years means that we have a host of institutions in international law alongside the International Court of Justice. These have developed a legal life and legal world of their own to engage with international laws and make authoritative claims about the content of international law.[84] International institutions are now increasingly tasked with both the application and the interpretation of international law either through explicit provisions in treaties[85] or by way of implicit power doctrines.[86] Either way, the line between the application of international law and the interpretation of international law is a thin one.[87]

Dynamic international law then refers to international law as interpreted by third parties. There is a growing body of literature on the necessity, growth, implications and at times, perils with dynamic international law.[88] The crux

[84] There are currently twenty-four international and regional courts and tribunals on the international plane. These are (i) International Court of Justice (ICJ), (ii) International Tribunal for the Law of the Sea (ITLOS), (iii) World Trade Organization Dispute Settlement Body (WTO DSB), (iv) Court of Justice of the European Communities (ECJ), (v) Benelux Court of Justice, (vi) European Free Trade Area (EFTA) Court, (vii) European Court of Human Rights (ECtHR), (viii) Inter-American Court of Human Rights (IACtHR), (ix) The Court of Justice of the Andean Community (TJAC), (x) Caribbean Court of Justice (CCJ), (xi) Central American Court of Justice (CACJ), (xii) African Union Court of Human and People's Rights (ACHPR), (xiii) African Court of Justice (ACJ), (xiv) Arab Maghreb Union Judicial Authority (AMUIJ), (xv) Court of Justice of the Common Market of Eastern and Southern African (COMESA), (xvi) Court of Justice of the East African Community (EACJ), (xvii) Court of Justice of the Economic Community of Central African States (ECCAS), (xviii) Court of Justice of the Economic and Monetary Community of Central Africa (CEMAC), (xix) Court of Justice of the Economic Community of West African States (ECOWAS CCJ), (xx) Court of Justice of the Organization for the Harmonization of African Business Law (OHADA), (xxi) Tribunal of the Southern African Development Community (SADC), (xxii) Court of Justice of the West African Economic and Monetary Union (WAEMU), (xxiii) International Criminal Tribunal for the Former Yugoslavia (ICTY), (xxiv) International Criminal Tribunal for Rwanda (ICTR), (xxv) International Criminal Court (ICC), (xxvi) Extraordinary Chambers in the Courts of Cambodia (ECCC), (xxvii) Programme of International Judges in Kosovo, (xxviii) Special Court for Sierra Leone (SCSL), (xxix) Special Panels for Serious Crimes in East Timor, and (xxx) Special Court for Lebanon.

[85] See for example Convention for the Protection of Human Rights and Fundamental Freedoms (European Convention on Human Rights, as amended) (ECHR).

[86] On the implicit power doctrine see *Reparation for injuries suffered in the service of the Nations (Advisory Opinion)* [1949] ICJ Rep 174 (*Reparations Case*).

[87] Throughout this section I will refer to all of these institutions generically as 'interpretive authorities'.

[88] See representatively, Georges Abi-Saab, 'The International Court as a World Court' in Vaughan Lowe and Malgosia Fitzmaurice (eds), *Fifty Years of the International Court of Justice: Essays in Honour of Sir Robert Jennings* (Cambridge: Cambridge University Press 1996);

of the tension between political authorities and dynamic international law is whether these third party actors that exist on the international plane can rightfully impose duties on political authorities through their interpretation of international law. In other words, can an actor other than the domestic political authority itself specify the duties generated by international law and demand a general attitude of deference when doing so? This is indeed what Mr Davis had in mind when he showed his dissatisfaction with the *Hirst* judgment.[89]

The skeptics of a general duty of deference to dynamic international law impose two types of qualifications to the dynamic authority of international law over political organs. These objections are, at their core, concerned with how an interpretative authority interprets international law. The central question here is whether the interpretive authority has interpreted international law in a sovereign-friendly manner to attract a duty of deference from political authorities.

In mainstream international law this concern has culminated in the 'restrictive interpretation' school of international law.[90] This school holds that, for international law as interpreted by a third party to attract a general duty of deference from the masters of international law (domestic political communities), it must impose a minimum level of constraint on a state sovereignty.[91] Restrictive interpretation is often contrasted against expansive, evolutive, or dynamic interpretation. The restrictive interpretation school of thought in international law is closely wedded to the voluntarism school of international law. Restrictive interpretation is highly valued as it is the form of interpretation that seeks to ensure that political authorities are not held responsible for more than they have initially consented to, or, presumably, intended to consent to.

In contemporary political theory approaches to international law, restrictive interpretation has gained a deeper normative orientation.[92] Those who

Jose E Alvarez, 'The New Dispute Settlers: (Half) Truths and Consequences' (2003) 38 *Texas International Law Journal* 405; Karen Alter, *The European Court's Political Power* (Oxford: Oxford University Press 2009); Karen Alter and Laurence Helfer, 'Nature or Nurture? Judicial Lawmaking in the European Court of Justice and the Andean Tribunal of Justice' (2010) 64 *International Organization* 563; Kristin Ainley, 'International Criminal Court on Trial' (2011) 24(3) *Cambridge Review of International Affairs* 309; von Bogdandy (n 30).

[89] See Chapter 1.

[90] Alexander Orakhelashvili, 'Restrictive Interpretation of Human Rights Treaties in the Recent Jurisprudence of the European Court of Human Rights' (2003) 14 *European Journal of International Law* 529 ; Crema (n 31).

[91] Crema (n 31).

[92] On the specification of the conflict in these terms, see Kristen Hessler, 'Equality, human rights, and political legitimacy' in Føllesdal (n 49); Andreas Føllesdal, 'Much ado about nothing?

hold special concerns about the authority claims of dynamic international law require that international law not only be interpreted in a generic sovereign-friendly manner, but also in a democratic state-friendly manner.[93] The proponents of the democratic state-friendly interpretation mount two arguments to support this view. First, it is held that democratic political authorities have better procedural qualities than international interpretive authorities. In democratic states, deliberations on matters of law take place in much more open and public fora where the interests of citizens can be adequately taken into account by the deliberative organ. In domains where international law and domestic law overlap, say in the case of human rights law and constitutional law, the skeptics of international interpretive authorities hold that democratic interpretive authorities are better placed to reach an outcome that would demand deference from their own citizens.[94] The second argument is a deeper one. It holds that, in particular where there is a domain overlap, democratic interpretive authorities are substantively better placed than any international court to have an authoritative claim on the interpretation of international law. This deeper normative claim links back to the idea of the self-determination of a political community or the right of a political community to choose whatever it wishes in matters that affect it. The decision of a democratic political community therefore is more authoritative because it is made by and for that community.

## In Defence of the Authority of Dynamic International Law

There are significant differences between the restrictive interpretation approach and the democracy-friendly approach to reject the authority of dynamic interpretation. The restrictive interpretation is reflexively an approach within international law. It does not distinguish between the types of states and political authorities on the international plane. It seeks to protect the domain of all political authorities vis-à-vis dynamic international law. The democratic-friendly school of thought on the other hand is either silent or willing to concede that even dynamic international law may have a strong authority claim when it

International judicial review of human rights in well-functioning democracies' in Føllesdal (n 49); Steven Wheately, 'On the legitimate authority of international human rights bodies' in Føllesdal (n 49).

[93] Richard Bellamy, 'The democratic legitimacy of international human rights conventions: political constitutionalism and the Hirst case' in Føllesdal (n 49).

[94] Hessler (n 30).

comes to non-democratic states, given that they lack procedural superiority over international law.[95]

What are the arguments in favour of a general attitude of deference even to dynamically interpreted international laws? I hold that continuous consent alongside initial consent to the binding qualities of the decisions of interpretive authorities have an important place in the argument for a general attitude of deference towards how interpretive authorities define strict, weak, and rebuttable duties for all types of political objections.

This view focusses on the centrality of two types of consent to the binding authority of international legal judgments. These are justified from the perspective of international law over three different dimensions: the need for a formal account of authority in international law, consent as an integral part of adjudication of the international legal system, and the interpretation as a holistic act performed by interpretive authorities in their own legal domains. I will discuss each in turn.

It is nothing remarkable to say that we have witnessed a democratic turn in international law in the recent decade. As I have discussed throughout this book, concern over the authority of international law has received its fair share of criticism, both from authors who are worried about the democratic legitimacy of international law and those who are worried about the democratic legitimacy of international courts and tribunals.[96] A key value of such criticism has been that international courts and tribunals have become sensitive to the concerns of their audiences and compliance constituents. An international court is best conceived as being part of an interdependent network of domestic, regional, and international norms and its composition, rules of access, transparency of processes, and interpretive attitudes have to be responsive to the demands and expectations of its public. Having said this, the democratic critique often focuses on what attitudes international courts should have towards democratic political power[97] and it is often silent on what these attitudes should be towards non-democratic states or transition states. In this respect, so long as democratic

[95] Buchanan (n 42).

[96] Madeline Morris, 'The Democratic Dilemma of the International Criminal Court', (2002) 5 *Buffalo Criminal Law Review* 591; Shotaro Hamamoto, 'An Undemocratic Guardian of Democracy—International Human Rights Complaint Procedures' (2007) 38 *Victoria University of Wellington Law Review* 199; Víctor Abramovich, 'From Massive Human Rights Problems to Structural Patterns: New Approaches and Classic Tensions in the Inter-American System' (2009) 11 *Sur International Journal on Human Rights* 6; Andreas Føllesdal, 'The Legitimacy of International Human Rights Review: The Case of the European Court of Human Rights' (2009) 40 *Journal of Social Philosophy* 595.

[97] Andreas Føllesdal and Reidar Maliks, 'Kantian Theory and Human Rights' in Andreas Føllesdal and Reidar Maliks (eds), *Kantian Theory and Human Rights* (London: Routledge 2014).

concerns are of a special type about the democratic state, they form part of an incomplete theory from the perspective of international law and its claim to be a co-ordinating and common value pursuing institution for all states in the international legal system. A fully developed account of the authority of international courts cannot be built on the partial concerns of a sub-set of states in the international legal system. This point is all the more pressing because there is no court in the international legal system that exclusively serves what are sometimes called 'advanced democracies'.[98] What is more, international courts seek to expand their jurisdiction to as many states as possible—regionally or internationally—to be as inclusive as possible in their legal domains.

These practical constraints on the membership of international courts require international law to develop an account of the authority they have over states that is formal and inclusive. If the special circumstances of a certain type of political power are regarded as an authority-qualifying feature, the claim of authority of international court judgments over all other types of states is undermined. A formal theory of the authority of international courts, therefore, is not merely a normative choice amongst other choices, but a theoretical and practical necessity. The initial and continuing consent to the authority of international courts currently offers the best foundation for grounding the authority of international court judgments.

This justification is linked to a second and even more practical justification. International courts in the international legal system are optional institutions, with, perhaps, the exception of the Security Council referral mechanism to the International Criminal Court. The initial and express consent to be part of the jurisdiction of an international court is a commonplace requirement. There are numerous examples that support the fact that states take the act of giving consent to an international court seriously. For example, even though there is an elaborate international human rights treaty mechanism and the right to individual petition before all United Nations treaty bodies, states have designed the individual complaints mechanism's decisions to have a legally, non-binding status.[99] That is, whilst UN Treaty bodies operate as

[98] Even in the case of the European Court of Justice, following the expansion of the EU to twenty-seven member states, this assumption may not hold.

[99] There are currently right to individual petition mechanisms before the Human Rights Committee (CCPR); the CEDAW Committee; Committee against All Forms of Racial Discrimination (ICERD); Committee against Torture (CAT); Committee on the Rights of Persons with Disabilities (CRPD); the individual petition mechanism of the ICESCR; Committee on Enforced Disappearances (CED). For two other treaty bodies (the Committee on Migrant Workers (CMW) and the Committee on the Rights of the Child (CRC)) the individual complaint mechanism have not yet entered into force. http://www.ohchr.org/EN/HRBodies/TBPetitions/Pages/HRTBPetitions.aspx).

international judicial bodies, the decisions of the bodies do not impose legally binding duties on the state parties.[100] Similar institutional designs are also at work in the regional courts of the Americas and Africa. In the Americas, the north American states—the US and Canada—have accepted the non-legally binding views of the Inter-American Commission on Human Rights, but they have not accepted the compulsory jurisdiction of the Inter-American Court of Human Rights. The African Court of Human and People's Rights also operates based on the same principle. Thus far, only seven states under the non-legally binding jurisdiction of the African Commission on Human and Peoples Rights accepted the compulsory jurisdiction of its Court.[101]

What these examples show is that there is a distinct value to accepting the jurisdiction of a court and its legally binding judgments in the international legal system. Not only do states intentionally create judicial organs that emit non-binding judgments, some states do not accept courts that emit legally binding judgments. States that do accept international legal adjudication proper, even at the time of initial consent, are aware that they are assigning authority to these organs. This is indeed a risk taken by political authorities. It is, however, a risk taken consciously and knowingly.

The final justification for the authority of international courts to emit authoritative judgments on strong, weak, or rebuttable duties concerns their interpretive functions. What is the authority claim of an international court that received initial consent from states, but then has leapt into making interpretations that state parties do not believe they initially consented to? Here, I submit that there are no generic answers that could apply to each and every court. This is not a cheap answer. It is an answer that is deeply rooted in the Vienna Convention on the Law of the Treaties and its interpretation provision under Articles 30 and 31.[102]

[100] The fact that these bodies do not impose legally binding duties does not suggest that they ought to be disregarded by the state parties that have accepted the right to individual petition. As the states have ratified the treaties, they remain to have a duty to deference towards the international treaties themselves. Clearly, the views of the Committees are the best aides to specify what a duty of deference to the treaty entails. For a defence of the legitimacy of UN Human Rights Treaty Bodies, see Başak Çalı, 'The Legitimacy of International Interpretive Authorities for Human Rights Treaties: An Indirect-Instrumentalist Defence' in Føllesdal (n 49) 141.

[101] See Protocol to the African Charter on Human and Peoples' Rights on the Establishment of the African Court on Human and Peoples' Rights (adopted 9 June 1998, entered into force 1 January 2004) OAU Doc OAU/LEG/EXP/AFCHPR/PROT(III) (Protocol on African Court).

[102] VCLT 1969 art 30 reads:

1. Subject to Article 103 of the Charter of the United Nations, the rights and obligations of States Parties to successive treaties relating to the same subject matter shall be determined in accordance with the following paragraphs.
2. When a treaty specifies that it is subject to, or that it is not to be considered as incompatible with, an earlier or later treaty, the provisions of that other treaty prevail.

The Vienna Convention approach instructs us to look at the wording, context, and the object and the purpose of the text in a holistic way.[103] The interpretive judgment concerning an international legal text is not pre-determined for any interpreter—including for international courts. To be the lawful interpreter of a text brings with it a responsibility to make value judgments about interaction amongst the wording, context, and the object and purpose of the text, where each of these elements have to be taken into account. The restrictive interpretation school, however, offers a pre-determined formula for sovereignty-friendly interpretations without due regard to the other elements of interpretation—namely, the context, the object, and the purpose. The holistic argument about international interpretation is not dynamic interpretation in disguise. It merely instructs the interpreter to formulate a fully-fledged argument about why a particular interpretive approach is the most rational. This must be developed uniquely for each interpretative domain.[104] A 'restrictive interpretation good, dynamic interpretation bad' axiom cannot be defended without intimately knowing the text, its context, object, and purpose and, in addition, the practice of states[105] after interpretations have been given by an international judicial body.[106]

The argument on subsequent practice, or what I call continuous consent, needs further elaboration. This argument suggests that there is a qualitative difference towards viewing the authority of international courts at their moment of inception and at the moment when they emit a reasonable amount of interpretation. When an international court carries out a holistic

3. When all the parties to the earlier treaty are parties also to the later treaty but the earlier treaty is not terminated or suspended in operation under Article 59, the earlier treaty applies only to the extent that its provisions are compatible with those of the later treaty.
4. When the parties to the later treaty do not include all the parties to the earlier one:
   (a) as between States Parties to both treaties the same rule applies as in paragraph 3;
   (b) as between a State party to both treaties and a State party to only one of the treaties, the treaty to which both States are parties governs their mutual rights and obligations.
5. Paragraph 4 is without prejudice to Article 41, or to any question of the termination or suspension of the operation of a treaty under Article 60 or to any question of responsibility which may arise for a State from the conclusion or application of a treaty the provisions of which are incompatible with its obligations towards another State under another treaty.

[103] Richard Gardner, *Treaty Interpretation* (New York: Oxford University Press 2008).

[104] George Letsas, 'Strasbourg's Interpretive Ethic: Lessons for the International Lawyer' (2010) 21(3) *European Journal of International Law* 509.

[105] VCLT 1969 art 31.

[106] Committee on International Human Rights Law and Practice, 'Final Report on the Impact of Findings of the United Nations Human Rights Treaty Bodies' in International Law Association Report (Berlin 2004) (International Law Association, Berlin 2004).

interpretation of the text before it, it will also form a unique domain specific general account of a general attitude for interpreting the text. In some instances, the interpretive attitude developed by the court can be squarely identified as a form of judicial activism: that is, the court may favour a restrictive or a dynamic attitude towards the text. At this point, it is important to consider what the reactions of the states (the secondary interpreters of the text) are to the court. Do they, for example, seek to shut down the court?[107] Do they, as state parties, convene to consider amendments to the original text of the court?[108] Do they, by and large, accept the interpretation imposed?[109] Do they seek to influence the interpretation of international law?[110] Does an individual state choose to the leave the compulsory jurisdiction of the court?[111] These options highlight that the possibility to react to the interpretations of courts as a collective always exists: ongoing consent alongside initial consent offers political authorities channels through which states may seek to influence the interpretations of international courts.

This analysis highlights that the risk of international courts emitting interpretations that are not favourable to a single political authority, domestic or otherwise, is always there. States often mediate this risk by not accepting the jurisdiction of international courts or not allowing institutions to have legally binding powers. But once states enter into an international adjudicatory system, they have distinct reasons to respect the delineation of strong, weak, and rebuttable duties imposed by these judicial institutions.[112] In cases of strong disagreement as to what general duty of deference is owed as a matter of international law and with respect to what outcomes the holistic interpretation brings in specific cases, political authorities, as interacting authorities, can react by leaving the judicial system, or by collectively seeking to redesign the judicial system.

[107] This has been the case of the Southern African Development Community (SADC) Tribunal.

[108] Brighton Declaration (2012) High Level Conference on the Future of the European Court of Human Rights available at: http://www.echr.coe.int/Documents/2012_Brighton_FinalDeclaration_ENG.pdf (accessed 26 December 2014).

[109] Cf the Council of Europe State parties' compliance records with *Tyrer v UK* (1978) 2 EHRR 1; *Marckx v Belgium* (1979) 2 EHRR 330; *Golder v UK* (1979–80) 1 EHRR 524. See also the OAS states' acceptance of the serious human rights violations case law of the Inter American Court of Human Rights.

[110] Anthea Roberts, 'Power and Persuation in Investment Treaty Arbitration: The Dual Role of States' (2010) 104 *American Journal of International Law* 179.

[111] More recently, even if perhaps not for legal interpretative reasons, Venezuela's denunciation of the Inter-American Convention on Human Rights.

[112] George Letsas 'The ECHR as a Living Instrument: its Meaning and Legitimacy' in Geir Ulfstein, Andreas Føllesdal, and Birgit Peters (eds), *Constituting Europe: The European Court of Human Rights in a National, European and Global Context* (Cambridge: Cambridge University Press 2013).

## Mr Davis Revisited

The European Court of Human Rights in its *Hirst* judgment did indeed ask the UK Parliament to reconsider its laws on the disfranchisement of prisoners. It did so within the context of the United Kingdom's legal obligations under the European Convention on Human Rights. In his response to the authority of the judgment, Mr Davis argued that the UK Parliament as a democratic institution representing the will of the British people enjoyed the sole authority to determine whether prisoners may vote.[113] In his view, the European Court of Human Rights had exceeded the authority initially assigned to it.

To put it differently, Mr Davis put forth two interrelated ideas. First, he advanced the idea that the authority of any interpretation of international law that goes beyond the restrictive interpretation of the treaty text is suspect. The second idea he put forward was the idea that an international court cannot enter into an authority competition with an omnipotent parliament. The parliament, by its democratic qualities and as the representative of the ongoing consent of the people, has a trumping authority claim over international law that was ratified in the distant past and has been interpreted in ways that arguably exceeded the original intentions of the state parties.

Following the scheme of duties developed in this study, the steps I would take to analyze Mr Davis's disapproval with developments brought by Mr Hirst's case start by asking whether we are within the sphere of the rebuttable authority of international law. That is, is Mr Davis justified in his disregard for international law in this particular instance. For this justification to hold, we have to investigate whether the final decision of the European Court of Human Rights generates rebuttable duties for domestic political authorities.

The European human rights system is a case of authority transfer. Political authorities allow the European Court of Human Rights to interpret and apply the European Convention on Human Rights and Fundamental Freedoms. It is well known that the European Court of Human Rights takes this task seriously and has signaled to member states of the Council of Europe that it will interpret the Convention to guarantee effective, and practical, and not illusory rights.[114] At the same time the European Court of Human Rights has proposed that it

[113] HC Deb 10 February 2011, vol 523, col 493.

[114] *Airey v Ireland* (App no 6289/73) (1981) 3 EHRR 305; *Tyrer v United Kingdom* (App no 5856/72) (1978) 2 EHRR 1, 15–16 [31]; *Chassagnou and others v France* (App no 25088/94, 28331/95, 28443/95) (1999) 29 EHRR 615 [100]; *Selmouni v France* (App no 25803/94) (1999) 29 EHRR 32 [101].

will invoke a judge-made doctrine of the margin of appreciation to domestic political and legal institutions when interpreting how the Convention interacts with the facts of each case and whether domestic institutions may be better placed to assess what specific actions must be taken in a specific case.[115] In effect, the margin of appreciation doctrine enabled the European Court of Human Rights to interpret some of the duties in the Convention as being rebuttable.

Since its first adjudication in 1960, the European Court of Human Rights' canon of interpretation has taken root in diverse European domestic jurisdictions. This has led both domestic political and legal authorities to adjust laws, policies, and case-law in accordance with the interpretations of the treaty text emitted by it.[116] It has also led to the emergence of regional customary remedy practices that states have developed in the shadow of the Court's interpretation.[117] This practice has a customary character, as most judgments of the European Court of Human Rights are declaratory and do not specify the kinds of actions that states need to take.[118] In 2004, members of the Council of Europe Committee of Ministers asked the European Court of Human Rights to offer more help to member states with the most appropriate remedies they could take in going beyond declaratory judgments.[119] Council of Europe member states, therefore, invited the European Court of Human Rights to interact more closely with their domestic political authorities. It is in this context that the European Court of Human Rights asked the United Kingdom to address its prisoners voting law before the British Parliament with the view of introducing (if this is what the UK Parliament elected to do) a reasoning to the law that explains why certain prisoners may and others may not vote. Whilst such reasoning may either depend on the type of crime or the length of sentence, the European Court of Human Rights did not suggest how the blanket ban could be turned into a non-blanket ban, or into less of a blanket ban.

[115] See Eva Brems, 'The Margin of Appreciation Doctrine in the Case-Law of the European Court of Human Rights' (1996) 56 *Zeitschrift für Auslandisches Offentliches Recht und Völkerrecht* 240; Yutaka-Arai Takahashi, *The Margin of Appreciation Doctrine and the Principle of Proportionality* (Antwerp: Intersentia 2002).

[116] Alex Stone Sweet and Hellen Keller, *A Europe of Rights* (Oxford: Oxford University Press 2008).

[117] Başak Çalı and Anne Koch, 'Foxes Guarding the Foxes: The Peer Review of Human Rights Judgments by the Committee of Ministers of the Council of Europe' (2014) 14(2) *Human Rights Law Review* 301.

[118] Ibid.

[119] CM Res(2004)3 on judgments revealing an underlying systemic problem, 12 May 2004, available at: wcd.coe.int/ViewDoc.jsp?id1/4743257&Lang1/4fr [last accessed 22 February 2015].

In this context, Mr Davis's argument that international law must be put aside when a ruling that goes to the heart of the democratic will of a parliament (ie voting laws) is misplaced. In this particular case, the European Court of Human Rights relied on its long-standing interpretive canon of interpreting rights effectively. This long-standing interpretive canon is a practice that has been endorsed by the members of the Council of Europe by delegating powers of interpretation of Convention rights to the Court, both initially and over time through their subsequent practice of collectively giving effect to the judgments of the Court, through their work at the Committee of Ministers and through their domestic internal practices. That is, members of the Council of Europe took away declaratory judgments made by the Strasbourg Court and considered their own legislation, policies, and case-law in the light of them. The minimalist deference to international law has found a meaningful practice in this region without explicit original rules to this effect.[120]

The rebellion organized in the UK Parliament by Mr Davis disregarded this body of practice—although it has been established through generations of British governments and parliaments participating in it. The one-directional conception of the politician as the guardian of democratic laws enacted domestically at the expense of the double role that they exercise domestically and internationally (or, in this case, regionally) is at the heart of Mr Davis's refusal to consider the judgment as one that could promote a debate on the quality of the UK's domestic laws. The substantive argument of Mr Davis, that international law ought to be displaced when it touches matters at the heart of domestic law, as a prima facie argument further undermines the conditions of rebuttal set out in this book. Such rebuttal cannot simply rely on the existence of a democratic regime. So long as the United Kingdom remains in the European human rights system the rebuttal ought to come in the form of an argument recognizable to all in the Council of Europe system. This rebuttal must explain to all what is essentially lost in making a blanket ban, into a ban with rational justifications attached and why such a loss overweighs going against the established practice of all states giving effect to Strasbourg judgments.

## Conclusion

This chapter has argued that conceiving the authority of international law as being grounded in a paradigm of minimal deference is richer than the

[120] In this respect the Council of Europe practice is distinct from the practice of the European Union, where there are institutionalized rules and penalties attached to non-conformity with the Court of Justice of the European Union.

standard view. Such flexibility has an important consequence for criticisms of the authority of international law over domestic political organs: the critical strategies that worry about either static or dynamic international laws cannot, by themselves, succeed against this richer understanding.

Minimalist deference to international law already accommodates these critiques. The first, exemplified by normative absolutism and primacy of democratic decision-making, alleges that the authority of international law fails to account for sovereignty. This variant fails. Jurisdictional limits to the authorities of sovereigns, and participation, implying active agency of sovereigns in the making of international laws demand that we conceive political authorities not as recipients of imposed international law, but as actors co-operating, albeit imperfectly, to create international regulation. These critiques also under appreciate the logic of existing international laws and the allowances they make for political authorities in negotiating the kinds of duties imposed by international law. The second variant, concerned by dynamic international laws and the rise of international legal judgments, alleges that international law has a tendency to expand once it is created. This argument ensues, but it loses its force because expansion of international law through dynamic interpretation is too participatory a process, within which the sovereign rights of modification of international law and even exiting it, still remain with the political authorities.

# 4

# Beyond Monism and Dualism

'Although international law is not binding upon Parliament or the provincial legislatures, a court must presume that legislation is intended to comply with Canada's obligations under international instruments and as a member of the international community. In choosing among possible interpretations of a statute, the court should avoid interpretations that would put Canada in breach of such obligations...'[1]

## Introduction

In the Chapter 3 I argued that political authorities were under an obligation to adopt a general attitude of deference towards international law and respond to duties imposed by either strong, weak, or rebuttable international law. I also argued that binding international court judgments attract an attitude of deference underpinned by the legal significance assigned to court decisions by political authorities, as opposed to institutions emitting non-legally binding decisions created by states. In this chapter, I turn to the authority of international law before domestic courts. In particular, I consider legal authority emitting domestic high courts, supreme courts, and constitutional courts. I seek to formulate and defend an argument for the following question: how should domestic courts situated in a web of commitments to domestic rule of law across diverse legal systems respond to the authority claims of international law?

My core aim here is to defend an overall coherent attitude towards international law for domestic judges that is neither relativistic in its approach to international law (suggesting that each legal system has its own rules for settling questions of authority) nor tout-court universalistic (holding that past

[1] *Ordon Estate v Grail SCC* [1998] 3 SCR 437, para 137.

domestic legal practices determined by political and judicial organs are of no consequence for international law to make authority claims). In line with the doctrinal conception of international law's authority developed in preceding chapters, I contend that the domestic judge's approach to the authority of international law must be informed by a reflective attitude towards international law's authority. This reflective attitude is both an extension of the duties that domestic political authorities have towards international law and is simultaneously required by the very purposes of judicial function, a concern for consistency of law as promulgated by political authorities to the extent that it is possible.[2]

In what follows I first clarify the core case to explain when international law generates legal duties that make domestic judges take international law into account. I then turn to why using both monism and dualism—our textbook approach—to settle questions of the authority of international law fall short and do not offer stable and clear guidance to domestic judges on the authority claims of international law. I then discuss the contours of the reflective approach that I argue is a better framework for settling the diversity of authority relationships imposed by strong, weak, and rebuttable duties imposed by international law and judgments of international courts and tribunals.

## The Domestic Judge and International Law

That domestic judiciaries are foremost a part of a domestic legal system entrusted with applying and interpreting domestic legislation is not a non-trivial statement. As part of the domestic legal system of a country, domestic judiciaries come into regular contact with international law and international judicial decisions.[3] Such contact takes place at different levels

[2] Theorists of the rule of law have formulated both narrow and broad conceptions of what the rule of law really requires from a judge. The search for consistency in the law is an aspect that figures in all such conceptions as a core requirement of judicial function. See Lon L Fuller, *The Morality of Law* (Oxford: Hart Publishing 1964), Joseph Raz, 'The Rule of Law and Its Virtue', in *The Authority of Law Essays on Law and Morality* (Oxford: Oxford University Press 1979) 210, 212–19; Jeremy Waldron, 'The Rule of International Law' (2006) 30 *Harvard Journal of Law and Public Policy* 15.

[3] See generally Christopher McCrudden, 'A Common Law of Human Rights?: Transnational Judicial Conversations on Constitutional Rights' (2000) 20(4) *Oxford Journal of Legal Studies* 499; Eyal Benvenisti and George W Downs, 'National Courts, Domestic Democracy, and the Evolution of International Law' (2009) 20(1) *European Journal of International Law* 59. Some scholars call this 'the globalization of judgment', Reem Bahdi, 'Globalization of

of intensity and has been subject to much literature under the rubrics of the internationalization or globalization of domestic judicial practice.[4]

Intensity of contact matters in assigning authority claims to international law before domestic courts. In particular, we must distinguish between three different levels of intensity of contact between international law and domestic judges. First is the contact that domestic judges have with the totality of the universe of international law. The general corpus of international law is the amalgamation of treaties and international judicial decisions that are emitted by institutions of international law. This is international law to which domestic political authorities have not consented through direct and participatory modes of international law making. Under this rubric we may place the contact the domestic judge has with treaties with which political authorities have not interacted at all,[5] treaties that have been negotiated but not signed,[6] international legal obligations that are considered merely soft law,[7] and international judicial decisions pronounced by international legal authorities with regard to third parties.

In the second layer is the domestic court's interaction with treaties that have been duly signed, but not ratified, or treaties that have yet not come into force even though they have been ratified by the state. This layer further includes nascent or emerging customary international law and international decisions of quasi-judicial bodies that are considered non-binding.[8] Here,

Judgment: Transjudicialism and the Five Faces of International Law in Domestic Courts' (2002) 34 *George Washington International Law Review* 555; 'a global community of courts' Anne-Marie Slaughter, 'A Global Community of Courts' (2003) 44 *Harvard International Law Journal* 191; or a 'globalized judiciary' Ken I Kersch, 'The New Legal Transnationalism, the Globalized Judiciary and the Rule of Law' (2005) 4(2) *Washington University Global Studies Law Review* 345, in order to capture the interactive nature of judicial decision-making challenging the role-orientation of domestic judges. It is helpful, however, to distinguish these from 'transnationalisation' of judicial decision-making, which more specifically refers to the use of foreign judgments as persuasive authority. See Bruce Carolan, 'The Search for Coherence in the Use of Foreign Court Judgements by the Supreme Court of Ireland' (2004–5) 12(1) *Journal of Comparative and International Law* 123; Jeremy Waldron, 'Foreign Law and the Modern Ius Gentium' (2005) 119(1) *Harvard Law Review* 129.

[4] Dinah Shelton, *International Law and Domestic Legal Systems: Incorporation, Transformation, and Persuasion* (Oxford: Oxford University Press 2011).

[5] For example, the position of the European Convention on Human Rights and Fundamental Freedoms (ECHR) with respect to the US judiciary.

[6] For example the situation of the United Kingdom with respect to the UN Sovereign Immunities Treaty of 2004.

[7] For example, domestic courts' interaction with the 2008 Declaration on the Rights of Indigenous Peoples in states that voted in favour of the Declaration.

[8] For example, the views of the Human Rights Committee of the United Nations, with regard to states that have not assigned any legal value to the views of the Human Rights Committee.

domestic judges come face-to-face with international law in the making of which their political authorities have directly participated, but to which they have not extended full, explicit consent as required by the Vienna Convention on the Law of the Treaties (VCLT), distillation of customary international law in its early stages to which a state may or may not have contributed actively and quasi-judicial treaty body obligations towards which states owe a good faith obligation to take due regard.

Third are the international treaties and customary international law that have been duly accepted and recognized by political authorities or fundamental norms of international law, ius cogens norms, that do not need an explicit formal recognition by domestic political authorities to enjoy a legally binding status as a matter of international law. Here we may also include decisions of international courts and tribunals that have been accepted as legally binding by political authorities.

In the fourth, albeit rare, layer are international treaties and international court judgments that are regarded as part of domestic law domestically, either through the incorporation of a treaty into domestic law[9] or through domestic precedent.[10] International law no longer looks like international law qua international law in this layer. It is part and parcel of domestic law due to the explicit place given to international law as a matter of domestic law.

Each of these four layers of intensity of contact between the domestic judge and international law signals the strength of intentions of the political authorities to domestic judges with regard to how domesticated international law is made by the political authorities in the domestic legal order. At the very outer layer, international law operates at the level of persuasive authority. A domestic judge does not have an unambiguous duty towards the whole universe of international law that their own political authorities have not participated or accepted in its making. At this level, we may also consider the relationship between the domestic judge and international law as one that generates imperfect moral duties and not legal duties per se. The further we move into the inner layers, the more the legal authority of international law becomes recognizable for the domestic judge and the general

[9] For example, the European Convention on Human Rights Act of 2003 of the Irish Parliament, incorporating the European Convention on Human Rights and Fundamental Freedoms.

[10] For example, the *Görgülü* Judgment of the German Constitutional Court, which said 'The Basic Law aims to integrate Germany into the legal community of peaceful and free states, but does not waive the sovereignty contained in the last instance in the German constitution. There is therefore no contradiction with the aim of commitment to international law if the legislature, exceptionally, does not comply with the law of international agreements, provided this is the only way in which a violation of fundamental principles of the constitution can be averted.' *Görgülü* Case, 111 BVerfGE 307, para 35.

duty to take international law into account as a matter of its legal authority increases. The further we move into the layers of intensity of contact we observe that domestic judges are dealing with international law *qua* international law. In other cases domestic judges may be dealing with international law *qua* domestic law or domestic law like international law. In cases where international law is fully domesticated clearly no questions about the authority of international law in the domestic legal order are raised. Those that are, are merely questions of the authority of one domestic law over the authority of another domestic law.

In this chapter, my attention is on the authority of international law that formally looks like international law in the domestic legal order. This excludes situations when the general corpus of international law generates moral duties that are not yet legal duties and when international law is no longer international law in the domestic legal system (such as when international law or international judicial decisions are fully domesticated through internal domestic rules). To return to our layers, the focus of this chapter, therefore, are layers two, three, and four and the interpretive problems found within.

Each time a domestic judge comes into contact with international law in one of these layers, standard interpretive questions arise about authority for the domestic judge regardless of the jurisdiction in which the domestic judge is located. Domestic judges face two analytical levels of questions in particular at the first point of contact with international law that makes legal authority claims in the domestic order. The first question is what attitude should they have towards the authority claims of international law that have not been fully domesticated, but have been acknowledged by the political authorities or are part of those very limited class of international laws that do not require acknowledgement? The second is what attitude should a domestic judge have towards the authority claims of international law in cases when the political organs of state refuses to accord due deference to that international law by their acts or omissions?

The first question lies at the heart of any conception of the legal authority of international law. The second question is properly a question of conflict of loyalty. It asks the extent to which a domestic judge, as part of their duties as a judge, has to be a follower of their political masters on the day of their judgment and the extent to which international law needs to be part of the interpretive domain. Both questions are highly doctrinal as well as highly practical. Authority claims of international law are heatedly debated across doctrinal divides in virtually all jurisdictions—civil and common law alike.[11] How

[11] Michael J Beloff, 'What Does It All Mean? Interpreting the Human Rights Act 1998' in L Betten (ed), *The Human Rights Act 1998—What It Means* (1998); Jutta Brunnee and Stephen J Toope 'A Hesitant Embrace: The application of international law by Canadian Courts' (2002) 40

domestic judges take their cues from such debates have practical consequences for each and every case in the domestic system.[12] Such practical consequences also extend to interpretive questions about the already existing corpus of ordinary domestic law[13] and constitutional law.[14] There is, therefore, much at stake when developing and defending a view on the authority claims of international law over domestic courts both for international law and domestic law.

## The Default Position: The Relativity of Monism and Dualism

Standard doctrinal international law literature on the authority of international law has long proposed that answers to questions of the authority of international law for the domestic judge are and must be of a relative nature as a matter of doctrine.[15] This is due to the two existing, competing

*Canadian Yearbook of International Law* 3; Gerrit Betlem and André Nollkaemper, 'Giving Effect to Public International Law and European Community Law before Domestic Courts—A Comparative Analysis of the Practice Consistent Interpretation' (2003) 14 *European Journal of International Law* 569; Roger P Alford, 'Foreign Relations as a Matter of Interpretation: The Use and Abuse of Charming Betsy' (2006) 67 *Ohio State Law Journal* 1339; Melissa A Waters 'The Creeping Monism: The Judicial Trend Toward Interpretive Incorporation of Human Rights Treaties' (2007) 107 *Columbia Law Review* 628.

[12] See for example, *Medellín v Texas* 552 US 491 (2008) (considerations of access to consular assistance for foreign criminal suspects); *A and B v Israel*, Appeal Decision, CrimA 6659/06, 1757/07, 8228/07, 3261/08, ILDC 1069 (IL 2008) 11 June 2008, Criminal Division (compatibility of domestic internment conditions with international humanitarian law); *Bekir-Ousta and ors*, Appeal in cassation, No 58/2006, (2006) 47 Elliniki Dikaiosyni 524, ILDC 831 (GR 2006), 10 January 2006 (freedom of association rights of persons belonging to minorities); *A and ors v Netherlands* (Ministry of Foreign Affairs and Ministry of Education, Culture, and Science), first instance judgment, Decision No LJN: BL1862/334949, ILDC 1463 (NL 2010), 3 February 2010, Netherlands (effects of the Security Council Resolution 1737 on the right to education of Iranians).

[13] A key debate that has ensued in the South American Countries has concerned the interpretation of amnesty laws against the backdrop of emerging right to truth and right to remedy interpretations that have emerged at the level of United Nations originated soft law and Inter-American Court of Human Rights originated remedy law. Cf *Caso Claude Reyes y otros v Chile* (Sentencia de 19 de septiembre de 2006. Serie C No 151); Sentencia sobre Excepciones Preliminares, Fondo, Reparaciones y Costas (Sentencia de 26 de septiembre de 2006. Serie C No 154).

[14] The interpretive attitude towards the Convention on the Elimination of Discrimination against Women, for example raises crucial interpretive questions with regard to the interpretation of gender equality clauses in Constitutions. See Ruth Rubio Marin, 'Constitutional Domestication of International Gender Norms: Categorizations, Illustrations and Reflections from the Nearside of the Bridge' with Martha I Morgan, in Karen Knopp (ed), *Gender and Human Rights* (Oxford: Oxford University Press 2004) 113–52.

[15] On a defense of the relativist position see Giorgio Gaja, 'Dualism: A Review' in Janne E Nijmann and André Nollkaemper (eds), *New Perspectives on the Divide between National and International Law* (Oxford: Oxford University Press 2007) 52–62.

frameworks used to answer them: monism and dualism. It has long been argued that without ascertaining the prior qualities of the legal order, either as a monist system or a dualist system, we cannot proceed. It is important to note that the necessity of this prior assessment is not only of descriptive value, but also of doctrinal and legal-normative value.

Relativism about the domestic legal effects of the authority of international law from the perspective of the domestic judge is deeply misguided. The oft invoked monism-dualism dichotomy that is built on the relativism of the authority relationship between international law and domestic judiciaries is unsatisfactory in the light of the scheme of authority conceptualization I developed in Chapter 2 and defended in Chapter 3.[16] The core weakness of the prior monism-dualism determination is that it directs the attention of the domestic judge away from directly engaging with schemes of authority imposed by the diverse duties present in international law. The standard discussion also collapses what I have posed as two questions into a single one. The guiding framework for the discovery of the authority relationship between international law and domestic courts is reduced to asking the kind of attitude the domestic judge should develop towards international law in general.[17] This stands in stark contrast to understanding international law as a system that imposes piecemeal duties on domestic political authorities and on domestic legal authorities.

Although they are conceptualized as two different world views about the relationship between international law and domestic law, monism and dualism share important, if not misleading similarities. Both accounts operate based on assumptions of a yes/no test for the authority of international law in the domestic order, at the expense of paying attention to the diversity of duty impositions inherent in international law as an institution made up of strong, weak, and rebuttable duties. The yes/no scheme is winner takes all. That is, if international law has authority all international law is to be obeyed. If international law has no authority it may be ignored in its totality. As discussed in Chapter 2, this either/or approach to the authority of international

[16] The descriptive and analytical literature on the same subject matter, as opposed to the doctrinal literature is much better developed. See generally, Eyal Benevisti, 'Judicial Misgivings Concerning the Application of International Law: An Analysis of Attitudes of National Courts' (1993) 4 *European Journal of International Law* 159; Yuval Shany, *Regulating Jurisdictional Relations between National and International Courts* (Oxford: Oxford University Press 2007); David Sloss *The Role of Domestic Courts in Treaty Enforcement: A Comparative Study* (Cambridge: Cambridge University Press 2009).

[17] Having said this, I must also note that there is a growing discontent with the automatic application of monism and dualism as the two frameworks exhausting the authority of international law in domestic courts. Most notably, see Ian Brownlie, *Principles of Public International Law* (5th edn, Oxford: Oxford University Press 1998) 33–4.

law is based on the false assumption that international law only imposes one type of duty towards its subjects, a strong duty to obey the dictates of the law. If we accept the assumption that international law generates a range of duties, then analytical frameworks that do not accommodate these offer us a misfocused lens through which to look at authority relationships and how domestic judges should treat international law in cases when the domestic executive or legislature dismiss it. Thus, the relationship between the monism versus dualism debate and its impact on the discussions on the authority of international law over domestic judges cannot be underestimated. The proposition that holds domestic law and international law as two separate legal orders, with no possibility of interaction between them, is antithetical to the authority of international law. The opposite proposition, that international law and domestic law are part of the same order, with no possibility of differentiation between them, over determines the authority of international law, and turns domestic judges into blind enforcers of international law.[18]

In what follows I first focus my attention on the two variants of the monism-dualism divide. The first is what I term the 'formal variant'. This is formal in that it allocates authority to international law by looking at its formal status in domestic legal orders. This status (with the exception of countries with written constitutions) is identified by analyzing the respective constitutions of individual states. This approach leads to characterizations of domestic legal orders simply as either monist or dualist, and says that the duty of a domestic judge is to follow their characterization when interacting with international law. The second variant is what I term as the 'ideological variant' to monism and dualism. This variant holds that what determines the authority of international law in domestic courts is the ideologies of the judges on the bench and how open or closed they are. I defend a different view. I defend a view that is beyond monism and dualism. In the light of the scheme of authority developed in the previous chapters, I frame this as a 'reflective approach' to the authority of international law before domestic courts. This reflective approach is admittedly one that is more challenging approach than either monism or dualism as a doctrinal construct. It demands the domestic law judge to both take due regard of the intensity of contact it

[18] This argument is often discussed in relation to Scelle and his theory of domestic judges as agents that carry out double functions. See Georges Scelle, 'Georges Scelle, *Précis de droit des gens: principes et systématique* (Paris: Recueil Sirey 1934) and also the discussion of this by Antonio Cassese and Pierre Marie Dupuy. Antonio Cassese, 'Remarks on Scelle's theory of "role splitting" (dédoublement fonctionnel) in international law' (1990) 1(1) *European Journal of International Law* 210; Pierre Marie Dupuy, 'The Unity of Application of International Law at the Global Level and The Responsibility of Judges', (2007) 2 *European Journal of Legal Studies* 1.

has with a specific international law as well as the scheme of duties that very international law imposes.

## Monism and Dualism: The Origins

The theoretical foundations of monism and dualism as worldviews about legal reality have been with us since international law originated in Europe and beyond.[19] Monism and dualism are best understood as worldviews that are dependent on more substantive (or to borrow a Rawlsian term, comprehensive)[20] doctrines about international law. To put it differently, monism and dualism are conclusive statements of larger and more substantive theories one adopts on the nature of law, the nature of international law, the overlap between international law and domestic law, constitutional law, and more importantly, on the authority of international law. It is for this reason that diverse sets of international lawyers[21] and domestic courts[22] have identified themselves either as monists or as dualists in different epochs and have referred back to plural theoretical foundations when defending their monist or dualist worldviews.

Historically, monism as a worldview predates dualism. The rise of dualism corresponds to the rise of positivism which sees international law as a contender to natural law conceptions.[23] After positivist international lawyers established a heavy grip on international law, the debate turned to what all recognize now as the 'monism versus dualsim' debate.[24] The theoretical

[19] As Von Bogdandy puts it 'The relationship between the norms of international law and those of domestic law is still understood in terms of concepts developed one hundred years ago: monism and dualism.' Armin von Bogdandy, 'Pluralism, Direct Effect and the Ultimate Say: On the Relationship between International and Domestic Constitutional Law' (2008) 6(3-4) *International Journal of Constitutional Law* 397, 399.

[20] John Rawls, *Political Liberalism* (New York: Columbia University Press 1996).

[21] The list of monists range from early Catholic international lawyers Suarez to Kelsen, from Scelle to contemporary Casesse. The famous dualists range from Triepel and Anzilotti to Prosper Weil. For a review of early monists see Joseph G Starke, 'Monism and Dualism in the Theory of International Law' (1936) 17 *British Yearbook of International Law* 66. See also Hans Kelsen, *Principles of International Law* (Robert W Tucker ed) (2nd edn, New York: Holt, Rinehart & Winston 1966) 551–2; Cassese, 'Towards a Moderate Monism: Could International Rules Eventually Acquire the Force to Invalidate Inconsistent National Laws?' in *Realising Utopia: The Future of International Law* (Oxford: Oxford University Press 2014) 187.

[22] The most well-known domestic example of this in the English speaking world is the US Supreme Court. David L Sloss, Michael D Ramsey, and William S Dodge (eds), *International Law in the US Supreme Court* (Cambridge: Cambridge University Press 2012).

[23] Starke (n 21) 68.

[24] All key textbooks of international law nod to the existence of this debate. See Brownlie (n 17); Peter Malanczuk, *Akehurst's Modern Introduction to International Law* (7th edn, London: Routledge

question for both classical and contemporary thinkers of international law since the establishment of this binary dichotomy has been whether international law and domestic law form part of the same legal reality or whether international law and domestic law form part of two separate, distinct legal realities. Famously, the idea of a unified legal reality has been labelled the monist worldview of international law. The latter has since been labelled the dualist worldview of international law.

Early Catholic natural lawyers were, by default, monists. For these lawyers, the divine or natural order was hierarchically above the sovereign order (ius gentium) of states.[25] By virtue of the non-derogability of the natural legal order by the sovereign, the laws of states could not exist separately from natural (international) law. Monism, therefore, was the conclusion early natural lawyers reached to explain the relationship between domestic law, international law, and natural law. Early natural law views on monism also advocated what we may term 'hierarchical monism'. It was not only that it was a unified legal order, but also that certain norms—binding on all states and their positive law—had a hierarchical relationship to positive law. The insertion of ius cogens norms into the VCLT certainly revived the debate on hierarchical monism in international law. It did not, however, clarify whether ius cogens norms also ought to have a hierarchical status when it interacted with domestic law.

The rise of will-based positivism in international law in the eighteenth century made dualism a strong theoretical competitor to hierarchical monist views of the legal order.[26] Just as positivism broke the link between divine law and posited law, it also shook assumptions about higher, superior law existing above domestic law. If the will of the state were supreme, as opposed to natural law, then international law as it did not originate through the will of the state, could not be part of the legal order of a sovereign state. International law, therefore, must exist in a different realm of legal reality to the domestic legal reality. For will-based positivism, international law is external and foreign to domestic law (ausseres Staatsrecht)[27] and is in constant need of domestication by the sovereign to have any recognizable authority for the domestic judge. The influence of positivism and its formulation of dualism, therefore,

1997) 63; Malcolm N Shaw, *International Law* (7th edn, Cambridge: Cambridge University Press 2014) 93.

[25] 'In universo humano genere potuerunt iuro gentium morbius introduci' Suarez cited in Starke (n 21) 68.

[26] Rafael Domingo, 'Gaius, Vattel, and the New Global Law Paradigm' (2011) 22(3) *European Journal of International Law* 621, 629.

[27] Albert Zorn, *Grundzüge des Völkerrechts* (Charleston: Nabu Press 2010).

based itself on the premise that the master of the domestic judge was the individual sovereign will of the state in which the judge operates. This view in its totality severs all contact between the domestic judge and international law and defines the domestic judge as the faithful applicant of domestic law. Instruction to the domestic judge by the political authority through domestic legislation becomes the only route through which international law can enter into decision making. Even then, what the judge applies is not international law, it is merely domestic law.

Whilst monism versus dualism originally developed as a byproduct of the natural law versus positivism debate, positivist international lawyers have proceeded to offer both substantive and legal pedigree based arguments in support of dualism becoming entrenched as an attitude towards international law, often at the expense of interpretive arguments focusing on the object and purpose of international law. Of these, the theoretical views of Triepel and Anzilotti are well-known. For Triepel, dualism was the right approach to the relationship between international law and domestic law not only because the single sovereign authority was supreme, but also because international law and domestic law regulated different fields.[28] That international law concerned itself with law between nations and domestic law within nations meant that these two bodies of law needed to be kept separate and the former did need to be a concern for domestic judges. Anzilotti reached a similar dualist conclusion by suggesting that the basis of legal obligation in international law and domestic law were not the same and, therefore, could not be enforced in the same way.[29] Dualists could embrace international law as a posited legal system between multiple sovereigns situated in parallel, but at the same time insist that it cannot be treated as a legal system as a matter of domestic law.[30]

Positivism also generated its own versions of monist thinking—with Kelsen the most famous positivist monist.[31] The central contribution Kelsen made to the monism versus dualism debate was his contribution to its relativity. For Kelsen, whether a positive domestic system was monist or dualist was a matter of choice by national law. Monism can be a fact of positive law. It was not a deeper theoretical discussion about the differences in the subject

[28] For a discussion of Treipel's writings in English see, AP Sereni, *The Italian Conception of International Law* (1943). Cf Giorgio Gaja, 'Positivism and Dualism in Dioniso Anzilotti' (1992) 3 *European Journal of International Law* 123.

[29] Gaja (n 28) at 134–5.

[30] Austin reached a similar conclusion to that of the continental dualists, but through a more radical assessment of the law-like qualities of international law. Cf Chapter 2.

[31] Kelsen (n 21).

matter or the basis of obligation between domestic and international law. As Kelsen famously states:

'The question as to whether in case of a conflict between national and international law the one or the other prevails can be decided only on the basis of the national law concerned; the answer cannot be deduced from the relation which is assumed to exist between international and national law. Since according to positive national law it is not excluded that in case of a conflict between this law and international law the former is to be considered as valid, we shall here assume that the state organs are bound to apply national law even if it is contrary to international law.'[32]

This paragraph and Kelsen's work has been influential in the formulation of constitutional statements on international law as well as shaping domestic judges' understanding of the authority of international law as it has reduced the authority of international law into a domestic debate about the nature of domestic legal systems and the doctrines of domestic judges.[33] Comparative constitutional law unassumingly adopted this Kelsenian position, analyzing domestic legal systems in terms of the degree to which they have adopted monist or dualist presumptions in relation to international law.

## The Formal Variant of Monism and Dualism

The journey from monist natural law to the positivist versions of monism and dualism has been most powerfully observed in the characterization of constitutional documents by international and constitutional lawyers. We are all accustomed to describing, characterizing, and teaching the constitutional arrangements of sovereign states as arrangements that take a firm view on the monism versus dualism debate. What is more, we hold that the very characterizations of constitutional documents by legal experts are action-guiding for the relationship between domestic judges and international law. This is foremost a formal positivist understanding of the authority relationship between these two bodies of law and an important legacy of Kelsen.

Under the formal variant, the monist characterization of constitutional norms suggests that international law has authority over domestic courts if such authority is expressly provided by a constitution. Dualist

[32] Ibid. 565–6.

[33] Even though Kelsen regarded both views to be possible, he in effect preferred a monist approach to the relationship between international law and domestic law, and he thought that international law should have primacy over domestic law. Kelsen (n 21).

characterizations suggest that international law has no authority over domestic courts if the national constitution of a state does not allow for an independent role for international law within the sphere of domestic law. Under the formal variant of monism and dualism, therefore, the authority of international law hinges on whether a state's constitution makes it subject to a constitutional order or to the will of parliaments.

For many, looking at constitutional texts to assign authority to international law before domestic judges is a straightforward and efficient way to settle authority questions from the perspective of domestic judiciaries. First, it reinforces the idea that domestic judges are primarily bound by domestic rule of law. Their duty to apply and interpret only extends to laws that they have been authorized to apply and interpret by political authorities. If political authorities formally ask domestic judges to apply and interpret international laws, then this becomes a legitimate task for a domestic court. If there is no such will expressed, then domestic judges have to stay away from international law, as it only exists for the regulation of inter-state relations. Second, a pre-existing rule in the domestic legal system allows domestic judges to engage with international law in a foreseeable and consistent manner. We would expect judges from monist-leaning countries to pay more attention to international law and those from dualist-leaning legal systems to await its domestication.

Whilst at first analysis a formal rule resolving authority questions of international law over domestic judges seems to solve difficult problems of domestic judges not acting ultra vires within a domestic hierarchy of laws, this relativistic and formal position has one central important weakness. This is the indeterminacy of constitutional texts and the inherently interpretative character of constitutional rules that assign some degree of significance to international law.

Constitutions seek to settle a diverse number of questions that have legal and political significance for a political community. When so doing, constitutions look at the present, and to the best of their ability, forward.[34] Constitutions are deeply interpretive documents. Even though the debate on constitutional interpretation is a long standing one, between originalists and teleological interpretivists,[35] the fact that constitutions beg interpretation

[34] Kersch, 'The New Legal Transnationalism, the Globalized Judiciary, and the Rule of Law' (2005) 4 *Washington University Global Studies Law Review* 345, 367; Bahdi, 'Globalisation of Judgment: Transjudicialism and the Five Faces of International Law in Domestic Courts' (2002) 34 *George Washington International Law Review* 555.

[35] Ronald Dworkin, A Matter of Principle (Cambridge: Harvard University Press 1985); Scott Douglas Gerber, To Secure These Rights (New York: New York University Press 1995); Robert Alexy and Julian Rivers, *A Theory of Constitutional Rights* (Oxford: Oxford University Press 2009).

in the light of their object and purpose is not disputed. What is more, at the core of constitutional interpretation lies the need for all interpretivists to remain loyal to a constitution that has sovereignty-respecting and sovereignty-limiting purposes.[36] To declare a constitution essentially monist or essentially dualist goes against the need of the constitution to be interpreted as a document as a whole. To the extent that a dualist view on the constitution conflict with other provisions of the constitution (say, for example, those provisions that guard the individual's rights and liberties) may lead to internal interpretive conflicts within. Equally, this is a risk for a strictly monist interpretation.

It is, therefore, no coincidence that there is no formal domestic constitutional text that openly declares a domestic constitutional system as expressly monist or dualist with regard to the authority of international law. The characterization of constitutions comes through recognizing their monist or their dualist inclinations. The assessment of constitutional texts, therefore, is an ex-post one made by domestic and international lawyers by imposing an interpretation on them. Unsurprisingly, in most domestic jurisdictions, there are long standing disagreements amongst jurists spatially and temporally over whether a constitutional system is monist or dualist and more importantly, to what degree.

Consider the following examples in order to highlight this textual indeterminacy.

Article VI of the US Constitution states: 'All treaties made, or which shall be made, under the authority of the United States, shall be the supreme law of the land.'

For an international lawyer not versed in the interpretive canons of the American legal system, a first reading of this article suggests a monist and even a monist hierarchical conception of the authority relationship between international law and domestic courts. Article VI explicitly grants 'all treaties' without any distinction to their character, the status of 'supreme law of the land'. The term supreme also suggests that the formal presumption of the authority of international law before domestic courts is a strong one. Despite this first reading, the US Supreme Court has, over time, offered a more nuanced interpretation of this article—one that has weakened this

[36] O'Cinneide, 'Human Rights and within Multi-Layered Systems of Constitutional Governance: Rights Cosmopolitanism and Domestic Particularism in Tension', University College Dublin Working Paper in Law, Criminology and Socio-Legal Studies Research Paper No 12/2009 (2009) 23–4.

presumption.[37] The US Supreme Court has developed a distinction between treaties that automatically have effect as domestic law, and those that—while they constitute international law commitments—do not by themselves function as binding federal law.[38] Non-self-executing treaty stipulations can only be enforced pursuant to legislation that carries them into effect.[39]

This example shows that the interpretation of the constitutional text that seeks to bring certainty to the formal authority of international law in the domestic courts is subject to interpretation by those very domestic courts. Its formal action-guiding role is subsequently altered by deeper doctrinal views held by domestic judges on the law-like qualities of international law in the domestic legal system.

The conundrum posed by the US Constitution and its subsequent interpretation is by no means an isolated incident.[40] It is often that domestic judges have significant disagreements on the formal rules of recognition of international law in the domestic system. This supports my initial premise that general constitutional rules on the action guiding status of the authority of international law under-determines authority questions attached to international law in domestic legal systems. This finding has led many to concede that formal determinations of international law's authority are indeterminate and such questions need to be resolved in relation to a wider web of concerns.

## The Ideological Variant of Monism and Dualism

The ideological variant of monism and dualism accepts the premise that constitutional documents have deeply indeterminate formal rules when discussing the relationship with international law and that domestic judges must appeal to deeper values when deciding on the authority claims that

[37] In a well-known early case, *Murray v The Schooner Charming Betsy* (1804) 6 US (2 Cranch) 64, the US Supreme Court held that interpretations of the acts of Congress, to the extent possible, ought not be construed to violate the law of nations. But Courts have continued to disagree over this. For example, in *Committee of US Citizens Living in Nicaragua v Reagan* (1988) 859 F 2d 929 (DC Cir) the DC Circuit Court held an opposing view altogether: 'Statutes inconsistent with principles of customary international law may well lead to international law violations. But within the domestic legal realm, that inconsistent statute simply modifies or supersedes customary international law to the extent of the inconsistency.'

[38] *Foster v Neilson* (1829) 2 Pet 253, 315.

[39] *Whitney v Robertson* (1888) 124 US 190, 194.

[40] Order of the German Constitutional Court, BVerfG, 2 BvR 1481/04 of October 14, 2004.

international law makes over them.[41] The ideological variant of monism and dualism is anti-formalist. It places the domestic judge, and their convictions, their understanding of law, as well as their formal training as a judge, at the heart of any decisions concerning an authority claim from international law.[42]

The ideological variant holds that monism and dualism continue to be helpful characterizations when pronouncing on outcomes of judicial decisions due to the values attached to monism and dualism by domestic judges. Kelsen's relativity theory still has an important grasp on the ideological variant. It has been held that some judges are monist or monist leaning. They are friends of international law and are prepared to act against the will of their political authorities through their willingness to consider international law as part of their interpretive legal domain.[43] Others are dualist or dualist leaning. They are international law skeptics either because they are, say, modern followers of Anzilotti or Triepel or because they feel that their foremost loyalty lies in giving effect to domestic legislation and, in cases of conflict between domestic law and international law, such conflict must be resolved in favour of domestic law.[44] They are unwilling to accord international law authority qua international law because they do not regard international law as a recognisable legal fact within their domain of interpretation.

In support of this judicial classification, under the ideological approach monist judges are sometimes also labelled internationalists and dualist judges as nationalists.[45] This variant of monism-dualism is at odds with the constitutional variant, as what the constitution says does not in and of itself

[41] The empirical evidence concerning the disagreements on the interpretation of constitutional documents further lends support to the ideological variant. David Sloss, 'Domestic Application of Treaties' (2011) 8–11 *Santa Clara University Legal Studies Research Papers Series* 3–10, esp 9 'Thus, just as judicial practice in some dualist states blurs the monist-dualist divide by applying unincorporated treaties as if they were incorporated, judicial practice in some monist states blurs the monist-dualist divide by handling formally incorporated treaties as if they were unincorporated.'

[42] Benevisti (n 16).

[43] Curtis A Bradley, 'Breard, Our Dualist Constitution and the Internationalist Conception' (1999) 51 *Stanford Law Review* 529, 530: '...the debate between monism and dualism is in part a debate about where one should look to determine international law's domestic status: Monism looks outward to the structure an content of international law; dualism looks inward to domestic standards and processes.'

[44] See, for example, *Federal Trade Comm'n v Compagnie de Saint-Gobain-Pont-a-Mousson* (1980) 636 F 2d 1300, 1323 where US courts 'obligated to give effect to an unambiguous exercise by Congress of its jurisdiction to prescribe even if such an exercise would exceed the limitations imposed by international law'.

[45] Bradley (n 43); Benevisti (n 16).

determine if judges become monist or dualist. It is for this reason that, empirically, we may encounter dualist judgments from a court in a legal system that is considered monist[46] and vice versa.[47]

In the ideological variant of monism there are divisions between strong monists and weak monists on the one hand, and hierarchical monists and conflict of law monists on the other. Strong monists are often hierarchical monists. They hold that international law must trump domestic law and domestic judges must apply international law directly or set aside domestic law when international law conflicts with it. This is often called the direct effect doctrine concerning international law. Strong monism that advocates the direct and hierarchical impact of international law has an authority-disregarding relationship with political authorities with respect to legislation that precedes a piece of international law. It also empowers domestic judges vis-à-vis their political counterparts as the interpretation of international law becomes a core component of applying and interpreting domestic law. Weak monists differ from strong monists. They do not subscribe to a strict hierarchical view and turn to international law when they see a clear authority pronouncement by international law or international court judgments, when, temporally, international law precedes domestic law or when it offers a *lex specialis* maxim to domestic law.[48] Weak monists, therefore, are concerned with finding the balance between respecting the integrity of domestic law and the authority of international law. They attempt this by identifying rules that mediate the ordering of authority between international law and domestic law.

In the ideological variant of dualism, too, one can be a strong dualist or a weak dualist. Strong dualists would be fully closed to according any authority to international law *qua* international law. Weak dualists, on the other hand, may regard international law as a domestic law 'gap filler'. They would only turn to international law created jointly by their own political authority with others when the political authority as a single actor has not enacted any legislation on the very same matter at all.

[46] Order of the German Constitutional Court, BVerfG, 2 BvR 1481/04 of October 14, 2004, especially §§ 49/50.

[47] Judgments—*R v Jones (Appellant) (On Appeal from the Court of Appeal (Criminal Division)) (formerly R v J (Appellant))* [2006] UKHL 16.

[48] In an interview I carried out with an Irish Constitutional Court Judge, this position, in particular with regard to the judgments of the European Court of Human Rights, was explained: 'If the guidance is not clear, it just means that we have to dig our heels in and we are not prepared to move until we are given a sound basis on which we feel we can proceed, and that is our right. I mean, we are entitled to do that.' Interview with Judge, Irish Constitutional Court (Dublin, Ireland, 3 March 2009).

The ideological variants of monism and dualism, and their branches in strong and weak forms, as a framework to settle authority questions of international law has important repercussions for the conceptualization of the authority of international law. It moves attention away from a direct and substantive engagement with the kind of authority claim that international law imposes on a domestic legal order to either ideological dispositions of judges as internationalists or nationalists or intermediate doctrines of clarity, temporality, or gap-filling in domestic law in order to assess the authority of international law. The move away from the substance of the authority claim blocks a reasoned engagement with international law. To hold that the worldview of a domestic judge is a core filter through which to understand authority claims of international law necessarily imposes a legal realist cloak on debates about the authority of international law. One then has to consider what other significant factors are at play other than the law when talking about the law. A deeply nationalist judge in a deeply nationalist political climate cannot be expected to produce an internationalist judgment. The power of reason that I have assigned to international law's claim even to qualified authority cannot then be expected to sway a judge with firm beliefs in the primary of that national constitution and statute.

## Beyond Monism and Dualism: Towards a Reflexive Authority of International Law before Domestic Courts

The previous section has shown that using a doctrinal outlook to explain the authority of international law before domestic courts under the banner of 'dualism versus monism' has significant short-comings. The indeterminacy of the application of this binary and its close association with extra-legal ideological commitments aside, the core doctrinal problem here is its insistence on furnishing categorical arguments about the relationship between international law and domestic law with insufficient attention paid to the norms of international laws at stake before the domestic judge.

This binary is unable to account for the diverse authority structures of international law. For a monist account, the authority of the prohibition of genocide and the authority of the duty to conduct neighbourly relations fall in the same camp. For a dualist, too, not incorporating the Convention against Torture and the Vienna Convention on Consular Relations has the same legal significance. The monist versus dualist binary, therefore, seeks to sign up a domestic legal system or a judge to one of the camps without any reflective understanding of what authority claims specific international laws make. This necessity to 'show one's monist or dualist colour' before taking into account the international law at stake obscures core questions of the authority of international law. Such questions are not about grand theories, but about the specific substantive claims that each international law makes with relation to legal and political authorities. It is on these subtle differences that the doctrinal development has to focus, rather than on pre-assigned titles.

To highlight the need to go beyond monism and dualism, I emphasize the need for a reflexive authority account of the authority of international law before domestic courts. Reflexive theories stand apart from categorical theories as they show concern for the substance of the authority claim at stake. By asking the domestic judge to first assess whether an international law makes a strong, weak, or a rebuttable authority claim, my account invites the domestic judge to adopt a reflexive understanding of the authority of international law.

## Domestic Judges and Strong Duties

If international law makes a strong authority claim, the reflexive approach to its authority would require a domestic judge to defer to the authority of international law. This is if it can be shown that political authorities have either consented to the formulation of a strong duty of international law or if the strong duty is such that it does not require a consensual grounding due to the jurisdictional disabilities of domestic authorities to the rule generating the strong duty.

The prohibition of torture in contemporary international law illustrates this well. That torture by state officials with the purpose of obtaining information or inflicting punishment is prohibited is constructed as an absolute norm that allows no exceptions in international law.[49] In addition, most states in the world have ratified a treaty that prohibits torture or have accepted that torture is part of customary international law and, even, ius cogens.[50] It is, therefore, not an exaggeration to state that for probably all domestic judges in all parts of the world, the prohibition of torture makes a strong authority claim and attracts a duty of obedience in the domestic adjudicatory process.

[49] See Convention Against Torture and Other Cruel, Inhuman, or Degrading Treatment or Punishment (adopted 10 December 1984, entered into force 26 June 1987) 1465 UNTS 112 (Convention Against Torture or UNCAT) art 1.

[50] Erika de Wet, 'The Prohibition of Torture as an International Norm of jus cogens and Its Implications for National and Customary Law' (2004) 15(1) *European Journal of International Law* 97.

If we seek to formulate this in the habitual language of monism versus dualism, the prohibition of torture ought not to attract any dualist inclinations from the domestic judge—even in jurisdictions where formal constitutional rules have a more dualist inclination.

In some jurisdictions, domestic judges formulate their duty towards international law in the form of doctrines of direct effect[51] or self-executing treaties.[52] For the purposes of our analysis, whether domestic judges, due to the peculiarities of their domestic systems and legal vernacular, offer mediatory doctrines to recognize the strong duties of international law is a matter for domestic judges to make sense of the authoritative weight of international law. Both the doctrine of the direct effect of international law as well as self-executing treaties allow for this. What is important, however, is that the domestic judge, when encountering a strong duty, is empowered to take due regard of it by that virtue, regardless of whether the domestic legal doctrinal vernacular also allows for other types of duties to be taken into account as a matter of direct effect.[53]

Alongside the requirement that strong duties imposed by international law necessitate domestic judges to take them into account as a matter of interpretive priority, strong duty classifications have two further implications.

First, strong duties imposed by international law empower domestic judges when dealing with domestic political authorities if the latter have not acted in accordance with the strong duty imposed by international law. A political authority's failure to act on a strong duty can take multiple forms. The political authority, contrary to its obligations under the Convention against Torture, for example, may fail to enact domestic legislation to incorporate

[51] Turkish Constitutional Court Application No 2013/187 Judgment of 19 December 2013.

[52] In *Medellin v Texas* (2008) 552 US 491 the US Supreme Court defined self-execution as follows: 'What we mean by "self-executing" is that the treaty has automatic domestic effect upon ratification. Conversely, a "non-self-executing" treaty does not by itself give rise to domestically enforceable federal law. Whether such a treaty has domestic effect depends upon implementing legislation passed by Congress.'

[53] For example, in the context of EU law, it has been discussed by the European Court of Justice that EU Law has direct effect over domestic law. This argument depends on a special deeper legal integration argument between EU Law and domestic law in EU member states. In the context of general international law, this constitutes a sui generis legal authority relationship in a sub-regional legal system and not on a general argument based on public international law. In the context of Inter-American Human Rights Law, too, the Inter-American Court of Human Rights advances a legal integration argument in support of its 'convention controlidad' doctrine which asks for direct and horizontal effect of all Inter-American Court of Human Rights' case-law for the parties to the San Salvador Protocol. The latter case is also a matter of debate in the Inter-American system. See Alexandra Huneaus, 'Rejecting the Inter-American Court: Judicialization, National Courts, and Regional Human Rights' in Javier Couso (ed), *Cultures of Legality Judicialization and Political Activism in Latin America* (Cambridge: Cambridge University Press 2010) 112.

the definition of torture into domestic law.[54] The political authority may also contravene its strong obligations by engaging in acts of torture.[55] Here, the domestic judicial authority is obligated to move against the political authority. The domestic judiciary should hold the political authority to account as it has failed in its unequivocal obligation to uphold the prohibition of torture. The strong duty classification in this respect overrides the democratic legitimacy of the single political organ as the (democratic) legitimacy of political authorities does not offer them carte blanche to disregard the strong duties imposed by international law.

Second, strong duties imposed by international law require the domestic judge to interpret existing, similar domestic law in ways harmonious with interpretations of international law. That is, the domestic judge ought not to take a simple shortcut because the same strong duty already exists in domestic law. In applying domestic law, they must ensure consistency between both domestic and international law.

This general duty, in practice, may be difficult when international interpretive organs further specify the strong duty in international law. As discussed in Chapter 3, international interpretive authorities with legally binding powers offer legally significant support for taking not only the law as stated in a treaty text into account, but also the law as interpreted by an international court when specifying the scope of the strong duty. In the case of the European Court of Human Rights, for example, the prohibition of torture extends to not extraditing someone to a jurisdiction where they face a real risk of torture,[56] as well as prohibiting domestically-sanctioned punishment that may amount to inhuman treatment.[57] Whilst the text of the ECHR does not specify these situations, the continuing consent of political authorities to the interpretive powers of the ECtHR invites domestic judges to include the textual prohibition of torture together with interpretations of Article 3 of the ECHR.

What attitude should a domestic judge have when a domestic political authority accepts the legal pronouncement of a strong duty, but then explicitly

[54] See for example, the Concluding Observations of the Convention against Torture on the second periodic report of Japan, adopted by the Committee at its fiftieth session (6–31 May 2013) UN Doc CAT/C/JPN/CO/2.

[55] Human Rights Committee Concluding Observations with respect to the United States of America (18 December 2006) UN Doc CCPR/C/USA/CO/3/Rev.1.

[56] *Chahal v UK* (1996) 23 EHRR 413; *Abdolkhani and Karimnia v Turkey* App no 30471/08 (ECtHR, 22 September 2009); *Othman v UK* (2012) 55 EHRR 1; *Nizomkhon Dzhurayev v Russia* App no 31890/11 (ECtHR 3 October 2013); *Al Nashiri v Poland* App no 28761/11 (ECtHR, 24 July 2014).

[57] *Soering v UK* (1989) 11 EHRR 439; *Trabelsi v Belgium* App no 140/10 (ECtHR, 4 September 2014).

disagrees with an evaluative or dynamic interpretation of the same principle as pronounced by an international interpretive authority with non-binding powers in international law? The doctrinal case for the strong duties as subsequently interpreted by interpretive authorities must be differentiated from the case of strong duties as interpreted by legally binding authorities. Here, the judge ought not to merely set aside the non-binding interpretations of international authorities for what is at stake is the specification of a strong duty, which through subsequent acquiescence or acceptance by states may also turn into a customary specification of the strong duty. Such interpretations, therefore, must be analyzed in tandem with the subsequent general practice of states asking whether the specific interpretation is part of customary international law. It is in this context that the domestic judge has a duty to assume active agency in confirming the scope of the strong duty in international law.[58] The domestic judge has a duty to make such a reflective assessment, weighing opposition from their political authority with the potential customary international law repercussions of the specification exercises carried out by non-binding interpretive legal authorities.

## Domestic Judges and the Duty to Respect

In the case of weak duties, reflectivity on the part of domestic judges first requires them to assess whether the duty imposed by international law is a weak duty—that is a duty that can be realized through multiple actions by the political authority at the domestic level through legalization, action, omission, or interpretation. The duty of the domestic judge, therefore, is not to directly apply international law (international law does not lend itself to direct application) or to ignore the duty domestic authorities have accepted as it does not contain specific action-guiding content. In the case of weak duties, the domestic judge has to take international law into account and conduct a compatibility analysis of the existing domestic legal framework with the weak duty. It is not the task of the domestic judge to declare what the specific steps that need to be taken to respect the authority of international law are, but to consider whether the steps taken are in harmony with the obligations imposed by way of international law or authoritative legal interpretations of the law.

[58] André Nollkaemper, *National Courts and the International Rule of Law* (Oxford: Oxford University Press 2011) at 267–71.

In international law, weak duties are often first directed towards political authorities, as they require them to achieve the common objectives set out by international law. Weak duties are duties that offer a spectrum of choices through which political authorities can choose to realize them.[59] This, however, does not suggest that domestic judges ought to wash their hands of weak duties. It merely changes the mode of engagement with the authority of international law. In particular, weak duties make domestic judges' interaction with international law take a form akin to compatibility review rather than direct international law application. In some respect, the task of the domestic judge is more onerous when it comes to interacting with weak duties as opposed to strong duties. They have to review whether the actions or omissions of political authorities, be they legislators or administrative organs, are compatible with the obligations of the weak duties they have agreed to under international law.

Consider Article 8 of the *Biodiversity Convention* to '[p]romote the protection of ecosystems, natural habitats and the maintenance of viable populations of species in natural surroundings'.[60] The provision is weak. It does not instruct the domestic judge to directly apply a specific international law prohibition, but to review whether a range of actions are compatible with the duty to promote the protections it lists. It asks the domestic judge to determine whether acts or omissions by political authorities are compatible with the maxim of 'promoting the protection of eco-systems [...] and the maintenance of viable populations of species'. The duty to promote, therefore, is guiding. It is not outcome-imposing in and of itself. When confronted with a weak duty construction such as this, the domestic judge has to show that the duty is a primary consideration, amongst other relevant considerations, when interpreting the adequacy of domestic law and actions. The primary consideration afforded to the weak duty will then operate as a determining factor of the outcome of the review of the actions of the political authority: this is how the authority of international law is imposed through weak duty.

A central difficulty of recognizing the authority of international laws imposed through weak duties for the domestic judge is the standard of review to be applied. If the wording of the international law treaty provision

[59] For a similar statement, see for example, *Colozza v Italy*, ECtHR, Series A, No. 89 (1985), at 15–16: 'The Contracting States enjoy a wide discretion as regards the choice of the means calculated to ensure that their legal systems are in compliance with the requirements of article 6 § 1 in this field. The Court's task is not to indicate those means to the States, but to determine whether the result called for by the Convention has been achieved.'

[60] 1992 Convention on Biological Diversity (adopted 5 June 1992, entered into force 29 December 1993) 1760 UNTS 79 (Biodiversity Convention).

or the content of the custom is unclear, the domestic judge is left to decide from a range of standards of judicial review—from manifestly unreasonable action by the political authorities (a weak form of review with a large margin of appreciation by domestic political organs) to stricter forms of review. In deciding the standard of review, the larger web of duties of which the weak duty forms part, as well as the object and purpose of the treaty and the context of the treaty will be important considerations for the domestic judge. If a weak duty is located within a broader context of international court judgments that the state has accepted as legally binding, for example, the way in which international courts interpret the strength of judicial review would be an important consideration. Equally, the domestic judge is entitled to look at transnational law (or foreign law) when deciding on the appropriate standard of judicial review of a weak duty. The domestic judge, therefore exercises important agency when interacting with weak duty constructions and directly contributes to the interpretation of both domestic law and international law.[61] In our example, the duty to 'promote' suggests a weak standard of review at first sight. Laws and policies that clearly undermine the ecosystem beyond reasonable doubt are well covered by a duty to promote. Any act or policy that may on a balance of probability undermine the eco-system but does not do so explicitly, however, cannot be deduced from the provision itself. The domestic judge must turn to a holistic interpretation[62] of the weak duty to specify what kind of compatibility analysis they will undertake.

## Domestic Judges and Rebuttable Duties

Rebuttable duties imposed by international law are duties that can be set aside when they are in conflict with other important domestic laws (or international laws that are legally binding for that matter) to the extent that they are required by those domestic laws. Whether a duty is rebuttable or not is not a question of whether there is a domestic law considered important by a domestic judge. It is a question of whether international law imposes the duty with the recognition that it can be rebutted under certain circumstances. In other words the general duty of deference to international law as a scheme of co-operation also applies to rebuttable duties imposed by international law. Furthermore, the rebuttable duty constructions recognize that state officials

[61] André Nollkaemper, *National Courts and the International Rule of Law* (Oxford University Press 2011).

[62] Richard Gardiner, 'The Vienna Convention Rules on Treaty Interpretation' in Duncan Hollis (ed), *The Oxford Guide to Treaties* (Oxford: Oxford University Press 2012) 475.

have aimed to collectively impose a qualified form of authority over domestic systems. They equally recognize that other legally pertinent considerations ought to enter the scheme of compliance advanced by rebuttable duties. Rebuttable duties of international law require the domestic judge to offer reasons for their inability to respect international law in specific circumstances. Such reasons cannot rely exclusively on the mere existence of domestic law arguments (or other pressing international law arguments) that point to the contrary. The duty is to specifically define considerations to act as a counterweight to the rebuttable duty and, in turn, balance these with the rebuttable duty imposed by international law. This is in the line with the spirit of the VCLT provision that domestic law cannot be a bar to carrying out international law obligations.[63] Rebuttable duties present the domestic judge with challenges other than weak duty constructions. In the latter case, the domestic judge is tasked with assessing the reason-blocking qualities international law has for the purposes of domestic legislation or action. In the former, the task is to carefully define and balance the rebuttable duty with countervailing legal obligations. A switch in the logic of assessing the authority of international law in the specific context, therefore, is needed.

To merely show that there is some domestic law that instructs contrary to international law when confronted with a rebuttable duty would illustrate creeping dualism in the judge's reasoning. The judge, however, must resist this and offer factual and situational arguments as to why the international duty cannot be fulfilled given the pressing weight of a counter obligation.

Consider Article 3(1) of the Convention on the Rights of the Child which states that 'in all actions concerning children, whether undertaken by public or private social welfare institutions, courts of law, administrative authorities or legislative bodies, the best interests of the child shall be a primary consideration.'[64] This convention enjoys near universal ratification from members of the United Nations.[65] Whilst this near-universal ratification points to the convention having strong legal authority, the duty imposed in Article 3(1) remains rebuttable as it specifies that the best interest of a child is a primary, but not exclusive consideration. Article 3(1) does not instruct the domestic judge to act in specific ways, or in reason-blocking mode. It rather instructs the domestic judge to identify whether a weighty consideration may exist as

[63] Vienna Convention on the Law of Treaties (adopted 23 May 1969, entered into force 27 January 1980) 1155 UNTS 331 (VCLT 1969) art 27.

[64] See Convention on the Rights of the Child (adopted 20 November 1989, entered into force 2 September 1990) 1577 UNTS 3, art 49.

[65] According to the United Nations Treaty Collection, the Convention on the Rights of the Child has 194 state parties as of 26 February 2015.

a matter of law or fact. This example is telling, as the primary consideration clause further indicates that the obligation to balance it with other legally relevant concerns sets a high threshold and points to a further layer of differentiation amongst different rebuttable duties. Whilst some rebuttable duties have a high threshold of rebuttal, others may have a more lax threshold.

The Supreme Court of the United Kingdom's handling of the case of *BH (AP) (Appellant) and another v The Lord Advocate and another (Respondents) (Scotland) KAS* demonstrates the challenge of applying a rebuttable international law duty and the process of balancing involved.[66] The case concerns the Court's tackling of the high threshold set by Article 3(1) in the context of a request to extradite a couple to the United States from the UK and the effect this would have on their children. The charges against the couple, Mr and Mrs H, were conspiracy and unlawfully importing chemicals used to manufacture methamphetamine into the US with the knowledge, or belief that they would be used for that very purpose. Mrs H is mother to six children whose ages, at the time of the case, ranged from one to 14. Mr H is the father of the four youngest children. In this case the Court recognized that the best interests of the children was 'a primary consideration', but not the primary consideration. The Court said that the UK also had obligations under its bilateral extradition treaty with the US. The case then went on to discuss fact-specific issues—including the lack of consistent contact between the father and the children and the father's history of sexual abuse. In making an assessment, whilst recognizing the importance of the best interest of the child and the prospective detention and, if found guilty, imprisonment of the parents in this case, the Court decided that the extradition request weighed heavier than the argument that the family should remain as a unit in the United Kingdom. For the purposes of our analysis, the Court approached the authority of the CRC as being rebuttable.

As in the case of weak duties, interlocking webs of commitments around a rebuttable duty are crucial markers for how domestic judges should identify how demanding rebuttal conditions are. For example, regional human rights courts that guard human rights conventions over time have developed higher thresholds of rebuttal for qualified rights.[67] They uniformly demand

[66] *BH (AP) (Appellant) and another v The Lord Advocate and another (Respondents) (Scotland) KAS or H (AP) (Appellant) v The Lord Advocate and another (Respondents) (Scotland) Trinity Term* [2012] UKSC 24, on appeal from: [2011] HCJAC 77.

[67] Brems & JH Gerards (eds), *Shaping Rights in the ECHR: The Role of the European Court of Human Rights in Determining the Scope of Human Rights* (Cambridge: Cambridge University Press 2014); Manuel Eduardo Gongora Mera, *Inter-American Judicial Constitutionalism: On the Constitutional Rank of Human Rights Treaties in Latin America through National and Inter-American Adjudication* (San Jose: Instituto Inter Americano de Derechos Humanos 2011); Frans Viljoen, *International Human Rights Law in Africa* (Oxford: Oxford University Press 2012).

that domestic courts provide relevant and sufficient reasons for their rebuttals when defending the weight domestic laws have or their actions against rebuttable duties imposed by international law. The now universally recognized 'necessity in a democratic society' test is one example of a demanding rebuttal condition, as applied in freedom of expression, freedom of assembly, or freedom of association case law.[68] Such demanding rebuttal conditions developed through the case law of human rights courts do not in essence touch the structure of the duties in international law. They do, however, play an attitude orientation role for domestic judges. The fact that a domestic judge's quality of rebuttal is now subject to judicial review in jurisdictions from the Council of Europe, to parts of the Americas and parts of Africa brings life to the general attitude defended here—at least in the case of international human rights law.

## Reflective International Law Authority and Domestic Law

The reflective approach to the authority of international law before domestic courts defended in this chapter inevitably has consequences for the conception of the authority of domestic law by domestic judges. The relative authority of international law that emerges through an analysis of the structure of the duties it imposes is a scheme of authority that co-exists with the authority of domestic law. It only asserts the right to fully displace domestic law when the duty imposed by international law is a strict duty and when political authorities have delayed in giving effect to their obligations of strict duty—either by amending domestic laws or by putting in place domestic laws that reflect the strict duty. As a matter of every day practice, the times in which international law imposes strict duties and political authorities undertake manifestly conflicting duties are relatively infrequent. In such rare situations (as an example, when the domestic political authority ratifies the Convention against Torture, but legalizes a form of torture as a matter of practice) the domestic judge is under a duty to disregard the domestic law that manifestly goes against a strict international law obligation. The authority of international law, therefore, is hierarchically above the authority of domestic law.

In most situations, however, international law imposes weak or rebuttable duties. It asks political authorities to strive to reach a collective goal (as in the case of weak duties) or recognize the existence of countervailing

[68] For a classical statment of this test, see, *Silver and others v United Kingdom* (1983) 6 EHHR 62.

concerns as a matter of conflicting law or practice. In these situations we no longer think of the relationship between the authority of international law and domestic law as a battle for having the ultimate say. We think of it as a matter of a good faith and transparent engagement. When weak duties are identified such transparent engagement may lead to outcomes that require declaring that the single will of the domestic political authority fell short of international promises. It may also lead the domestic judge to set aside the authority of a particular international law on balance of argument. In the case of weak duties, the domestic law may in some instances continue to have primacy if it respects the spirit of international law. In other words, whether the authority of international law remains intact is not given—even in what may transpire to be a strong and hierarchical monist system in the formal sense. Equally, the authority of domestic law does not remain intact solely by the simple virtue of its existence. The reflective approach advanced in this thesis demands that the overall attitude of the domestic judge to the authority of domestic law cannot be separated from the scheme of duties imposed by international law.

## Conclusion

In this chapter I have argued that the domestic judge's attitude towards the authority of international law must be primarily determined by the differentiated scheme of authority imposed by international law on domestic legal systems rather than short-hand characterizations of domestic legal systems or judicial attitudes either as monist or dualist. I have highlighted that moving from the characterization of a domestic legal system to the authority of international law has serious deficiencies as it remains blind to diverse (and constantly evolving) international law and how particular international laws set out to interact with domestic law. It is incoherent to insist that a rebuttable duty must be obeyed because a domestic legal system is monist. This is because a rebuttable duty does not generate a law to be obeyed, but specifies a modality to engage with international law. It is equality incoherent to assert that a strict duty in international law has no legal relevance in a legal system dubbed as dualist. Domestic legal systems are made up of powers as well as disabilities. The presumption that political authority needs to be viewed as an actor that seeks coherent governance (and not enacting highly disparate laws domestically and internationally) further acts against the impulses of dualism.

The reflective approach that I advance here takes a clear position between what Jeremy Waldron has framed as a tension between 'law as will and law as reason'.[69] The dualist and monist positions approach law as a matter of will. They do not see why they should reflectively engage with the content of a law when deciding its authority. Those who see law as a matter of reason, however, are able to approach the authority of international law in a reflective spirit. The reflective spirit does not rely purely on the personal reasoning of the judge about what is right or wrong, but on a rational relationship between the schemes of authority in international law and how they then interact with the efforts of political authorities to regulate them.

[69] Jeremy Waldron, 'Is the Rule of Law an Essentially Contested Concept?' (2002) 21 *Law and Philosophy* 137.

# 5

# The Practical Authority of International Law: An Appraisal

'The problem of extending the subjection of states to international law is one of great practical difficulty, but it is not one of intrinsic impossibility.'[1]

## Introduction

In what preceded, I aimed to defend the relational authority of international law with respect to political and legal authorities. In particular, I advanced three types of argument. First, I held that an attitude of taking international law into account must be common amongst state officials—be they political or judicial—as contributing to a larger scheme of co-operation and striving for consistency of legal regulation is part and parcel of their duties. This attitude is grounded in the commonalities of risks faced by politically organized communities and individuals living in these communities regardless of differences in history, culture, and politics they may have. Second, I argued that this common attitude does not determine which laws must be viewed as legally authoritative for what reasons, to what extent, and in what form. For such a screening to be carried out one has to appeal and reflect on to the pluralist foundations of the authority of international law, which is informed both by pre-consent considerations and consent (both initial and ongoing) as well as the normative demands of particular legal norms. Matters that in particular fall within the jurisdictional disabilities of domestic political orders do not attract consent-based grounding concerns. Third, I argued that the attitude of deference does not determine how the authority of international law manifests itself. Importantly, the authority of international law generates duties ranging from strict duties to weak or rebuttable ones. Each of

[1] James Brierly, *The Law of Nations: An Introduction to the International Law of Peace* (6th edn, Oxford: Oxford University Press 1963) 55.

these structures requires the domestic political and legal authority to reflect on how they give due effect to the authority of international law.

In this final chapter, I focus on the appeal of the doctrinal account of the relative authority of international law. I seek to investigate the following questions: Is the relational authority of international law a better, a more feasible, and more desirable understanding of the legal authority of international law than the standard account of authority? Does it advance the standard account of the authority of international law? Does it respond well to critics of the authority of international law? Does this formal account in the final analysis tilt towards more foundationalist analyses proposed by constitutionalist approaches or is it more compatible with pluralism? Have I in effect argued for disguised monism? My central aim here is to identify a range of potential problems as well as objections to the doctrinal account of authority I have put forward and to consider whether the overall account developed stands up against them.

## A Better Account than the Standard Account?

In the authority account I develop here, the binding/non-binding categorization of international law, which acts as the exclusive determinant of the authority of international law, is replaced by both a hybrid view grounding the authority of international law and a more content specific analysis of binding international laws. Consent, I argue, is neither tout court sufficient nor necessary. Turning to the content of specific international laws, rather than only to their source of validity as seen through the lens of consent, enables us to distinguish between different demands that international law makes on domestic legal and political orders. This, I submit, is a better account through which to understand the practical authority of international law for three important reasons.

First, this revised account is better connected to the substantive and particular nature of international laws. This allows us to see that international law cannot be a system of tyranny or systematic coercion over domestic political and legal orders in its totality because the duties it imposes on domestic systems are diverse. Many duties that international law impose are reflective and dialogical, where the domestic political, and, in turn, legal authority has to exercise independent political and judicial agency. Much has been written about why international law and domestic law are different from one another.[2] One of the major concerns about why international law is different

[2] Ranging from why international law is not law to why international law cannot command authority like domestic law. John Austin, *The Province of Jurisprudence Determined*

is its level of generality and the vagueness of what it says to those either following or interpreting the law.[3] This has often been contrasted against the much more detailed and specific nature of domestic statutes with the implication that these are much more amenable to application as law, whilst international law is more interesting as a process.[4] In the account I advance in this book, the vagueness of some international law obligations do not, in and of themselves, undermine the authority of international law. They simply instruct domestic actors to reflect on how they best give effect to those obligations. The core issue at stake is the range of freedoms political and legal authorities enjoy in giving effect to the authority of international law. The relative authority of international law asserts that such freedom is neither fully constrained nor fully accorded. The range of freedom accorded to domestic legal systems is precisely to what we must turn our attention when assigning authority to international law.

That international laws are significantly variable in terms of their authority supports the more fundamental view that international law as an institution offers multiple routes for political authorities to collectively achieve their aims in a horizontally organized system. International law is neither world legislation nor merely conversation. Whilst international law can certainly operate like a legislative power for all states in areas that fall within the jurisdictional disabilities of domestic systems or when domestic systems offer unanimous consent, it can also be a horizon to sail towards and a consideration that can be rebutted in case of a conflict with a weighty concern. Once we move away from the either/or paradigm to this differentiated one, we are also closer to the practice of everyday international law.

Second, the image supporting the idea that the authority of law is a yes/no affair sits uneasily with the relative authority of international law. However, even the most well established accounts of authority in philosophical terms concede that a key characteristic of authority is that it is piecemeal.[5] The standard account advances the 'authority as a binding text' paradigm both at the expense of the everyday norms we have in international law and against the intuition that not all international laws can claim full authority over its subjects. The idea of the piecemeal authority of international law, however,

(Wilfrid E Rumble ed) (Cambridge: Cambridge University Press 1995) (1832) 30–1, 117, 122–4, 171; Jeremy Bentham, *Of Laws in General* (HLA Hart ed, London: Athlone Press 1970) (1782) 16, 70.

[3] On a more recent discussion of this point, see Joshua Kleinfeld, 'Skeptical Internationalism: A Study of Whether International Law Is Law' (2010) 78 *Fordham Law Review* 2451.

[4] Cf W Michael Reisman, 'International Lawmaking: A Process of Communication' (1981) 75 *American Society of International Law Proceedings* 75, 101, 107, 113.

[5] Raz *The Morality of Freedom* (Oxford: Oxford University Press 1986), 80.

does not go too far in terms of giving us doctrinal clarity for specifying when and how it is piecemeal. Here, the relative authority of international law argues that piecemeal authority cannot be a matter of self-assessment by domestic political and legal authorities if all that does is to reiterate the supremacy of domestic law over international law. It is acceptable in so far as the norm of international law allows and domestic legal and political authorities offer reasons that would be justifiable to the international legal community as a whole. The very idea of offering justifiable reasons to a community holding plural values is rooted in the domestic theories of Hobbes and Kant and also, more recently, Rawls.[6] It forms an important part of the public reason tradition. Rawls, in particular, views the condition of public reason as stemming from the political culture of a constitutional democracy.[7] Whilst public reason has a unique place in theories of democratic polity, the practice of giving reason to a collection of political communities that are also pluralistic in their make-up builds on the idea. It asks that collectively decided norms can only be set aside by offering reasons to the remainder of the norm makers. Such reasons, therefore, must be recognisable to all who take part in the institution of international law. The requirement for offering reasons for how the authority of international law is respected, in the case of weak and strong duties, to a wider audience than just the domestic one further offers a chance to air conflicts between domestic law and international law, with an attempt to reach a solution through balancing such conflicts in particular circumstances.

## Hybrid Consent and the Authority of International Law

Here I have taken a hybrid view on consent as the basis for the authority of international law. I have not insisted, as some classical positivists and rational international scholars do, that the will of the state is the basis for authority.[8] I have, however, also not advocated a view that asks for consent to be disregarded as a basis for the authority of international law.[9] Those who

[6] John Rawls, 'The Idea of Public Reason Revisited' (1994) 64(3) *University of Chicago Law Review* 765.

[7] Ibid.

[8] There is a long judicial and academic tradition regarding this starting from *SS Lotus/Bozkurt* (Fr v Turk), 1927 PCIJ (ser A) No 9, at 18 (7 September) ('The rules of law binding upon States...emanate from their own free will.'). See also, *Barcelona Traction* (Belg. v. Spain), 1970 ICJ 3, 47 (5 February) and *Military and Paramilitary Activities in and Against Nicaragua* (Nicar v US), 1986 ICJ 14, 135 (27 June).

[9] Fernando R Teson, *A Philosophy of International Law* (Boulder: Westview Press 1998); Anne Peters, *Global Constitutionalism Revisited* (2008) 11 *International Legal Theory* 39, 51.

hold strongly to one view or the other, therefore, may find my hybrid view unsatisfactory.

I follow a hybrid view because this is the best one possible to explain how international law comes about in the contemporary international system. I do not, therefore, look at consent through a normative lens, but through a practical one. The contemporary international law system hosts a vast range of norms that have been either created through the individual consent of a certain number of states or by way of the tacit or active participation of a group of states, or they are norms that do not need collective validation by individual members, some members, or all members. So, full individualized consent, some consent, and no consent are all capable of generating particular international laws. The most well-known of these is pacta sunt servanda.[10] In contemporary international law, however, we hold that certain acts that deeply harm the well-being of individuals are also prohibited in international law without any need for state officials to consent to this collectively. The *Restatement on Foreign Relations of the United States* defines ius cogens to include, at a minimum, the prohibition of genocide; slavery or the slave trade; murder or disappearance of individuals; torture or other cruel, inhuman, or degrading treatment or punishment; prolonged arbitrary detention; systematic racial discrimination; and 'the principles of the United Nations Charter prohibiting the use of force' in this category. This is without making any reference to whether states have signed treaties in these issue areas or have explicitly consented to the generation of customary international law.[11]

Many specific norms within the international legal system, however, exhibit conscious choices for a specific frame of regulation or they are implementing norms for what we come to regard as non-consensual norms. For example, the General Agreement on Tariffs and Trade or the United Nations Convention on the Law of the Sea represents the choices of a large number of states in regulating trade and the sea. Whether a norm requires the consent of the individual state or not is an important discussion,[12] however it cannot determine the authority of a specific particular law in and of itself. Whilst we assume that consent does not bar the authority of international laws that are constitutive or deeply harming to the survival of a political community, it still plays a role in making more regulative norms of international law

[10] Duncan Hollis, 'Introduction' *Oxford Guide to Treaties* (Oxford: Oxford University Press 2012) 2.

[11] Restatement (Third) of Foreign Relations of the United States (1987) ALI.

[12] For a recent discussion of this, see, Andrew Guzman, 'Against Consent' (2012) 52 *Virginia Journal of International Law* 747.

cognizable in domestic legal systems. Consent has an instrumental value for making regulative norms enter into the deliberations of legal and political actors. This is how we understand which regulation is preferred by a collection of states and how the norm is shaped through collective agreement. Making a norm cognizable as a matter of law, however, is different from ascertaining the authoritative weight of that norm. It is for this reason that we cannot simply search for or disregard the consent of states. We also need to ascertain what a norm *really says* to domestic state officials.

## Indeterminacy and Multiple Authority Claims

So far what I have articulated may sound to some as a project aimed at undermining the authority of international law rather than advancing it, as the whole account relies on a pre-determination of the strength of authority prior to making a claim concerning the authority of international law. If one carves out exceptions for respecting the authority of international law, what prospect, if any, does international law have in pushing for compliance in a world where respect for its authority is at best partial? Would these exceptions not open the floodgates to abuse where states that have ratified treaties would simply refuse to follow them, arguing that the obligation to obey in the strict sense simply does not exist? By asking domestic political and legal authorities to be aware of their differentiated obligations towards international law, are we not contributing to making international law indeterminate, fluid, and vague?

In response to these legal-policy considerations that argue that the authority structure of international law would be better posited as having constant and pre-emptive consent, I submit that a more accurate conceptual account of the authority of international law (including potential cases for the rebuttal of its authority) would lead to better interpretation and compliance, not undermine it. The legal policy preference of calling international law pre-emptive only appeals to domestic political officials and judges who already identify themselves as internationalists. The pre-emptive characterization of international law, therefore, can only succeed for a cadre of state officials who have a pre-legal or an ideological commitment to international law.[13] The relative

[13] In the US legal culture, for example, the zero sum game discussions of the authority of international law are regarded as a function of whether a judge is a liberal or a conservative. This ideological framework leaves not much room for a doctrinal debate on the authority of international law divorced from ideological commitments. On the consequences of this conflict, see Jens David Ohlin, *The Assault on International Law* (New York: Oxford University Press 2015).

authority of international law appeals to a much wider doctrinal audience and asserts that the authority of international law can be settled by a commitment to a shared doctrine rather than an appeal to pre-legal commitments concerning internationalism or nationalism. In other words, the doctrine is nuanced enough for a nationalist judge to conduct a compatibility analysis of a weak duty under international law and for an internationalist judge to conduct a rebuttal analysis. By setting out the kinds of situations in which a strict duty to follow a rule of international law exists, the relative authority scheme further helps by pointing out and protesting against clear cases of violation of the authority of international law by domestic legal orders. By pointing out that international law does not demand blind obedience, the concern that international law undermines domestic integrity and predictability of laws and democratic processes is also better addressed. From a perspective of legal policy, therefore, holding that international law's authority is variable makes a more forceful claim for compliance with strict duties and is able to respond to the critics of international law's claim to domination of political life in single political communities.

Even if we accept that setting out on a path to identify the strength with which demands are made on a domestic legal system is a more sound approach, there could, however, also be a deeper criticism of the norm-focussed account of authority I advance here. My account of the authority of international law asks the relevant domestic authority, be they a political official or a judge, to take into account what is imagined as a single norm making an authoritative claim on the international legal system. The deeper criticism here is that this is not always the case. The domestic political authority is at times in a position to consider the demands of multiple international laws making authoritative claims on the domestic legal system. The critic may also highlight that, given the multiple international law obligations imposed by multiple international law treaties, the distinction between strong, weak, and rebuttable duties is all the more complicated for the domestic judge or the politician. A judicial problem is not often about applying or interpreting a single rule of international law, but about being pulled between a number of international laws and domestic laws at the same time. The authority conundrum, therefore, is not always about a single norm of domestic law against a single norm of international law, but about multiple norms of international law making demands on the domestic legal system. How far then is the general attitude to take into account international law and the corresponding task of identifying the strength of the authority of international law able to address the multiplicity of norms or, as some now phrase it, the 'fragmentation' of international law?

We need to unpack this question further. The central question here is whether my scheme of authority in and of itself can offer a way out of the multiple authoritative demands problem, or a guiding framework for it. I must first concede that my purpose here has not been to answer the multiple authoritative demands of international laws for *any* interpreter of international law.[14] My focus is 'domestic official centric' in the sense that my interest remains with the dominant authority problem of international law, the authority of international law over domestic legal systems. Whilst there are other authority problems, such as the authority of the UN Security Council over the European Union or the authority of the European Court of Human Rights over the European Union, the state-centric case remains the core, standard case.

My response to this question is, of course, positive. The authority scheme of international law over the domestic legal systems that I defend in this book can alleviate some of the problems associated with multiple claims to authority debates in two important ways. First, the variable authority scheme assists in sorting out whether international law is made up of genuine normative conflicts, where reasonable domestic or international interpretive authorities may disagree, or whether we may in effect be faced with the problem of the lack of an assignment of proper authority. Second, expressing a genuine disagreement concerning what weight an international law should enjoy vis-à-vis another international law actively contributes to the interpretation of international law by domestic actors. Neither of the advantages of variable authority may do away with reasonable disagreements on what norm has what kind of authority over domestic legal systems. It does, however, play both a clarification and a structuring role when talking about international law's authority competition from within.

Let me discuss how an approach that instructs assigning weights to specific international laws offers a better way out of what may at first seem to be a 'head-on conflict' by way of an illustrative example. I will then return to cases where a 'genuine head-on conflict' may be at stake as well as the added value of a relative authority scheme.

For a recent example of how, by assigning weights to the authority of international law, we may overcome some problems that at first seem insurmountable we can consider the case of *Nada v Switzerland*.[15] Mr Youssef Moustafa Nada is an Italian/Egyptian national, who had been living in Campione d'Italia,

[14] For studies that focus on that see Mattias Kumm, 'The Cosmopolitan Turn in Constitutionalism: An Integrated Conception of Public Law' (2013) 20(2) *Indiana Journal of Global Legal Studies* 605.

[15] *Nada v Switzerland* (GC) (2013) 56 EHRR 18 (*Nada*).

a small Italian exclave surrounded by Swiss territory, since the 1970s. Following the addition of his name to the United Nations blacklist run by the Security Council Sanctions Committee Switzerland froze all Mr Nada's financial assets and imposed a travel ban on him. Due to these restrictions on his freedom of movement, Mr Nada was unable to leave Campione d'Italia for over six years.[16] This case concerns both domestic and Strasbourg litigation by Mr Nada. He argues that the sanctions, in particular the travel ban, imposed on him by Security Council Resolution 1390 (2002) were in violation of his right to privacy and family life protected by the Swiss Constitution as well as by the European Convention on Human Rights and Fundamental Freedoms (ECHR).

The case was first litigated before domestic courts in Switzerland and subsequently before the European Court of Human Rights. In this case, the Swiss Federal Court pursued a pedigree-focussed analysis of the authority of international law, whereas the European Court of Human Rights pursued a norm-focussed analysis.

In its judgment of 14 November 2007, the Federal Court of Switzerland denied Mr Nada's claim, holding that the duty to comply with a Security Council Resolution was strict under international law.[17] The Federal Court, in particular, regarded Article 25 of the United Nations Charter as imposing strong duties on member states in terms of accepting and carrying out the decisions of the United Nations Security Council.[18] The Swiss Court then turned to its obligations in relation to the ECHR, which guarantees the right to fair trial under Article 6. It observed that Article 103 of the Charter made the strict duty formulation undisputable: obligations arising from the UN Charter must prevail both over the domestic law of member states and also over obligations under all other international agreements.[19] If we had one clear rule in international law concerning the conflict of competition amongst international treaties, Article 103 was it. By concluding that Article 25 obligations extended to all Security Council Resolutions, Article 103 played a central role in the reasoning of the Federal Court.

The Grand Chamber of the European Court of Human Rights took a different route. It classified the obligation imposed by the specific wording of Security Council Resolution 1390 as a weak duty.[20] For the European Court of Human Rights, the United Nations Charter Article 25:

> 'does not impose on States a particular model for the implementation of the resolutions adopted by the Security Council under Chapter VII. Without prejudice to the

[16] Ibid. para 156.

[17] Federal Court judgment as quoted by the European Court of Human Rights, *Nada* paras 41–52.

[18] Ibid. para 42. [19] Ibid. paras 175–80. [20] Ibid.

binding nature of such resolutions, the Charter in principle leaves to United Nations member States a free choice among the various possible models for transposition of those resolutions into their domestic legal order. The Charter thus imposes on States an obligation of result, leaving them to choose the means by which they give effect to the resolutions Security Council Resolutions.'[21]

The European Court of Human Rights, then is able to argue that Article 103 of the UN Charter does not, and cannot, place any Security Council Resolution on top of a hierarchy of obligations requiring strict duties of obedience. In turn, going back to the wording of the resolution, the European Court of Human Rights argues that Switzerland had not respected its obligations to take into account the ECHR adequately when fulfilling its weak duty to give effect to resolutions of the Security Council.[22] This analysis of the European Court of Human Rights further suggests that the ECHR imposes strong duties to take into account Convention rights as a matter of Article 1 of the Convention which states 'The High Contracting Parties shall secure to everyone within their jurisdiction the rights and freedoms defined in Section I of [the] Convention.'[23] According to Strasbourg, then, the correct analysis of the multiplicity of duties imposed on the Swiss Federal Courts is that the Convention imposes a strong duty by way of 'shall secure' and Security Council resolutions impose weak duties given that the UN does not specify any means for them to be implemented. It is not, then surprising that the 'strong duty' prevails over the 'weak one'.

Departing from this example, we may conclude that the classification of multiple duties imposed by international law with regard to the strength of their authoritative demands as a matter of judicial reasoning has the important advantage of bringing transparency and a better understanding of the content of the norms of international law. Here, the heart of the matter is not simply that 'human rights' are more important than 'counter-terrorism' or the Strasbourg Court is superior to the Security Council. Rather, what is demanded by two different, but equally important regimes is a better way of understanding the issue. The Swiss Federal Court's reasoning is incomplete as it does not consider how to categorize the demands of each norm placed on itself. The Strasbourg Court on the other hand makes an explicit effort to do so, bringing in a more transparent understanding of duties under Article 1 of the ECHR and Article 25 of the UN Charter.

What about cases where we are unable to decipher whether what is at stake may be a mistaken assignment of authority to one international law? The

[21] Ibid. para 176. [22] Ibid. para 198.
[23] Cf art 1 of the European Convention on Human Rights and Fundamental Freedoms (ECHR).

distinction between strong, weak, and rebuttable duties is not always clear amongst the norms that are present in the international legal system.[24] There are two types of concern here. First there may be a genuine disagreement about whether specific international laws that are in conflict with one another demand strict, weak, or a rebuttable duties.[25] Second, there may be a genuine agreement that conflicting norms both make similar authority demands. Both sets of problems are particularly acute when ascertaining the authority of customary international laws over treaty obligations or other customary international laws. To complicate matters further, a domestic norm created by a single political authority may weigh in from the perspective of one jurisdiction to define one norm as strict and another international law norm as rebuttable or weak. In such cases, by moving away from the yes/no paradigm of binding international laws, we are in fact opening up the authority of international law to be interpreted in different ways by different interpreters across different domestic contexts in the light of how they view one international law as having more authority than another. How does this then differ from and advance the relativist approach of monist/dualist characterizations of domestic legal systems or judges?

In fact, disagreements about what duties diverse sets of international law impose is a prevalent discussion of judicial dialogue that takes place between review courts and low instance courts as well as between final courts and international courts.[26] Judicial exchanges between the Italian courts and the International Court of Justice illustrate this tellingly.[27]

[24] Furthermore, the system is open to the classification of duties imposed by international laws to change over time, for example, through making new treaties or through the decisions of international courts and tribunals. The international law of armed conflict is one area where the community of states, multilaterally have moved from weak duties to more strict duties through the acceptance of prohibitive rules in armed conflict, in particular with regard to the prohibition of different types of weapons. This move towards stronger duties in international law has been famously dubbed the 'humanization' of humanitarian law by Theodor Meron, 'The Humanization of Humanitarian Law' (2000) 94(2) *American Journal of International Law* 239.

[25] The fact that the international legal system is becoming more and more sophisticated, but also complicated is a well-accepted fact of international law. States are taking on multiple obligations, availing themselves to accept opposing strong, weak, or rebuttable duties. The literature on head-on conflicts between international human rights law and international investment law or international trade law and international environmental law are abound with examples of norm conflicts in international law.

[26] For some of the cases that attracted significant attention from this perspective, see Woodhouse, *The Pinochet Case: A Legal and Constitutional Analysis* (Oxford: Hart Publishing 2000); Pasquale De Sena and Francesca De Vittor, 'State Immunity and Human Rights: The Italian Supreme Court Decision on the Ferrini Case' (2005) 16 *European Journal of International Law* 89–112; Juliane Kokott and Christoph Sobotta, 'The Kadi Case—Constitutional Core Values and International Law—Finding the Balance?' (2012) 23 *European Journal of International Law* 1015–24.

[27] The Italian Constitutional Court Judgment No 238 of 22 October 2014 and *Jurisdictional Immunities of the State (Germany v Italy: Greece Intervening)* [2012] ICJ Rep 99 (*Jurisdictional Immunities*).

In its decision of 2004, the Italian Constitutional Court decided that arrest, deportation, and forced labour during the Second World War was within the jurisdiction of Italian courts.[28] This decision led to Germany litigating against Italy before the International Court of Justice. In its judgment, the International Court of Justice had to address the norm conflict between the sovereign immunity of states and the right of access to judicial proceedings in international human rights law. As the domain of sovereign immunity is largely governed by customary international law, the International Court of Justice had to decide what kind of a duty is present under customary international law towards the sovereign immunity of states for civil claims concerning the actions of their armed forces. The International Court of Justice concluded that the international law on sovereign immunity attracted strong duties in international law.[29]

In 2014, the Italian Constitutional Court, amongst others,[30] was asked to review the constitutionality of the 'norm created in (our) legal order by the incorporation, by virtue of Article 10, para 1 of the Constitution', of the international custom, as found by the International Court of Justice (ICJ) in its Judgment of 3 February 2012, insofar as it denies the jurisdiction (of civil courts) in the actions for damages for war crimes committed jure imperii by the Third Reich by the Tribunal of Florence.[31] The Italian Constitutional Court declared that it regards the absolute guarantee to judicial protection as imposing a strong obligation in Italian Constitutional law. It, however, did not stop there as we may have expected the dualist to do. It also held that the guarantee of judicial protection was a general principle of international law.[32] Based on assigning strong duties to the protection of judicial protection, it then held,

[28] *Ferrini v Germany* (2006) 128 ILR 658, Corte di cassazione [Italian Court of Cassation], No 5044/2004, 11 March 2004 ('*Ferrini*').

[29] *Jurisdictional Immunities* (n 27).

[30] The Tribunal of Florence also asked to review the constitutionality of 'Article 1 of Law No 848 of 17 August 1957 (Execution of the United Nations Charter, signed in San Francisco on 16 June 1945), insofar as, through the incorporation of Article 94 of the U.N. Charter, it obliges the national judge to comply with the Judgment of the ICJ, which established the duty of Italian courts to deny their jurisdiction in the examination of actions for damages for crimes against humanity, committed jure imperii by the Third Reich, at least in part in Italian territory; of Article 1 (recte: Article 3) of Law No. 5 of 14 January 2013 (Accession by the Italian Republic to the United Nations Convention on Jurisdictional Immunities of States and their Property, signed in New York on 2 December 2004, as well as provisions for the amendment of the domestic legal order), insofar as it obliges the national judge to comply with the Judgment of the ICJ, even when it established the duty of Italian courts to deny their jurisdiction in the examination of actions for damages for crimes against humanity, committed jure imperii by the Third Reich in Italian territory, in relation to Articles 2 and 24 of the Constitution.'

[31] *The Italian Constitutional Court Judgment No 238* of 22 October 2014.

[32] Ibid. p 2.

contrary to the International Court of Justice, that state immunity in domestic jurisdictions is rebuttable.[33] This was in response to the International Court of Justice's decision that the customary norm of state immunity attracted strong duties.[34]

It is clear that the disagreement between the Italian Constitutional Court and the International Court of Justice concerns the assessments of the authoritative demands of different sets of international law. The Italian Constitutional Court also viewed the wishes of its own constitutive community to be fully in sync with the norm of access to courts in international law. Sovereign immunity in the eyes of the Italian Constitutional Court is rebuttable. More significantly, the Italian Constitutional Court makes use of the doctrine that holds that constitutional courts as a genre of domestic courts are not passive recipients of customary international law, but active participants in it. By asserting its views on the rebuttability of sovereign immunity, the Italian Constitutional Court is asserting its right to participate in assigning weights to a core norm of international law.

## Constitutionalism and Pluralism Revisited

In the final analysis, does my doctrinal account of the authority of international law tilt towards a constitutionalist or a pluralist conception of the nature of the international legal system? In order to answer this we must differentiate between the levels of analysis constitutionalism and pluralism have and the doctrinal analysis I have aimed to advance here. I would characterize my account of authority as a middle range theory.[35] Middle range theories are propositions that bridge the gap between empirical observation

33 *The Italian Constitutional Court Judgment No 238* of 22 October 2014 ('The principle of absolute guarantee of judicial protection is a supreme principle of the Italian constitutional order and, as such, constitutes a limit to the introduction [in the domestic legal order] of generally recognized norms of international law (under Article 10, para 1 of the Constitution), as well as of norms contained in treaties establishing international organizations furthering the ends envisaged by Article 11 of the Constitution, or deriving from such organizations.')

34 *Jurisdictional Immunities of the State (Germany v Italy: Greece Intervening)* [2012] ICJ Rep 99 (*Jurisdictional Immunities*) para 78 ('customary international law continues to require that a State be accorded immunity in proceedings for torts allegedly committed on the territory of another State by its armed forces and other organs of State in the course of conducting an armed conflict', even if [the foreign State] is accused of serious violations of international human rights law).

35 Middle range theory originates in sociology. It is concerned with theoretical knowledge generation that is sufficiently abstract to allow behavioral generalization, and yet are satisfactorily grounded in reality, so that they could be empirically verified. Robert K Merton, *Social Theory and Social Structure* (New York: Free Press 1949).

and broad, often abstract and untestable, general or high-level theories. It seeks to chart the difficult waters between imposing a normative vision on reality and empirically describing singular phenomena. In this analysis, my starting point has been a practice-based view of international law. This view asserts that there are ranges of rules that bind any single domestic authority through consensual or non-consensual forms. This approach is open to the idea that some domestic systems are more bound by some international laws than others. According to the relative scheme of authority, this does not, however, mean that international law asserts more authority on a single domestic system by virtue of the fact that it may have ratified a large number of treaties. It also is open to the idea that the normative content of some international laws (for example, human rights law) is more specified by some states than others depending on the specific obligations they have undertaken. My second contention is that state officials and judges are able to recognize or discover through legal analysis—on most occasions—the kinds of demands that international law makes on them through interacting with broad range of consensual and a more limited range of non-consensual obligations that exist on the international plane. Once identified, they must seek to act in harmony with them. This line of analysis, therefore, is concerned both with ordinary and positive international laws and ius cogens norms of international law.

Based on this, I do not have a direct engagement with the more high level disputes that have been pitted against variants of constitutionalism and pluralism[36] as theories of the international system. My concern is not whether, for example, human rights are a core foundation of the international legal order. I am more interested in how established and specific international human rights laws may impose duties on domestic authorities. Despite the normative force of 'human rights' as a more abstract concern, such duties do come in the form of strong, weak, and rebuttable duties. If what we understand from constitutionalism is a clear commitment to a pre-defined set of international laws that imposes strict duties in relation to domestic legal systems, my relative account of the authority of international law is in agreement with this to the extent that strict duties exist in international law. International law is capable of generating strict duties both through consent and through non-consensual ways. My account, however, does not rely on

[36] See for recent debates, M Loughlin, 'Constitutional Pluralism: An Oxymoron?' (2014) 3 *Global Constitutionalism* 9; Gráinne de Búrca and Joseph Weiler (eds), *The Worlds of European Constitutionalism* (Cambridge: Cambridge University Press 2012); Jeffrey L Dunoff and Joel P Trachtman (eds), *Ruling the World? Constitutionalism, International Law, and Global Governance* (Cambridge: Cambridge University Press 2009).

constitutionalism to ground such duties and recognizes that strict duties do not have to be constitutional values. It further holds that weak and rebuttable duties may also be generated both by what is regarded as having deeper constitutional significance, such as human rights, as well as at the level of ordinary international law making.

The account I provide in this book also overlaps with some of the insights of pluralist accounts. Pluralism promotes the insight that there is an interaction among the different legal orders. The concept of interaction for pluralism, however, has far-reaching consequences for the understanding of the normative order of international law. Any given constitutional system (domestic or international) does not have its own contained normative space, but becomes part of a 'normative *pluriversum*'.[37] My reflective account agrees with this proposition, but does not hold that the interactions between domestic law and international law are open-ended. First, the authority structures of international law ask international judges to order these interactions. Second, domestic judges are duty-bound to respond to such authority structures in ways that are demanded of them. This, of course, as a matter of practice, may not lead to identical outcomes in each and every jurisdiction due to the specifities of each and every international law application and the background domestic laws that exist alongside international law. I, however, demand more than open mindedness from the domestic judges. They ought to operate in ways that are sensitive to the duties imposed by international laws.

In sum, whilst my practical account of the authority of international law is compatible with some tenets of both constitutionalism and pluralism, due to its interest in the authority structures of specific international laws, it can part ways both with closed constitutional views and more open-ended pluralist views when domestic judges interact with international law.

## Is Relative Authority Monism in Disguise?

A final concern of the original contribution of this practical view of authority is whether it is in effect disguised monism. Despite its insistence of overcoming the monist-dualist worldview competition, it ultimately takes the side of monism. The question of whether the relative authority is disguised monism hinges on what we ascribe to monism as a worldview of the international system. If the relative authority of international law is qualified as disguised

[37] Armin Von Bogdandy, 'Pluralism, direct effect, and the ultimate say: On the relationship between international and domestic constitutional law' (2008) 6 *International Journal of Constitutional Law* 397, 401.

monism, this suggests a very nominal conception of monism in the first place. The paradigm of the attitude of minimalist deference to international law is not grounded in a strict conception of the unity of legal systems of international law and domestic law. It is rather grounded in the social condition of political authorities as interdependent communities who ultimately share common risks to the welfare of individuals residing in their jurisdictions. The post-Second World War consensus on the need for co-ordination, confirmed by the United Nations Charter, recognizes these common risks.[38] It also takes a step further in underlying the need for continuous co-operation to respond to the shape and scale of common risks both through legal and political measures.[39] That the United Nations Charter makes reference to good faith co-operation is how we translate this underlying concern to the vocabulary of international law.[40]

Given this background, any concern for minimalist deference is not to advocate a unity of legal systems, but the inescapable necessity of taking international law into account as agents of international law. International laws that we have devised since the end of the Second World War do not pursue the agenda of displacing all domestic laws with international laws. Rather, they make forceful demands to insist that some domestic laws ought to be present in all domestic jurisdictions in order, in particular, to protect individuals against common risks. The model legislation requests of the Convention Against Torture, the Convention against All Forms of Discrimination against Women, the Convention on the Elimination of All Forms of Racial Discrimination, and the Statute of the International Criminal Court, for example, are means of fighting common risks rather than pronouncements to drive domestic legal systems towards a monist international legal order. In

[38] This spirit is reflected in the wording of UN Charter art 1(3) which identifies one of the purposes of the United Nations as: 'To achieve international co-operation in solving international problems of an economic, social, cultural, or humanitarian character, and in promoting and encouraging respect for human rights and for fundamental freedoms for all without distinction as to race, sex, language, or religion.'

[39] UN Charter art 55 is the most notable of these: 'With a view to the creation of conditions of stability and well-being which are necessary for peaceful and friendly relations among nations based on respect for the principle of equal rights and self-determination of peoples, the United Nations shall promote: (a) higher standards of living, full employment, and conditions of economic and social progress and development; (b) solutions of international economic, social, health, and related problems; and international cultural and educational cooperation; and universal respect for, and observance of, human rights and fundamental freedoms for all without distinction as to race, sex, language, or religion.'

[40] UN Charter art 2(2): 'All Members, in order to ensure to all of them the rights and benefits resulting from membership, shall fulfill in good faith the obligations assumed by them in accordance with the present Charter.'

other areas of international law, such as the international law of the environment and the international law of trade, the logic of differentiated duties is more prevalent. Thus, international law recognizes the need for a monist drive as a means to fight common risks in some issue areas. In other areas, regulation comes in the form of weak and rebuttable duties. The account I developed caters for this structural condition of international law: the joint use of both unity and diversity as tools of co-ordination.

If we call this structural condition 'monist' and subsequently the account in this book as monist or disguised monist, monism becomes a catch-all phrase for all contemporary international law underpinned by the United Nations Charter. This is a category error as the value of minimalist deference and reflective doctrines that correspond with it do not always advocate a monist attitude towards international law in domestic legal systems. A strict advocate of monism has a teleological edge that the minimalist deference paradigm does not share.

## Conclusion

What I have outlined places a greater burden on domestic political and legal authorities compared to treating all international laws as having an effect in the domestic system or as having no effect at all. A lot of responsibility is placed on domestic actors to take international law into account. These demands are not only reflective in relation to a single norm of international law in the domestic legal system, but also reflective with regard to the proliferation of international law and the shifting strength of duties in the system. Taking international law into account is indeed a complex and deliberative task and not a mechanical task. My view is that the burden placed on the interpreter to reflectively engage with international law is a more productive route doctrinally even if it may still produce conflicting accounts of the authority of international law across different institutions. The value of this doctrine lies in removing authority of international law debates from an exclusively domestic law analysis and creating a common form of engagement with international law's authority through the use of reasons recognizable by all participants—domestic and international alike.

# Conclusion

'International Law? It is a bargain.'[1]

This book focused on an old school problem of international law: what is its authority over domestic legal systems? In so doing, it aimed to claim decidedly legal-doctrinal territory as opposed, in particular, to moral, normative, or empirical territory. The core argument here has been that international law as it exists in contemporary legal and political conditions enjoys a form of practical authority over domestic legal systems. This authority, however, is neither supreme nor obvious in each and every instance when authority over domestic legal systems is claimed. I disagree in this respect with the Permanent Court of International Justice, the authority of international law is not self-evident.[2] The specific authority of international law is something that needs to be discovered, and, in some instances, reconstructed by the domestic authorities themselves.

The legal-doctrinal way of approaching the authority of international law has made me focus on our existing corpus of international law. When advocating for the relative authority of international law I have relied on existing international laws and their diversity as my starting point. Taking cue from what we have in the form of positive international law has enabled me to rethink and revise the standard view of international lawyers, who view the authority of international law as self-evident when it is binding.

I have two key concerns with the standard view. First, the doctrine has not had an internal consistency within itself. International law is abound with references that indicate that states are free to choose the means to discharge their obligations. This doctrine of 'freedom to enforce' sits side by side with the bindingness account of the authority of international law. The gap between the assumed authority of international law and the freedom

[1] Interview, Judge, Karlsruhe, April 2009.

[2] *Exchange of Greek and Turkish Populations*, Advisory Opinion of the Permanent Court of International Justice, 21 February 1925, Series B no 10 at 20.

to choose to respect it, I argue, is in need of reconciliation, and needs to be shown in a better light. The standard authority of international law is also too focused on consent. This underestimates its role when political authorities do not have too much space to consent and over-estimates its role when consent does not lead to the automatic authority of international law.

My second concern is that the standard view of the authority of international law has been under sustained criticism and attack from neighboring disciplines for the past two decades. This ranges from political science to political theory and constitutional law. In the face of such sustained attack—even if it does not always reach the international law audience—to insist that international law has authority when it is binding does not seem to be a well-versed defense. On the contrary, it is more repeating a mantra and stating a conclusion than forming an argument against staunch critiques.

In response to these twofold weaknesses of the standard view of the authority of international law, I formulated a view that both revises the internal inconsistencies of the standard view and that aims to make it argumentatively defensible against the skeptics of authority of international law based on initial and ongoing consent. This culminated in grounding the doctrine of minimalist deference to international law and the authority account that takes its cue from the differentiation of duties imposed by international laws on domestic legal orders.

In this conclusion, I seek to reflect on two broader implications of the relative account of the authority of international law. The first concerns the contingency of this view and whether this account is largely responsive to certain historical periods in international law's development. Second, is how the relative authority of international law relates to our understanding of compliance with international law.

The account developed and defended in this book is informed by the current historical circumstances of international law. These historical circumstances are marked by the recognition of international law as a tool of co-operation to combat common risks to collective human communities as well as individuals residing in states. The proliferation of international law opens up difficult questions of complexity. How can an international legal system that still largely relies on the consent of states for the formulation of international laws in terms of binding commitments and is also reliant on international interpretive authorities for further differentiation and specification of fine grained duties make a claim to authority? I have argued that in these historical circumstances state officials, be they political officials or judiciaries, play an important role for reflectively engaging with the authority of specific international laws. Furthermore, the proliferation of international law, coupled with the proliferation of international courts has not diminished the role of the agency of such authorities. They have made the role of such agency more demanding. More international law and more international judicial decisions have led to the rise of strict duties in international law across its various branches. International legal interpretive authorities, too, have been sensitive in identifying weak and rebuttable doctrines, in particular through developing margin of appreciation doctrines. The consolidation of international law since 1945, therefore has not made international law into a blunt tool of international governance, but into a sophisticated and interlinked web of obligations whose specification requires our views regarding both the grounds of authority and the form and shape they take to be sophisticated.

The account of practical authority I developed in this book is flexible towards future changes in the historical circumstances of international law. Whether more duties can be placed in the category of strict duties, whether the compatibility of domestic obligations with weak duties can exclude a wider range of options and whether rebuttable duties may require stricter conditions of rebuttability are open-ended and case-sensitive questions. In a few decades from now, with more international law obligations introduced on the international plane,[3] and with more refined accounts of inter-branch interactions,[4] domestic judges need to revise the structure of duties imposed by specific international laws. Without imposing a telos on what may emerge, we already see potential shifts in our understanding of duties imposed by various international laws.[5]

What are we to make of the relationship between the authority of international law and compliance with it? The relative authority of international law has some important implications for how we theorize compliance. First, similar to demands it makes on our conception of authority, it asks us to view compliance not as an either/or concept.[6] Whilst compliance with strict duties imposed by international law corresponds with the vision of an either/or conception, weak and rebuttable duties do not view compliance in terms

[3] See for example, the coming into force of the Arms Trade Treaty in 24 December 2014 with 62 ratifications. http://www.un.org/disarmament/ATT/ accessed on 25 February 2015.

[4] *Suez, Sociedad General de Aguas de Barcelona SA and Vivendi Universal SA*, ICSID Case No ARB/03/19, Decision on Liability, para 262 (30 July 2010); WW Burke-White & A von Staden, 'Investment Protection in Extra-Ordinary Times: The Interpretation and Application of Non-Precluded Measures Provisions in Bilateral Investment Treaties' (2008) 48 *Virginia Journal of International Law* 307.

[5] Marko Milanovic, *Extra-Territorial Application of Human Rights Treaties: Law, Principles and Policy* (Oxford: Oxford University Press 2011).

[6] This view is also echoed in international relations literature. See Jana von Stein, 'The Engines of Compliance' in Jeffrey L Dunoff and Mark A Pollack (eds), *Interdisciplinary Perspectives in International Law and International Relations: The State of the Art* (Cambridge: Cambridge University Press 2012) 477.

of the outcome of the actions taken by domestic political or legal authorities. In the case of weak duties, the compliance can be corroborated if the political authority takes steps in good faith to devise a policy option that is in line with the obligations foreseen by weak duties. The judicial compliance in this case turns to whether judicial authorities have duly considered the compatibility of the measure taken by political authorities. Clearly, no engagement with the duty, and no review of the measure by judicial authorities would be indicators of non-compliance. If there is some level of engagement with the weak duty, however, any assessment of compliance becomes more fact-specific. In the case of rebuttable duties, compliance verification turns to the assessment of the appropriateness and proportionality of the rebuttal that is mounted by political authorities. In this case, whether the rebuttal takes place under the shadow of a body of international legal judgments or in the more opaque field of customary international law will also matter when passing a compliance view on the ultimate outcome of the political action or the judicial pronouncement.

The relative authority of international law, therefore, is able to propose a way of understanding what we may mean by the relative spectrum of compliance. It also asserts that the empirical assessments with compliance of international law must directly engage with the kinds of demands international law makes from domestic authorities.

Could or would this view have a positive effect on compliance with international law? The conception of duties imposed by international law as differentiated schemes of duties has the potential of offsetting what we may call 'reactionary non-compliance' with international law. If a political or judicial authority is under the impression that international law (unfairly) always imposes strong duties on them and, for that reason, they view themselves as being entitled to disregard it to protect their democratic order or judicial integrity, I hold that the conception of differentiated duties would act as a corrective. The active agency left to domestic authorities to attune their policies with weak duties and to defend domestic laws and policy under conditions of rebuttability, goes some way to convince domestic authorities to revise reactionary views against international law *tout court*. For the same reason the account also has the potential to prevent the entrenchment of defensive dualism and nationalism towards international law. For those in favour of insisting on an isolationist view of political communities and a purely domestic view of law, however, the relative practical authority of international law, or any other vision of international law, will remain impertinens. That, however, is ultimately a political failing of international law and not the doctrine of its authority.

# *Bibliography*

Abi-Saab G, 'The International Court as a World Court' in Vaughan Lowe and Malgosia Fitzmaurice (eds), *Fifty Years of the International Court of Justice: Essays in Honour of Sir Robert Jennings* (Cambridge: Cambridge University Press 1996)

Abramovich, V, 'From Massive Human Rights Problems to Structural Patterns: New Approaches and Classic Tensions in the Inter-American System' (2009) 11 *SUR International Journal on Human Rights* 6

Ainley K, 'International Criminal Court on Trial' (2011) 24(3) *Cambridge Review of International Affairs* 309

Akehurst M, 'Custom as a Source of International Law' (1975) 47(1) *British Year Book of International Law* 1

Alford RP, 'Foreign Relations as a Matter of Interpretation: The Use and Abuse of Charming Betsy' (2006) 67 *Ohio State Law Journal* 1339

Alter K, *The European Court's Political Power* (Oxford: Oxford University Press 2009)

Alter K and Helfer L, 'Nature or Nurture? Judicial Lawmaking in the European Court of Justice and the Andean Tribunal of Justice' (2010) 64 *International Organization* 563

Alvarez JE, *International Organizations as Law-makers* (Oxford: Oxford University Press 2006)

Alvarez JE, 'The New Dispute Settlers: (Half) Truths and Consequences' (2003) 38 *Texas International Law Journal* 405

Alvarez JE, 'The Once and Future Foreign Invesment Regime' in M H Arsanjani and others (eds), *Looking to the Future: Essays in the Honour of W Michael Reisman* (Leiden: Nijjhoff 2011)

Amann DM and Sellers MNS, 'The United States of America and the International Criminal Court' (2002) 50 *American Journal of Comparative Law Supplement* 381

Anzilotti D, *Cours de Droit International* (Paris: Sirey 1929)

Arai Y, *The Margin of Appreciation Doctrine and the Principle of Proportionality in the Jurisprudence of the ECHR* (Antwerp: Intersentia 2002)

Arambulo K, *Strengthening the Supervision of the International Covenant on Economic, Social and Cultural Rights: Theoretical and Procedural Aspects* (Antwerp: Intersentia 1999)

Aristotle, 'Nicomachean Ethics' in Jonathan Barnes (ed), *The Complete Works of Aristotle: The Revised Oxford Translation*, vol 2, (rev Oxford trans, Bollingen Series 1984)

Austin J, *The Province of Jurisprudence Determined* (1832) (ed W Rumble) (Cambridge: Cambridge University Press 1995)

Bahdi R, 'Globalization of Judgment: Transjudicialism and the Five Faces of International Law in Domestic Courts' (2002) 34 *George Washington International Law Review* 555

Barzun CL, 'Legal Rights and the Limits of Conceptual Analysis: A Case Study' (2013) 26(2) *Ratio Juris* 215

Baumgold D, *Contract Theory in Historical Context: Essays on Grotius, Hobbes and Locke* (Leiden: Brill Academic Publishers 2010)

Beckett J, 'Behind Relative Normativity: Rules and Process as a Prerequisite of Law' (2001) 12 *European Journal of International Law* 627

Beitz CR, *The Idea of Human Rights* (Oxford: Oxford University Press 2009)

Bellamy R, 'Democracy as Public Law' (2013) 14(8) *German Law Journal* 1017

Bellamy R, 'Interview' in Morten Ebbe Juul Nielsen (ed), *Political Questions: 5 Questions on Political Philosophy* (London: Automatic Press 2006)

Bellamy R, *Political Constitutionalism: A Republican Defence of the Constitutionality of Democracy* (Cambridge: Cambridge University Press 2007)

Bellamy R, 'Political Constitutionalism and the Human Rights Act' (2011) 9(1) *International Journal of Constitutional Law* 86

Bellamy R, 'The Democratic Legitimacy of International Human Rights Conventions: Political Constitutionalism and the Hirst Case' in Andreas Follesdal, Karlsson Schaffer, and Geir Ulfstein (eds), *The Legitimacy of International Human Rights Regimes: Legal, Political and Philosophical Perspectives* (Cambridge: Cambridge University Press 2013) 242–71

Beloff MJ, 'What Does It All Mean? Interpreting the Human Rights Act 1998' in L Betten (ed), *The Human Rights Act 1998—What It Means* (1998) (The Hague: Nijhof)

Benedetti F, Bonneau K, and Washburn J, *Negotiating the International Criminal Court* (Leiden: Brill 2014)

Benvenisti E, 'Judicial Misgivings Concerning the Application of International Law: An Analysis of Attitudes of National Courts' (1993) 4 *European Journal of International Law* 159

Benvenisti E and Downs GW, 'National Courts, Domestic Democracy, and the Evolution of International Law' (2009) 20(1) *European Journal of International Law* 59

Berman PS, *Global Legal Pluralism: A Jurisprudence of Law Beyond Borders* (Cambridge: Cambridge University Press 2012)

Besson S, 'The Authority of International Law-Lifting the State Veil' (2009) 31(3) *Sydney Law Review* 343

Besson S, 'Sovereignty, International Law and Democracy' (2011) 22(2) *European Journal of International Law* 37

Betlem G and Nollkaemper A, 'Giving Effect to Public International Law and European Community Law before Domestic Courts—A Comparative Analysis of the Practice Consistent Interpretation' (2003) 14 *European Journal of International Law* 569

Bodin J, *The Six Books of the Commonwealth* (first published 1576, R Knowles tr, KD McRae ed, (Cambridge: Harvard University Press 1962)

Bogdandy A von, 'Pluralism, Direct Effect and the Ultimate Say: On the Relationship between International and Domestic Constitutional Law' (2008) 6(3–4) *International Journal of Constitutional Law* 397

Bogdandy A von and Venzke I, *In Whose Name? A Public Law Theory of International Adjudication* (Oxford: Oxford University Press 2014)

Bogdandy A von and Venzke I, 'In Whose Name? An Investigation of International Courts' Public Authority and Its Democratic Justification' (2012) 23(1) *European Journal of International Law* 7

Bradley C A, 'Breard, Our Dualist Constitution and the Internationalist Conception' (1999) 51 *Stanford Law Review* 529

Brems E, 'The Margin of Appreciation Doctrine in the Case- Law of the European Court of Human Rights' (1996) 56 *Zeitschrift fur Asulandisches Offentiliches Recht und Volkrecht* 240

Brems E and Gerards JH (eds) *Shaping Rights in the ECHR: The Role of the European Court of Human Rights in Determining the Scope of Human Rights* (Cambridge: Cambridge University Press 2014)

Brierly JL, *Laws of Nations* (6th edn, Oxford: Oxford University Press 1963)

Brierly JL, *The Basis of Obligation in International Law* (Oxford: Clarendon Press 1958)

Bronckers M, 'The Relationship of the EC Courts with Other International Tribunals: Non-committal, Respectful or Submissive?' (2007) 44(3) *Common Market Law Review* 601

Brownlie I, *Principles of Public International Law* (6th edn, Oxford: Oxford University Press 2006)

Brownlie I, *Principles of Public International Law* (7th edn, Oxford: Oxford University Press 2008)

Brunnee J and Toope S J, 'A Hesitant Embrace: The application of international law by Canadian Courts' (2002) 40 *Canadian Yearbook of International Law* 3

Buchanan A, *Justice, Legitimacy, and Self-Determination: Moral Foundations for International Law* (Oxford: Oxford University Press 2003)

Buchanan A, 'The Legitimacy of International Law' in Samantha Besson and John Tasioulas (eds), *The Philosophy of International Law* (Oxford: Oxford University Press 2010)

Buchanan A and Keohane R O, 'The Legitimacy of Global Governance Institutions' (2006) 20(4) *Ethics and International Affairs* 405

Buchanan A and Powell R, 'Survey Article: Constitutional Democracy and the Rule of International Law: Are They Compatible?' (2008) 16(3) *Journal of Political Philosophy* 326

Bull H, *The Anarchical Society: A Study of Order in World Politics* (London: Macmillan 1977)

Búrca G de, 'The European Court of Justice and the International Legal Order After Kadi' (2010) 51(1) *Harvard International Law Journal* 1

Búrca G de and Weiler JHH (eds), *The Worlds of European Constitutionalism* (Cambridge: Cambridge University Press 2011)

Burke-White WW and von Staden A, 'Investment Protection in Extra-Ordinary Times: The Interpretation and Application of Non-Precluded Measures Provisions in Bilateral Investment Treaties' (2008) 48 *Virginia Journal of International Law* 307

Çalı B, 'On Interpretivism and International Law' (2009) 20(3) *European Journal of International Law* 805

Çalı B, 'The Legitimacy of International Interpretive Authorities for Human Rights Treaties: An Indirect-Instrumentalist Defence' in Andreas Follesdal, Karlsson Schaffer and Geir Ulfstein (eds), *The Legitimacy of International Human Rights Regimes: Legal, Political and Philosophical Perspectives* (Cambridge: Cambridge University Press 2013) 141

Carolan B, 'The Search for Coherence in the Use of Foreign Court Judgements by the Supreme Court of Ireland' (2004–5) 12(1) *Journal of Comparative and International Law* 123

Cassese A, *International Law* (2nd edn, Oxford: Oxford University Press 2004)

Cassese A, *Realizing Utopia: the Future of International Law* (Oxford: Oxford University Press 2012)

Cassese A, 'Remarks on Scelle's theory of 'role splitting' (dédoublement fonctionnel) in international law' (1990) 1(1) *European Journal of International Law* 210

Cassese A, *Self-Determination of Peoples: A Legal Reappraisal* (Cambridge: Cambridge University Press 1995)

Charney J, 'Universal International Law' (1993) 87 *American Journal of International Law* 529

Chayes Abr and Chayes Ant, *The New Sovereignty: Compliance with International Regulatory Agreements* (Cambridge: Harvard University Press 1998)

Chimni BS, 'The Past, Present and Future of International Law: A Critical World Approach' (2007) 8 *Melbourne Journal of International Law* 499

Chinkin C M, 'The Challenge of Soft Law: Development and Change in International Law' (1989) 38 *International and Comparative Law Quarterly* (1989) 850

Christiano T, 'Democratic Legitimacy and International Institutions' in Samantha Besson and John Tasioulas (eds), *The Philosophy of International Law* (Oxford University Press 2010)

Clapham A, *Brierly's Law of Nations* (7th edn, Oxford: Oxford University Press 2012)

Coleman J, *The Practice of Principle: In Defence of a Pragmatic Approach to Legal Theory* (Oxford: Oxford University Press 2001)

Coleman J and Kraus J, 'Rethinking the Theory of Legal Rights' (1986) 95(7) *Yale Law Journal* 1335

Condorelli L and Cassese A, 'Is Leviathan still holding sway in International Dealings' in Casesse (ed), *Realising Utopia: The Future of International Law* (Oxford: Oxford University Press 2012)

Cottier T and Mavroidis P C and Blatter P, (eds) *Regulatory Barriers and the Principle of Non-Discrimination of World Trade Law: Past, Present and Future* (Ann Arbor, Michigan University Press 2000)

Craven M, *The Decolonization of International Law: State Succession and the Law of Treaties* (Oxford, Oxford University Press 2007)

Craven M, 'Unity, Diversity and the Fragmentation of International Law' (2005) 14 *Finnish Yearbook of International Law* 3

Crawford J, *The Creation of States in International Law* (2nd edn, Oxford: Oxford University Press 2006)
Crawford J, *The International Law Commission's Articles on State Responsibility: Introduction, Text and Commentaries* (Cambridge: Cambridge University Press 2002)
Crema L, 'Disappearance and New Sightings of Restrictive Interpretation(s)' (2010) 21(3) *European Journal of International Law* 681
Dai X, *International Institutions and National Processes* (Cambridge: Cambridge University Press 2007)
Daly M, 'Effective Judicial Review: Necessary because of Bad Governance' in Christopher Forsyth and others (eds), *Effective Judicial Review: A Cornerstone of Good Governance* (Oxford: Oxford University Press 2010)
d'Aspremont J, *Formalism and the Sources of International Law: A Theory of the Ascertainment of the Legal Rules* (Oxford: Oxford University Press 2011)
Devins N and Fisher L, *The Democratic Constitution* (Oxford: Oxford University Press 2004)
Dobson L, 'Legitimacy, institutional power, and international human rights institutions: a conceptual enquiry' in Andreas Follesdal, Karlsson Schaffer, and Geir Ulfstein (eds), *The Legitimacy of International Human Rights Regimes: Legal, Political and Philosophical Perspectives* (Cambridge: Cambridge University Press 2013) 190–211
Donnely J, *Realism and International Relations* (Cambridge: Cambridge University Press 2000)
Downs GW, Rocke DM, and Barsoom PN, 'Is the Good News About Compliance Good News About Cooperation?' (1996) 50 *International Organization* 379
Durkheim E, *The Rules of Sociological Method* (W D Halls tr, Steven Lukes ed, The Free Press 1982)
Dworkin R, 'A New Philosophy for International Law' (2013) 41(1) *Philosophy and Public Affairs* 2
Dworkin R, *A Matter of Principle* (Cambridge: Harvard University Press 1985)
Dworkin R, '"Natural" Law Revisited' (1982) 34 *University of Florida Law Review* 165
Dupuy PM, 'The Unity of Application of International Law at the Global Level and the Responsibility of Judges' (2007) 2 *European Journal of Legal Studies* 1
Fassbender B, 'The UN Charter as the Constitution of the International Community' (1998) 36(3) *Colombia Journal of Transnational Law* 529
Fassbender B, 'We the Peoples of United Nations: Constituent Power and Constituent Form in International Law' in Martin Louhglin and Neil Walker (eds), *The Paradox of Constitutionalism: Constituent Power and Constitutional Form* (Oxford: Oxford University Press 2007)
Fearon JD, 'Bargaining, Enforcement, and International Cooperation' (1998) 52 *International Organization* 269
Fitzmaurice GG, 'The Foundations and the Authority of International Law and the Problem of Enforcement' (1956) 19 *Modern Law Review* 1

Fitzpatrick P, *The Mythology of Modern Law* (Routledge 1992)
Flathman RE, *The Practice of Political Authority: Authority and the Authoritative* (Chicago: University of Chicago Press 1980)
Follesdal A, 'Much ado about nothing? International judicial review of human rights in well-functioning democracies' in Andreas Follesdal, Karlsson Schaffer, and Geir Ulfstein (eds), *The Legitimacy of International Human Rights Regimes: Legal, Political and Philosophical Perspectives* (Cambridge: Cambridge University Press 2013)
Follesdal A, 'The Legitimacy of International Human Rights Review: The Case of the European Court of Human Rights' (2009) 40(4) *Journal of Social Philosophy* 595
Follesdal A and Reidar Maliks, 'Kantian Theory and Human Rights' in Andreas Follesdal and Reidar Maliks (eds), *Kantian Theory and Human Rights* (London: Routledge 2014)
Fox G and Roth BR (eds), *Democratic Governance and International Law* (Cambridge: Cambridge University Press 2000)
Franck TM, *Fairness in International Law and Institutions* (Oxford: Clarendon Press 1995)
Franck TM, 'The Emerging Right to Democratic Governance' (1992) 86 *American Journal of International Law* 46
Franck TM, *The Power of Legitimacy Among Nations* (Oxford: Oxford University Press 1990)
Friedman RB, 'On the Concept of Authority in Political Philosophy' in Richard E Flathman (ed), *Concepts in Social and Political Philosophy* (London: Macmillan 1973)
Friedman W, *The Changing Structure of International Law* (New York: Columbia University Press 1964)
Fuller C, 'Legal Anthropology, Legal Pluralism and Legal Thought' (1994) 10(3) *Anthropology Today* 9
Fuller, L, *The Morality of Law* (Oxford: Hart Publishing 1964)
Gaja G, 'Dualism: A Review' in Janne E Nijmann and André Nollkaemper (eds), *New Perspectives on the Divide between National and International Law* (Oxford: Oxford University Press 2007) 52–62
Gardiner R, 'The Vienna Convention Rules on Treaty Interpretation' in Duncan Hollis (ed), *The Oxford Guide to Treaties* (Oxford: Oxford University Press 2012) 475
Gardiner R, *Treaty Interpretation* (Oxford: Oxford University Press 2008)
Gauri V and Brinks M (eds), *Courting Social Justice: Judicial Enforcement of Economic and Social Rights in the Developing World* (Cambridge: Cambridge University Press 2010)
Gerber SD, *To Secure These Rights* (New York: New York University Press 1995)
Giegerich T, 'The *Is* and *Ought* of International Constitutionalism: How Far Have We Come on Habermas's Road to a "Well Considered Constitutionalization of International Law"?' (2009) 10(1) *German Law Journal* 31
Ginsburg T, 'The Global Spread of Constitutional Review' in Gregory A Caldeira, R Daniel Kelemen, and Keith E Whittington (eds), *The Oxford Handbook of Law and Politics* (Oxford: Oxford University Press 2008)

Goldsmith J and Posner E, *The Limits of International Law* (Oxford: Oxford University Press 2005)

Gongora-Mera ME, *Inter-American Judicial Constitutionalism: On the Constitutional Rank of Human Rights Treaties in Latin America through National and Inter-American Adjudication* (San Jose: Instituto Inter Americano de Derechos Humanos 2011)

Goodman R, 'Human Rights Treaties, Invalid Reservations, and State Consent' (2002) 96 *American Journal of International Law* 531

Green L, 'Law and Obligations' in Jules Coleman and Scott Shapiro (eds), *The Oxford Handbook of Jurisprudence and Philosophy of Law* (Oxford: Clarendon Press 2002)

Greenwood C, 'Law of Weaponry at the Start of the New Millennium' in Michael N Schmitt and Leslie C Green (eds), *The Law of Armed Conflict: Into the Next Millennium* (Newport: Naval War College 1998)

Grewal DS, *Network Power: The Social Dynamics of Globalization* (New Haven: Yale University Press 2008)

Griffiths J, 'What is legal pluralism?' (1986) 24(1) *Journal of Legal Pluralism* 2

Gross L, *States as Organs of International Law and the Problem of Auto-Interpretation* (Berkley: University of California Press 1953)

Groudine CJ, 'Authority: H.L.A. Hart and the Problem with Legal Positivism' (1980) 4(3) *Journal of Libertarian Studies* 217

Guzman A T, *How International Law Works: A Rational Choice Theory* (Oxford: Oxford University Press 2008)

Habermas J, 'The Crisis of the European Union in the Light of a Constitutionalisation of International Law' (2012) 23(2) *European Journal of International Law* 335

Halberstam D, 'Constitutionalism and Pluralism in Marbury and Van Gend' in Miguel Poiares Maduro and Loïc Azoulai (eds), *The Past and Future of EU Law: Revisiting the Classics on the 50th Anniversary of the Rome Treaty* (Oxford: Hart Publishing 2008)

Hamamoto, S 'An Undemocratic Guardian of Democracy—International Human Rights Complaint Procedures', (2007) 38 *Victoria University of Wellington Law Review* 199

Harris D, *Cases and Materials on International Law* (7th edn, London: Sweet & Maxwell 2010)

Hart HLA, *The Concept of Law* (Oxford: Oxford University Press 1961)

Hart HLA, *The Concept of Law* (2nd edn, Oxford: Clarendon Press 1994)

Hathaway OA, 'Why Do Countries Commit to Human Rights Treaties?' (2007) 51 *Journal of Conflict Resolution* 588

Henckaerts J and Doswald-Beck L, *Customary International Humanitarian Law* (Cambridge: Cambridge University Press 2005)

Henkin L, *How Nations Behave: Law and Foreign Policy* (New York: Frederick A Praeger 1968)

Henkin L, 'International Law: Politics, Values and Functions: General Course on Public International Law' (1989) 216 *Recueil des Cours* 1

Henkin L, *International Law: Politics and Values* (Leiden: Brill 1995)

Hershovitz S, 'The Role of Authority' (2011) 11(7) *Philosophers Imprint* 1
Hessler K, 'Equality, human rights, and political legitimacy' in 'in Andreas Follesdal, Karlsson Schaffer, and Geir Ulfstein (eds), *The Legitimacy of International Human Rights Regimes: Legal, Political and Philosophical Perspectives* (Cambridge: Cambridge University Press 2013)
Hessler K, 'Resolving Interpretive Conflicts in International Human Rights Law' (2005) 13(1) *Journal of Political Philosophy* 29
Higgins R, *Problems and Process: International Law and How We Use It* (Oxford: Clarendon Press 1994)
Hobbes T, *Leviathan* (first published 1651) (Richard Tuck (ed)) (Cambridge: Cambridge University Press 1991)
Hollis DB (ed), *Oxford Handbook on Treaties* (Oxford: Oxford University Press 2012)
Hollis DB, 'Why Consent Still Matters—Non-State Actors, Treaties, and the Changing Sources of International Law' (2005) 23 *Berkeley Journal of International Law* 137
Hollis DB and Newcomer J, 'Political Commitments and the Constitution' (2009) 49(3) *Virginia Journal of International Law* 507
Hollis M and Smith S, *Explaining and Understanding International Relations* (Oxford: Clarendon Press 1990)
Huneeus A, 'Rejecting the Inter-American Court: Judicialization, National Courts and Regional Human Rights' in Javier Couso, Alexandra Huneeus, and Rachel Sieder (eds), *Cultures of Legality: Judicialization and Political Activism in Latin America* (Cambridge: Cambridge University Press 2010)
Hurd D, *The Search for Peace* (London: Little, Brown 1997)
International Law Commission, 'Guide to Practice on Reservations to Treaties, Adopted by the International Law Commission at its sixty-third session' (2011) Vol II Part 2 *Yearbook of the International Law*
Jennings R and Watts A (eds), *Oppenheim's International Law*, vol 1 (9th edn, Harlow: Longman 1992)
Kant I, *Perpetual Peace* (trans Lewis White Beck 1797, Indianapolis: Library of Liberal Arts 1957)
Kavanagh A, *Constitutional Review under the Human Rights Act* (Cambridge: Cambridge University Press 2009)
Kelsen H, *General Theory of Law and State* (New York: Russell & Russell 1961)
Kelsen H, *Principles of International Law* (New York: Rinehart, 1952)
Kelsen H, *Principles of International Law* (Robert W Tucker edn, 2nd ed, New York: Holt, Rinehart & Winston 1966)
Kersch KI, 'The New Legal Transnationalism, the Globalized Judiciary and the Rule of Law' (2005) 4(2) *Washington University Global Studies Law Review* 345
Kingsbury B, 'Legal Positivism as Normative Politics: International Society, Balance of Power and Lassa Oppenheim's Positive International Law' (2002) 13 *European Journal of International Law* 401
Kirgis FL, 'Custom on a Sliding Scale' (1987) 81 *American Journal of International Law* 146

Klabbers J, 'On Rationalism in Politics: Interpretation of Treaties and the World Trade Organization' (2005) 74 *Nordic Journal of International Law* 405

Klabbers J, 'The Redundancy of Soft Law' (1996) 65(2) *Nordic Journal of International Law* 167

Klabbers J, Peters A, and Ulfstein G, *The Constitutionalization of International Law* (Oxford: Oxford University Press 2009)

Klabbers J, *The Concept of Treaty in International Law* (The Hague: Kluwer Law International 1996)

Kleinlein T, 'Alfred Verdross as a Founding Father of International Constitutionalism?' (2012) 4(2) *Goettingen Journal of International Law* 385

Kokott J and Sobotta C, 'The Kadi Case-Constitutional Core Values and International Law-Finding the Balance?' (2012) 23(4) *European Journal of International Law* 1015

Koskenniemi M, *From Apology to Utopia: The Structure of International Legal Argument* (Cambridge: Cambridge University Press 2006)

Koskenniemi M and Leino P, 'Fragmentation of International Law? Postmodern Anxieties' (2002) 15(3) *Leiden Journal of International Law* 553

Krisch N, *Beyond Constitutionalism: The Pluralist Structure of Post-National Law* (Oxford: Oxford University Press 2010)

Kumm M, 'The Cosmopolitan Turn in Constitutionalism: An Integrated Conception of Public Law' (2013) 20(2) *Indiana Journal of Global Legal Studies* 605

Kumm M, 'The Cosmopolitan Turn in Constitutionalism: On the Relationship between Constitutionalism in and Beyond the State' in JL Dunoff and JP Trachtman (eds), *Constitutionalism, International Law and Global Government* (Cambridge: Cambridge University Press 2009)

Kumm M, 'The Legitimacy of International Law: A Constitutionalist Framework of Analysis' (2004) 15(5) *European Journal of International Law* 907

Lacey N, 'Analytical Jurisprudence versus Descriptive Sociology Revisited' (2006) 84(4) *Texas Law Review* 945

Lamond G, 'Persuasive Authority in the Law' (2010) 17(1) *Harvard Review of Philosophy* 16

Lau H, 'Comment, Rethinking the Persistent Objector Doctrine in International Human Rights Law' (2005) 6 *Chicago Journal of International Law* 495

Lauterpacht H, *Function of Law in the International Community* (Oxford: Clarendon Press 1933)

Leiter B, 'Beyond the Hart/Dworkin Debate: The Methodology Problem in Jurisprudence' (2003) 48(1) *American Journal of Jurisprudence* 17

Letsas G, 'Strasbourg's Interpretive Ethic: Lessons for the International Lawyer' (2010) 21(3) *European Journal of International Law* 509

Letsas G, 'The ECHR as a Living Instrument: its Meaning and Legitimacy' in Geir Ulfstein, Andreas Follesdal, and Birgit Peters (eds), *Constituting Europe: The European Court of Human Rights in a National, European and Global Context* (Cambridge: Cambridge University Press 2013)

Loughlin M, 'Constitutional Pluralism: An Oxymoron?' (2014) 3(1) *Global Constitutionalism* 9

Loughlin M, *Public Law and Political Theory* (Oxford: Clarendon Press 1992)

Loughlin M, 'Why Sovereignty?' in Richard Rawlings, Peter Leyland, and Alison Young (eds), *Sovereignty and the Law: Domestic, European and International Perspectives* (Oxford: Oxford University Press 2013)

Loughlin M and Walker N (eds), *The Paradox of Constitutionalism: Constituent Power and Constitutional Form* (Oxford: Oxford University Press 2007)

Malanczuk P, *Akehurst's Modern Introduction to International Law* (7th edn, Routledge 1996)

Marks S, 'What has become of the emerging right to democratic governance?' (2011) 22 (2) *European Journal of International Law* 507

Martin M, 'Raz's *Morality of Freedom*: Two Models of Authority' (2010) 1 *Jurisprudence* 1

Martinico G, 'Is the European Convention Going to Be 'Supreme'? A Comparative-Constitutional Overview of ECHR and EU Law before National Courts' (2012) 23(2) *European Journal of International Law* 401

McCrudden C, 'A Common Law of Human Rights?: Transnational Judicial Conversations on Constitutional Rights' (2000) 20(4) *Oxford Journal of Legal Studies* 499

Merry SE, *Colonising Hawai'i: The Cultural Power of Law* (Princeton: Princeton University Press 2000)

Merton RK, *Social Theory and Social Structure* (New York: Free Press 1949)

Milanovic M, *Extra-Territoral Application of Human Rights Treaties: Law, Principles and Policy* (Oxford: Oxford University Press 2011)

Moravcsik A, 'The Origins of Human Rights Regimes: Democratic Delegation in Postwar Europe' (2000) 54(2) *International Organization* 217

Morgenthau H, *Politics Among Nations: The Struggle for Power and Peace* (2nd edn, New York: Knopf 1954)

Morgan MI and Rubio-Marin R, 'Constitutional Domestication of International Gender Norms: Categorizations, Illustrations and Reflections from the Nearside of the Bridge' in Karen Knopp (ed), *Gender and Human Rights* (Oxford: Oxford University Press 2004)

Morris, M 'The Democratic Dilemma of the International Criminal Court' (2002) 5 *Buffalo Criminal Law Review* 591

Nollkaemper A, *National Courts and the International Rule of Law* (Oxford: Oxford University Press 2011)

Opsahl T, 'An "International Constitutional Law"?' (1961) 10 *International and Comparative Law Quarterly* 760

Orakhelashvili A, *Peremptory Norms in International Law* (Oxford: Oxford University Press 2006)

Orakhelashvili A, 'Restrictive Interpretation of Human Rights Treaties in the Recent Jurisprudence of the European Court of Human Rights' (2003) 14(3) *European Journal of International Law* 529

Pahuja S, *Decolonising International Law* (Cambridge: Cambridge University Press 2013)

Parker R, 'The Historic Basis of Administrative Law: Separation of Powers and Judicial Supremacy' (1957–8) 12 *Rutgers Law Review* 449

Paulus AL, '*Jus Cogens* in a Time of Hegemony and Fragmentation—An Attempt at a Re-appraisal' (2005) 74(3–4) *Nordic Journal of International Law* 297

Pauwelyn J, *Conflict of Norms in Public International Law: How WTO Law Relates to Other Rules of International Law* (Cambridge: Cambridge University Press 2003)

Payandeh M, 'The Concept of International Law in the Jurisprudence of H.L.A Hart' (2010) 21(4) *European Journal of International Law* 967

Peers S, 'Banana Split: WTO law and Preferential Agreements in the EC Legal Order' (1999) 4(2) *European Foreign Affairs Review* 195

Pellet A, '1969 Vienna Convention, Article 19 Formulation of reservations' in Olivier Corten and Pierre Klein (eds) *The Vienna Conventions on the Law of Treaties: A Commentary* (Oxford: Oxford University Press 2011)

Pellet A, Seventeenth report on reservations to treaties, by Mr Alain Pellet, Special Rapporteur, A/CN.4/647, General Assembly International Law Commission Sixty-third Session, 26 May 2011

Pellet A, 'The ILC Guide to Practice on Reservations to Treaties, A General Presentation by the Special Rapporteur', (2012) Jean Monnet Working Paper 15/12, The Jean Monnet Program, NYU

Perry S, 'Interpretation and Methodology in Legal Theory' in Andrei Marmor (ed), *Law and Interpretation* (Oxford: Clarendon Press 1995)

Peters A, 'Compensatory Constitutionalism: The Function and Potential of Fundamental International Norms and Structures' (2006) 19(3) *Leiden Journal of International Law* 579

Peters A, 'Global Constitutionalism Revisited' (2005) 11 *International Legal Theory* 39

Posner E, *The Perils of Global Legalism* (Chicago: Chicago University Press 2009)

Poulliot V, 'The Essence of Constructivism' (2004) 7 *Journal of International Relations and Development* 319

Rawls J, *Lectures on the History of Political Philosophy* (Samuel Freeman ed, Cambridge: Harvard University Press 2007)

Rawls J, *The Law of Peoples* (Cambridge: Harvard University Press 1999)

Rawls J, *Political Liberalism* (New York: Columbia University Press 1996)

Rawls J, 'The Idea of Public Reason Revisited' (1994) 64(3) *University of Chicago Law Review* 765

Raz J, *Ethics in the Pubic Domain: Essays in the Morality of Law and Politics* (Oxford: Oxford University Press 1995)

Raz J, 'Liberty and Trust', in RP George (ed), *Natural Law, Liberalism and Morality* (Oxford: Oxford University Press 1996)

Raz J, *The Authority of Law* (Oxford: Clarendon Press 1979)

Raz J, *The Morality of Freedom* (Oxford: Oxford University Press 1986)

Raz J, Joseph Raz, 'The Obligation to Obey: Revision and Tradition' (1984) 1 *Notre Dame Journal of Law Ethics & Public Policy* 139

Raz J, *Authority* (New York: New York University Press, 1990)
Raustiala K, 'Form and Substance in International Agreements', (2005) 99 American Journal of International Law 581
Redgewell C, 'Universality or Integrity? Some Reflections on Reservations to General Multilateral Treaties' (1993) 64 *British Yearbook of International Law* 245
Robert A, 'Power and Persuasion in Investment Treaty Arbitration: The Dual Role of States' (2010) 104 *American Journal of International Law* 179
Robert A and Rivers J, *A Theory of Constitutional Rights* (Oxford: Oxford University Press 2009)
Roberts AE, 'Traditional and Modern Approaches to Customary International Law: A Reconciliation' (2001) 95 *American Journal of International Law* 757
Rodley N and Çalı B, 'Kosovo Revisited: Humanitarian Intervention on the Fault Lines of International Law' (2007) 7(2) *Human Rights Law Review* 275
Scelle G, *Précis de droit des gens: principes et systématique* (Paris: Recueil Sirey 1934)
Schabas W, 'Invalid Reservations to the International Covenant on Civil and Political Rights: Is the United States Still a Party?' (1995) 21 *Brooklyn Journal of International Law* 277
Schaffer G, 'A Transnational Take on Krisch's Pluralist Postnational Law' (2012) 23(2) *European Journal of International Law* 565
Scharf MP, *Customary International Law in Times of Fundamental Change Recognizing Grotian Moments* (Cambridge: Cambridge University Press 2013)
Schreuer C and Kriebaum U, 'From Individual to Community Intertest in International Investment Law' in Ulrich Fastenrath and others (eds), *From Bilateralism to Community Interest: Essays in Honour of Bruno Simma* (Oxford: Oxford University Press 2011)
Shany Y, *Regulating Jurisdictional Relations between National and International Courts* (Oxford: Oxford University Press 2007)
Shaw MN, *International Law* (7th edn, Cambridge: Cambridge University Press 2014)
Shelton D, *International Law and Domestic Legal Systems: Incorporation, Transformation, and Persuasion* (Oxford: Oxford University Press 2011)
Simma B, 'From Bilateralism to Community Interest in International Law' (1994) 250 *Recueil des Cours* 217
Simma B, 'The International Community: Facing the Challenge of Globalization' (1998) 9(2) *European Journal of International Law* 266
Simma B and Paulus AL, 'The Responsibility of Individuals for Human Rights Abuses in Internal Conflicts: A Positivist View' (1999) 93(2) *American Journal of International Law* 302
Simmons B, 'Treaty Compliance and Violation' (2010) 13(1) *Annual Review of Political Science* 273
Simmons BA, *Mobilizing for Human Rights: International Law in Domestic Politics* (Cambridge: Cambridge University Press 2009)
Simmons J, *Moral Principles and Political Obligations* (Princeton: Princeton University Press 1979)

Sloss DL, 'Domestic Application of Treaties' (2011) 8–11 *Santa Clara University Legal Studies Research Papers Series* 3

Sloss DL, Ramsey MD, and Dodge WS (eds), *International Law in the US Supreme Court* (Cambridge: Cambridge University Press 2012)

Slaughter A-M, 'A Global Community of Courts' (2003) 44 *Harvard International Law Journal* 191

Sousa Santos B de, *Towards a New Common Sense* (London: Routledge 1995)

Starke JG, 'Monism and Dualism in the Theory of International Law' (1936) 17 British *Yearbook of International Law* 66

Sweet AS, *Constitutionalism, Legal Pluralism, and International Regimes*, (2009) 16(2) *Indiana Journal of Global Legal Studies* 633

Tasioulas J, 'In Defence of Relative Normativity: Communitarian Values and the Nicaragua Case' (1996) 16(1) *Oxford Journal of Legal Studies* 85

Tasioulas J, 'The Legitimacy of International Law' in Samantha Besson and John Tasioulas (eds), *The Philosophy of International Law* (Oxford: Oxford University Press 2010)

Tomuschat C, 'International Law: Ensuring the Survival of Mankind on the Eve of a New Century, General Course on Public International Law' (1999) 281 *Recueil des Cours* 9

Tushnet M, 'The Relation Between Political Constitutionalism and Weak-Form Judicial Review' (2013) 14 *German Law Review* 2249

Tzanakopoulos A, *Disobeying the Security Council Countermeasures against Wrongful Sanctions* (Oxford: Oxford University Press 2011)

Valentini L, 'Coercion and (Global) Justice' (2011) 105(1) *American Political Science Review* 205

Verdross A, *Die Einheit des rechtlichen Weltbildes auf Grundlage der Völkerrechtsverfassung* [The Unity of the Legal Order on the Basis of the International Constitution] (Tübingen: JCB Mohr 1923)

Verdross A, 'Droit international public et droit interne' (1954) 32(3) *Revue de Droit International de Sciences Diplomatiques et Politiques* 219

Viljoen F, *International Human Rights Law in Africa* (Oxford University Press 2012)

von Bogdandy A, 'Pluralism, direct effect, and the ultimate say: On the relationship between international and domestic constitutional law' (2008) 6(3–4) *International Journal of Constitutional Law* 397

von Stein J, 'Do Treaties Constrain or Screen? Selection Bias and Treaty Compliance' (2005) 99 *American Political Science Review* 611

von Stein J, 'The Engines of Compliance' in Jeffrey L. Dunoff and Mark A. Pollack (eds), *Interdisciplinary Perspectives in International Law and International Relations: The State of the Art* (Cambridge: Cambridge University Press 2012)

Voyiakis E, 'Customary International Law and the Place of Normative Considerations' (2010) 55(1) *American Journal of Jurisprudence* 163

Waldron J, 'Foreign Law and the Modern Ius Gentium' (2005) 119(1) *Harvard Law Review* 129

Waldron J, 'Is the Rule of Law an Essentially Contested Concept?' (2002) 21 *Law and Philosophy* 137

Waldron J, *Law and Disagreement* (Oxford: Oxford University Press 1999)

Waldron J, 'The Core of the Case Against Judicial Review' (2006) 115 *Yale Law Journal* 1346

Waldron J, *The Dignity of Legislation* (Cambridge: Cambridge University Press 1999)

Waldron J, 'The Rule of International Law' (2006) 30(1) *Harvard Journal of Law and Public Policy* 15

Walker N, 'Beyond boundary disputes and basic grids: Mapping the global disorder of normative orders' (2008) 6(3–4) *International Journal of Constitutional Law* 373

Walker N, 'Postnational Constitutionalism and Postnational Public Law: A Tale of Two Neologisms' (2012) 3 *Transnational Legal Theory* 61

Waters MA, 'The Creeping Monism: The Judicial Trend Toward Interpretive Incorporation of Human Rights Treaties' (2007) 107 *Columbia Law Review* 628

Weber M, *On Law in Economy and Society* (Max Rhinstein ed, Edward A Shils trans) (Cambridge: Harvard University Press 1954)

Weil P, 'Towards Relative Normativity in International Law?' (1983) 77(3) *American Journal of International Law* 413

Weiler JHH, 'A Constitution for Europe? Some Hard Choices' (2002) 40(4) *Journal of Common Market Studies* 563

Weiler JHH (ed), *The EU, the WTO, and the NAFTA: Towards a Common Law of International Trade* (Oxford: Oxford University Press 2000)

Weiner and others, 'Why a new journal on global constitutionalism? Global Constitutionalism—Human Rights, Democracy, and the Rule of Law' (2012) 1(1) *Global Constitutionalism* 1

Wet E de, 'The International Constitutional Order' (2006) 55(1) *International and Comparative Law Quarterly* 51

Wet E de, 'The Prohibition of Torture as an International Norm of jus cogens and Its Implications for National and Customary Law' (2004) 15(1) *European Journal of International Law* 97

Wet E de and Vidmar J, *Hierarchy in International Law: The Place for Human Rights?* (Oxford: Oxford University Press 2012)

Wheately S, 'A Democratic Rule of International Law' (2011) 22(2) *European Journal of International Law* 425

Wheately S, 'On the legitimate authority of international human rights bodies' in Follesdal, Karlsson Schaffer, and Geir Ulfstein (eds), *The Legitimacy of International Human Rights Regimes: Legal, Political and Philosophical Perspectives* (Cambridge: Cambridge University Press 2013)

Wheately S, *The Democratic Legitimacy of International Law* (Oxford: Hart Publishing 2010)

Wheately S, 'The Security Council, Democratic Legitimacy and Regime Change in Iraq' (2006) 17(3) *European Journal of International Law* 531

Wheeler NJ, *Saving Strangers: Humanitarian Intervention in International Society* (Oxford: Oxford University Press 2000)

Witte B De, 'The European Union as an international legal experiment' in Gráinne de Búrca and Joseph H H Weiler (eds), *The Worlds of European Constitutionalism* (Cambridge: Cambridge University Press 2011)

Wolff RP, *In Defense of Anarchism* (Berkeley: University of California Press 1998)

Wolfke K, *Custom in present International Law* (2nd rev edn, The Hague: Martinus Nijhoff 1993)

Wood, M, Second report on identification of customary international law by Michael Wood, Special Rapporteur of 22 May 2014, (2014) International Law Commission Sixty-sixth session, A/CN.4/672

Yourow HC, *The Margin of Appreciation Doctrine in the Dynamics of European Human Rights Jurisprudence* (The Hague: Kluwer Law International 1996)

Zorn A, *Grundzüge des Völkerrechts* (Charleston: Nabu Press 2010)

# Index

The manufacturer's authorised representative in the EU for product
safety is Oxford University Press España S.A. of El Parque Empresarial
San Fernando de Henares, Avenida de Castilla, 2 - 28830 Madrid
(www.oup.es/en or product.safety@oup.com). OUP España S.A. also acts
as importer into Spain of products made by the manufacturer.
Printed and bound by CPI Group (UK) Ltd, Croydon, CR0 4YY
14/09/2026
02216308-0006